The Economics of Space Sustainability

DELIVERING ECONOMIC EVIDENCE TO GUIDE GOVERNMENT ACTION

OECD
BETTER POLICIES FOR BETTER LIVES

Please cite this publication as:
OECD (2024), *The Economics of Space Sustainability: Delivering Economic Evidence to Guide Government Action*, OECD Publishing, Paris, https://doi.org/10.1787/b2257346-en.

ISBN 978-92-64-77780-4 (print)
ISBN 978-92-64-54808-4 (PDF)
ISBN 978-92-64-78291-4 (HTML)
ISBN 978-92-64-82773-8 (epub)

Photo credits: Cover © Frame Stock Footage/shutterstock.com.

Corrigenda to OECD publications may be found on line at: www.oecd.org/about/publishing/corrigenda.htm.

Foreword

In the last ten years, the number of satellites launched into space annually has multiplied twelve-fold, from 200 satellites in 2013 to more than 2 600 in 2023. This massive deployment of space infrastructure reflects its growing role in society, supporting critical societal functions such as telecommunications, energy grids, financial transactions and air transportation, as well as essential government services. It also reflects the democratisation of space activities, with a shift from mainly public to mainly commercial operators, and a remarkable geographic expansion, with currently more than 90 countries having operated a satellite in space.

The key driver of current growth is the rollout of multiple commercial constellations for satellite broadband in the low-earth orbital region, with proposed projects numbering hundreds of thousands of satellites. This could be a game changer for bridging the digital divide, providing broadband connectivity to hundreds of millions of people in under-served remote and sparsely populated regions.

But it also raises concerns about the environmental sustainability of space activities, including harmful effects on Earth's atmosphere and the brightening of the night sky. The most pressing question is how this intensified activity will affect the access to space for future generations. Once in orbit, satellites occupy an increasingly limited and congested space, whose regulation and supervision are geopolitically, legally and technologically complex. Satellites and inhabited space stations face the growing threat of space debris, created from routine space operations, collisions and anti-satellite tests. If the number of debris collisions spins out of control and they become self-generating (the so-called Kessler's Syndrome), certain orbits of high socio-economic value could eventually become unusable. Satellites in the most exposed orbits are mainly public and play a key role in weather and climate monitoring, science, disaster management and defence.

Adequately assessing the costs of space debris and the benefits of these space activities is a challenge because there may be large societal effects, harder to quantify than economic impacts. In 2019, the OECD Space Forum launched a project on the economics of space sustainability to address these issues, inviting researchers worldwide to assess, and where possible quantify, the effects generated by the accumulation of space debris, as well as their mitigation or potential remediation. Preliminary findings were published in 2022, in *Earth's Orbits at Risk: The Economics of Space Sustainability*.

This follow-up publication provides valuable information to decision makers about the extent and nature of risks posed by space debris and offers new evidence on the value of space infrastructure for public and private end users. For the first time, guidance is also available on policy options for debris remediation and their possible socio-economic effects.

Acknowledgements

Marit Undseth (Policy Analyst) led the development of this publication with support from Claudia Abdallah (Junior Economist), James Jolliffe (Economist) and Barrie Stevens (Senior Advisor), under the leadership of Claire Jolly (Head of Unit) in the OECD Space Forum.

The authors of individual chapters were the following: Marit Undseth (Chapters 1 and 2). Chapters 3-8 were authored by participants in the OECD project on the economics of space sustainability. Chapter 3 was authored by Chanhee Lee, Jong Ho Hong, Keewon Kim, Habin Kim, Heeyoung Seo (Seoul National University in Korea) and Jinyoung Kang (National Research Council for Economics, Humanities, and Social Sciences, Korea) and the work was supported by the Ministry of Science and ICT of Korea under [NRF-2023M1A3B6A02061456]. Chapter 4 was authored by Yui Nakama, Quentin Verspieren (University of Tokyo, Japan) and Aya Iwamoto (Astroscale, Japan). Chapter 5 was authored by Gelsomina Catalano (Csil, Italy) and Valentina Morretta (University of Milan, Italy). Chapter 6 was authored by Alessandro Paravano, Giorgio Locatelli and Paolo Trucco (Polytechnic University of Milan, Italy). Chapter 7 was authored by Erika Scuderi (Vienna University of Economics and Business, Austria). Chapter 8 was authored by Xiao-Shan Yap and Emmanuelle David (Swiss Federal Institute of Technology Lausanne, Switzerland). Furthermore, Box 2.2. is based on a paper written by Nonthaphat Pulsiri and Victor Dos Santos Paulino (Toulouse Business School). Box 2.3. is based on a paper authored by a team of students and researchers in the United Kingdom: Marek Ziebart, Santosh Bhattarai, Charles Constant, Indigo Brownhall, Wei Lai, Zhaoqun Zhang, Logan Scott, Barnaby Jupp, Xueru Hao (University College London, United Kingdom), Johnathan Wolff (University of Oxford, United Kingdom) and Joanne Wheeler (Alden Legal, United Kingdom).

The Secretariat warmly thanks the authors as well as all the other participants, for their inputs and their engagement throughout the project, without which this publication would not be possible.

The Secretariat further wishes to acknowledge with sincere thanks the support provided by the organisations forming the Steering Group of the OECD Space Forum: the Canadian Space Agency (CSA), Canada; the National Centre for Space Studies (CNES), France; the German Aerospace Centre (DLR), Germany; the Italian Space Agency (ASI), Italy; the Korea Aerospace Research Institute (KARI), Korea; the Netherlands Space Office (NSO), Netherlands; the Norwegian Space Agency (NOSA) and the Ministry of Trade, Industry and Fisheries, Norway; the Swiss Space Office, Switzerland; the UK Space Agency (UKSA), United Kingdom; the Office of Technology, Policy and Strategy at the National Aeronautics and Space Administration (NASA), United States; and the European Space Agency (ESA).

Finally, we thank our OECD colleagues in the Directorate for Science, Technology and Innovation for their contributions to this report, notably Sylvain Fraccola for publication support and Alessandra Colecchia, Head of the Science and Technology Policy Division, Hanna-Mari Kilpelainen, Senior Counsellor, and Jens Lundsgaard, Deputy Director, for their comments and careful review.

Table of contents

Tables

Figures

Boxes

Abbreviations and acronyms

ADR	active debris removal
ASAT	anti-satellite testing
ASI	Italian Space Agency (Italy)
	Agenzia Spaziale Italiana
CAO	Cabinet Office (Japan)
CHBR	Combined hard body radius
CI	Critical infrastructure
CIP	Critical infrastructure protection
CNES	National Centre for Space Studies (France)
	Centre National d'Études Spatiales
CSA	Canadian Space Agency (Canada)
CV	Contingent valuation
DLR	German Aerospace Center
	Deutsches Zentrum für Luft- und Raumfahrt
DoT	Department of Transportation (United States)
EARSC	European Association of Remote Sensing Companies
EO	Earth observation
EPFL	Swiss Federal Institute of Technology Lausanne
	Ecole Polytechnique Fédérale de Lausanne
ESA	European Space Agency
EU	European Union
EUSPA	European Union Agency for the Space Programme
FAA	Federal Aviation Administration (United States)
FCC	Federal Communication Commission (United States)
GDP	Gross domestic product
GEO	Geostationary orbit
GNSS	Global navigation satellite systems

GPS	Global Positioning System
IADC	Inter-Agency Space Debris Coordination Committee
IAU	International Astronomical Union
ICT	Information and communication technology
IDA	International Dark-Sky Association
ISS	International Space Station
ITU	International Telecommunication Union
JAXA	Japan Aerospace Exploration Agency (Japan)
LEO	Low-earth orbit
MEO	Medium-earth orbit
MIC	Ministry of Internal Affairs and Communication (Japan)
NASA	National Aeronautics and Space Administration (United States)
NEREUS	Network of European Regions Using Space Technologies
NGSO	Non-geostationary orbit
OCST	Office of Commercial Space Transportation (United States)
ODT	Orbiting debris tax
OST	Outer Space Treaty
OUF	Orbital-use fee
PC	Personal computer
PHS	Personal Handyphone System
PDA	Personal digital assistant
PMD	Post-mission disposal
PNT	Positioning, navigation and timing
R&D	Research and development
SBDC	Single-bounded dichotomous choice
SDG	Sustainable Development Goal
SDMFS	Space debris mitigation fiscal scheme
SeBS	Sentinel Economic Benefits Studies
SSA	Space situational awareness
SSR	Space Sustainability Rating
TraCSS	Traffic Coordination System for Space
UCS	Union of Concerned Scientists
UNIDIR	United Nations Institute for Disarmament Research
UNOOSA	United Nations Office for Outer Space Affairs
WTP	Willingness-to-pay

Executive summary

The accumulation of debris in Earth's orbits is one of the most pressing threats to the long-term sustainability of space infrastructure and the services it provides to modern societies. Together with space organisations and researchers worldwide, the OECD is supporting mitigation efforts by exploring economic aspects of space sustainability and policy options for ensuring responsible use of the space environment.

How does growing traffic in Earth's orbits affect long-term space sustainability?

Earth's orbits have never been more crowded, with 9 500 operational satellites in early 2024.Most of them privately operated and concentrated in a small number of orbits. Growth is driven by the deployment of satellite broadband and hundreds of thousands of satellites could be launched in the next decade. The 500-600 km orbital region poses traffic co-ordination challenges, with more than 4 000 active satellites and over 260 public, private and amateur/university operators from 51 countries. Some 66% of commercial satellites and 27% of government and military satellites are found at these altitudes.

The orbital environment is already polluted by more than 100 million pieces of debris from past space activities that not only pose a collision threat for active satellites but also generate additional debris when colliding with each other. In a worst-case scenario, high debris density could trigger an irreversible chain reaction of collisions, rendering certain orbits of great socio-economic value unusable. Mathematical models show that this tipping point may have already been reached in selected regions and that the debris population is now slowly growing. Policy action is therefore required to stabilise the orbital environment and ensure continued access to space for future generations.

How to assess the value of space infrastructure and the costs of space debris?

This publication summarises the state of the art so far (Chapter 2) and provides new evidence. All satellites and space stations are exposed to space debris, but the risk of collision varies greatly. The total global value of economic activity at risk is estimated to be USD 191 billion with the bulk of the value concentrated in orbits at 500-600 km altitude. The orbits with the highest exposure to debris (at around 850 km altitude and 70-80 degrees inclination) are mainly occupied by publicly funded satellites, vital for scientific research, climate monitoring, weather forecasting and national security. Practically all the risk (97%) is associated with defunct objects, with two-thirds (65%) coming from spent rocket bodies.

The value of space infrastructure and its associated signals and data can be expressed in multiple ways. A Korean willingness-to-pay study assesses the value of public earth observation satellites at risk from space debris at USD 388.7 million over ten years for Korea, indicating not only the importance of the societal services provided by these satellites but also broad popular support to preserve essential public services and conduct space debris mitigation (Chapter 3). A Japanese study uses growth theory to explore how space technology contributes to economic growth in sparsely populated prefectures in Japan

(Chapter 4). More qualitatively, an Italian survey finds that over half of its respondents from public bodies (72%), have used earth observation services to enhance the quality of their products and services, expand research and development capabilities and increase the efficiency of their production and service processes (Chapter 5). In contrast, European private sector users (in Chapter 6) often perceive a gap between the potential of satellite data and its practical utility in strategic product decisions. For many of these end users, exploiting satellite data products fully necessitates considerable investments in both resources and specialised skills.

How to formulate effective policy responses to address space debris issues?

National and international measures for debris mitigation have existed for several decades. However, compliance rates would need to approach 100% to reach desired outcomes, but in 2022 only 55% of satellites and 85% of rocket bodies respected orbit clearance recommendations. Additional measures are necessary to improve compliance. Several missions to actively remove debris from orbit are under development, but this solution is expensive and technologically and legally challenging.

Policy options for space sustainability include command-and-control regulations, incentive-based mechanisms and voluntary approaches.

- Incentive-based measures, such as launch and orbital taxes and performance bonds for post-mission disposal, could bring considerable long-term positive environmental outcomes and economic efficiency gains. However, there are questions about how binding measures could be introduced and co-ordinated, and how increased regulatory stringency would affect the growth of the space economy.
- The design of a fair and equitable fiscal measure compatible with national domestic tax systems and constitutional frameworks is further explored in this publication, where operators first pay a tax that is subsequently refunded upon evidence of compliance with a specific action (Chapter 7).
- Meanwhile, voluntary schemes will continue to play an important role in space activities, and good design is critical to ensure they are effective. Setting up a successful environmental rating system for space sustainability will rely on its recognition as a transparent, credible third-party rating body (Chapter 8). Furthermore, it would be important to combine it with other measures, such as packaging it with an insurance model and creating financial incentives such as access to corporate loans or public funding.

OECD research on the general effects of environmental regulations finds that they stimulate innovation, with overall minor negative impacts on the jobs and profits of regulated firms. Still, more research is needed to explore concrete applications of these findings to the space economy.

Policy implications and next steps

The growing body of evidence on the state of the space environment, the growing risks of collision in orbit and the wider impact of space debris incidents call for responses from both public and private actors. International co-operation is essential to adapt the international legal framework to the threats facing the orbital environment. At the national level, existing measures should be used more extensively – a promising first step is the first-ever fine issued to a non-compliant US operator in 2023.

Future avenues of research could involve delving deeper into the effects of different policy options and exploring how specific objectives affect policy design; the interaction and effects of policy mixes for space sustainability; and how international and domestic administrative and legal arrangements may affect outcomes. The OECD Space Forum will continue supporting these efforts by producing economic evidence on these emerging policy themes and beyond.

1 Space sustainability at the OECD

Today's unprecedented use of Earth's orbits coincides with increasingly unsustainable levels of space debris. Too much debris in orbit could disrupt the use of space as we know it, which would affect today's critical government services and infrastructures, as well as burgeoning private activity. This chapter provides the overall background on the issues of space debris and space sustainability and introduces the OECD project on the economics of space sustainability and its many contributors.

Introduction

Today's unprecedented use of Earth's orbits coincides with increasingly unsustainable levels of space debris. Space debris already pose a direct collision risk to operational satellites and other spacecraft such as the International and Chinese space stations. This risk is expected to grow in the future, with planned projects numbering hundreds of thousands of satellites.

The ultimate threat is that debris density reaches such levels that it could disrupt the use of space as we know it, with impacts on the functioning of critical government services and infrastructures, such as communications and transportation, that increasingly rely on space assets. It would also strongly affect commercial activity, a key source of growth in the sector.

As a useful complement to other efforts at the international level, the OECD Space Forum launched a project in 2019 on the economics of space sustainability. The objective was to explore specific economic aspects, such as the current and future costs generated by space debris and the value of space infrastructure at risk. In the past five years considerable progress has been made on the topic. This publication presents the latest findings.

This first chapter provides background on the issues of space debris, space sustainability and the OECD project, also introducing the academic contributions to the project that constitute the bulk of this publication.

Growing concerns about the state of the orbital environment

Figure 1.1. Number of tracked objects in Earth's orbits by object type

Historical increase of the catalogued objects based on data available on 3 February 2024

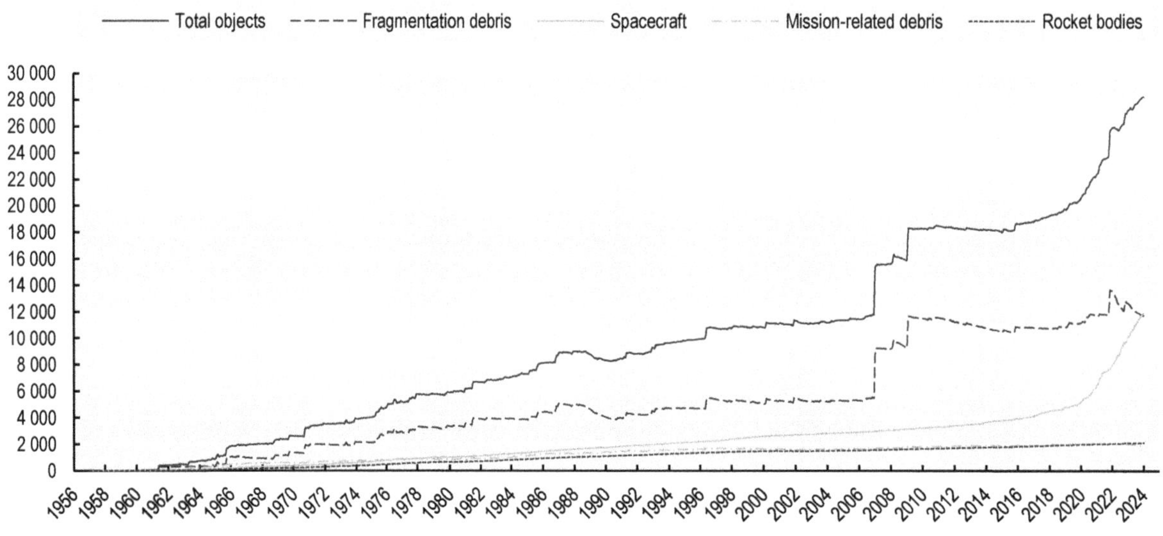

Notes: This chart displays a summary of all objects in Earth orbit officially catalogued by the US Space Surveillance Network. "Fragmentation debris" includes satellite breakup debris and anomalous event debris, while "mission-related debris" includes all objects dispensed, separated or released as part of the planned mission.
Source: NASA (2024[11]), "Monthly total of objects in orbit by object type", as of 3 February 2024.

There has been a notable jump in the number of space debris objects since 2007, as demonstrated in Figure 1.1, which shows the total number of satellites and different types of debris in space as tracked by the US Space Force. This debris growth can largely be attributed to two specific events: one anti-satellite test conducted by the People's Republic of China [hereafter 'China'] in 2007 and a collision in 2009 between two communications satellites, one operational, one defunct.

The accelerated launch activity to the low-earth orbit since 2019 is leading to an unprecedented number of new human-made objects in the space environment. In early 2024, there were some 9 500 active satellites in orbit (McDowell, 2024[2]).

The increased density of objects on orbits increases the risk of collisions: between active (operational) satellites; between active satellites and debris; and, most importantly, between debris objects themselves. The longer-term key concern associated with space debris is a self-generating chain reaction of collisions between debris objects referred to as Kessler's Syndrome (Kessler and Cour-Palais, 1978[3]), which could effectively disrupt the access to and use of orbits of high socio-economic value (Adilov, Alexander and Cunningham, 2018[4]; Undseth, Jolly and Olivari, 2020[5]). Mathematical models of the space environment indicate that the orbital debris population is already growing of its own accord in certain regions, albeit slowly (ESA, 2023[6]).

According to data from the National Aeronautics and Space Administration (NASA) Orbital Debris Program, debris resulting from intentional or accidental break-ups account for some 47% of the current tracked debris population. This is followed by defunct spacecraft (34%), mission-related debris and rocket bodies (both 8%) (Anz-Meador, Opiela and Liou, 2022[7]). It is important to note that most catalogued debris objects can be attributed to the limited number of government actors launching objects into space before 2000. The vast majority of the more than 15 000 debris objects catalogued and tracked by the US Space Force can be attributed to the Russian Federation [hereafter 'Russia'] (35% of currently tracked debris objects), the United States (32%) and China (28%) (US Space Force, 2024[8]) (Figure 1.2). Russia also dominates the count of "high-risk" objects with a potential for generating a lot of additional debris, combining several high-mass risk factors such as very large rocket bodies, orbit, inclination, etc. (McKnight et al., 2021[9]).

Figure 1.2. A few actors are responsible for most catalogued space debris objects

Counts of catalogued rocket bodies and orbital debris objects, as of 22 February 2024

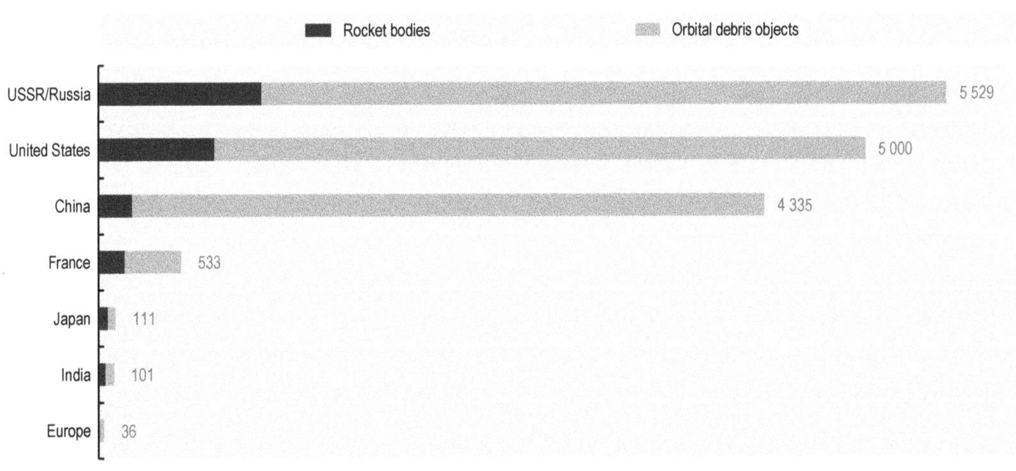

Source: US Space Force (2024[8]), *Space-track website*, https://www.space-track.org/#launchData, data accessed 22 February.

Another important point is that tracked debris objects account for only about 4% of the estimated harmful debris population (greater than 1 cm), with the total estimated debris population surpassing 100 million objects (ESA, 2024[10]), as shown in Table 1.1. This could skew perceptions of risks among space system operators, insurers and investors, creating a false sense of security and artificially lowering the costs of operating safely in the orbital environment.

Today, many of these debris objects result from a lack of end-of-life strategies, e.g. no passivation (removal of stored energy such as unused propellant or batteries) or post-mission disposal. Urgent implementation of more stringent mitigation and remediation measures to all missions, particularly in LEO, is necessary to avoid an exponential acceleration in the number of debris objects in orbit.

Table 1.1. Space debris by the numbers

Estimated number of break-ups, explosions, collisions or anomalous events resulting in fragmentation	More than 640[1]
Total mass of all space objects in Earth orbit	More than 11 500 metric tonnes[1]
Estimated number of debris objects greater than 10 cm	36 500[2]
Estimated number of debris objects smaller than 10 cm and greater than 1 cm	1 million[2]
Estimated number of debris objects smaller than 1 cm and greater than 1 mm	130 million[2]

1. Data as of 6 December 2023, 2. Estimation based on statistical model MASTER-8, future population 2021.
Source: ESA (2024[10]), "Space debris by the numbers", https://www.esa.int/Space_Safety/Space_Debris/Space_debris_by_the_numbers.

Increasing international awareness about space sustainability

Calls for government action and regulation to limit the risks associated with space debris are multiplying due in part to an improved understanding of the importance of space-based infrastructure and assets to society (OECD, 2023[11]). Over recent decades, international organisations and bodies (e.g. the United Nations Committee on the Peaceful Uses of Outer Space, the Inter-Agency Space Debris Coordination Committee), national administrations and space agencies have carried out extensive work on space debris mitigation and the sustainability of space activities (as defined in Box 1.1). This work has mainly concentrated on the technical aspects of space debris and specific guidelines for the most congested regions in the low-earth orbits and the geostationary orbit.

Box 1.1. What is "space sustainability"?

In 2019, the United Nations Committee on the Peaceful Uses of Outer Space (UN COPUOS) reached an international agreement on guidelines for the "long-term sustainability of outer space activities", that would ensure:

"[...] the ability to maintain the conduct of space activities indefinitely into the future in a manner that realises the objectives of equitable access to the benefits of the exploration and use of outer space for peaceful purposes, in order to meet the needs of the present generations while preserving the outer space environment for future generations."

This agreement reflects increased awareness about the negative externalities associated with activities in space and particularly of the unrestricted use of certain orbits of value for activities on Earth. To fully capture these effects both on Earth and in space, the term "earth-space sustainability" is sometimes used (Yap and Truffer, 2022[12]).

While space debris is considered the most urgent challenge, it is worth noting that there are also other dimensions to environmental space sustainability, such as the management of space traffic, the allocation and use of the electromagnetic spectrum, the brightening of the night sky, the environmental terrestrial and atmospheric impacts of space activities, etc. These issues will become increasingly important as the space economy grows both in scale and in scope.

Sources: UN COPUOS (2018[13]) *Guidelines for the Long-term Sustainability of Outer Space* and OECD (2022[14]) *Earth's Orbits at Risk: The Economics of Space Sustainability*, https://doi.org/10.1787/16543990-en.

Governments also need other types of evidence to make informed decisions on space debris mitigation or alleviation with effective outcomes. First, in order to identify the overall risks generated by space debris in the short-, medium- and long term, decision makers need to know which orbits and activities are directly and/or indirectly exposed to space debris; the probabilities of different space debris-related events occurring (ranging from collisions with very small objects to a dramatically worsened space environment); and the estimated socio-economic impacts of such events. Second, more evidence is needed on the effects of different policy options to mitigate space debris, including an ability to "test" such effects *ex ante*, e.g. modelling the effects of reducing post-mission disposal guidelines from 25 to 5 years after mission completion), their potential effectiveness, as well as feasibility of implementation and success. These are points that the OECD tries to address.

The OECD project on the economics of space sustainability

The OECD Space Forum, within the OECD Directorate for Science, Technology and Innovation, sits at the intersection between the space sector, science and technology policy and economic and industrial policy and is uniquely placed to address this multidimensional issue of space sustainability. On the initiative of several of its Steering Group members, the OECD Space Forum launched a project on space sustainability and the economics of space debris in 2019.

The initial phase of the project focused on the economics of space debris and was informed by inputs from several OECD Space Forum members – notably the Canadian Space Agency, the US NASA and the UK Space Agency – and space debris experts from the French National Centre for Space Studies (CNES) and the German Aerospace Centre (DLR). Commercial satellite operators were also consulted to inform policy discussions of industry perspectives on the issues of space debris mitigation. The work was presented in Undseth, Jolly and Olivari (2020[5]), providing a first-time comprehensive economic analysis of space debris and a stepping stone for further research.

In the next phase of the project, the OECD Space Forum launched an initiative to bring in the perspectives of the academic world and spur new research internationally. Young researchers – master's and PhD students – and faculty members in universities and other research organisations from OECD member countries and beyond were invited to author research papers and provide initial answers to three fundamental questions: 1) what is the value of space-based infrastructure?; 2) what are the potential costs of space debris?; and 3) what are the benefits and costs of different policy options? Their work was then reviewed by experts from space agencies and ministries from ten countries, as well as the European Space Agency and the OECD Space Forum. Several partnering space agencies have further supported the work by launching their own calls for research proposals or providing financial support to participants in the OECD project.

Over Phase 1 in 2020-21 and Phase 2 in 2022-23, almost 30 research teams from 11 different countries submitted extended abstracts or final papers on the topics (Table 1.2). These multi-disciplinary and geographically diverse contributions brought together research from engineering, law, environmental management and economics. All teams were able to present their work and share their perspectives during the project, and the OECD thanks them warmly for their engagement. After peer review, only a few were selected for publication, based on the novelty of findings and practical applicability.

Table 1.2. Participating institutions in the OECD Project on the Economics of Space Sustainability

Country	Affiliation	Project participation	Leading research discipline	Number of long abstracts
Austria	Wirtschaftsuniversität Wien	Phase 2	Law	1
Canada	University of McGill	Phase 1	Law	1

Country	Affiliation	Project participation	Leading research discipline	Number of long abstracts
France	École Polytechnique	Phases 1 and 2	Management	2
	University of Franche-Comté	Phase 2	Economics	1
	Toulouse Business School	Phase 2	Business	1
Italy	Politecnico Milan	Phase 2	Management	1
	CSIL, University of Milan	Phases 1 and 2	Economics	2
	Bocconi School of Management	Phase 1	Economics	1
	Politecnico di Bari	Phases 1 and 2	Engineering	2
	Mediterranean University of Reggio Calabria	Phase 1	Economics	1
Japan	University of Tokyo, Astroscale	Phase 2	Public policy	1
Korea	Seoul National University	Phases 1 and 2	Environmental studies	2
Norway	University of Oslo	Phase 2	Law	1
South Africa	University of Pretoria	Phase 2	Engineering	1
Spain	University of Basque Country and the Aeronautical Technologies Centre (CTA)	Phases 1 and 2	Economics	2
Switzerland	Swiss Federal Institute of Technology Lausanne	Phase 2	Engineering, social sciences	1
United Kingdom	University College London, University of Oxford	Phase 2	Engineering	1
	University of Aberdeen	Phase 2	Law	1
	Cranfield University	Phase 1	Engineering	1
	University of Plymouth	Phase 1	Business	2

- Selected findings from Phase 1 were published in the OECD report *Earth Orbits at Risk* (2022[14]). Themes included: valuing selected space activities and modelling the effects of disrupted space services on other sectors; introducing better categories of costs for inclusion in satellite impact assessments, modelling operator behaviour and incentives as well as the effects of different debris mitigation policies; exploring the active debris removal market; and assessing satellite mission efficiency.
- The present publication presents six selected papers from Phase 2, in addition to references to the other researchers' work. They offer new evidence on the value of space infrastructure for public and private end users, as well as for the first time, on policy options and their possible effects (notably fiscal measures and environmental certification schemes). The latter rely on methodologies that range from contingent valuation and qualitative surveys to scenario building. Also, Phase 2 of the project coincided with an initiative to fund specific socio-economic research on orbital debris and space sustainability by NASA, involving leading research organisations. The joint findings were presented at an OECD workshop on 14 December 2023 in Paris (see Box 1.2).

Box 1.2. NASA-funded projects on space sustainability important enablers of further research

In parallel with OECD's international efforts, in 2022 the US National Aeronautics and Space Administration awarded funds to three university-based teams to analyse the economic, social, and policy issues associated with space sustainability (NASA, 2022[4]).

The first project produced a sophisticated open-source space debris model that allows users to model the long-term future space environment to understand growth in space debris and assess the effectiveness of debris prevention mechanisms (Liberty, 2024[5]). This could encourage more policy research in this domain. The MIT Orbital Capacity Assessment Tool was released at an OECD Space Forum space sustainability workshop in December 2023. The project ("Adaptive Space Governance and Decision-Support using Source-Sink Evolutionary Environmental Models") was submitted by Richard Linares and Danielle Wood of the Massachusetts Institute of Technology and Moriba Jah of the University of Texas-Austin. Privateer Space of Maui, Hawaii, and the Aerospace Corporation of El Segundo, California, verified and validated the project's modelling tool.

The second project developed an experimental integrated assessment model for satellites and orbital debris that combines the astrodynamics of the orbital population and the economic behaviour of space actors (Rao et al., 2023[6]). This is a particularly useful tool for evaluating the effects of policy options on orbital congestion. The proposal "An Integrated Assessment Model for Satellite Constellations and Orbital Debris," was submitted by Akhil Rao of Middlebury College, Daniel Kaffine of the University of Colorado-Boulder and Brian Weeden of the Secure World Foundation.

The third proposal uses a similar methodology to the one employed in Chapter 3 of this publication, studying the public's willingness to pay for space debris mitigation (Wells, 2022[7]). Such research collaboration improves the international comparability of data and could make overall findings more robust. The proposal "Communication and Space Debris: Connecting with Public Knowledges and Identities" was submitted by Patrice Kohl, Sergio Alvarez, and Philip Metzger of the University of Central Florida.

The Economics of Space Sustainability: Delivering Economic Evidence to Guide Government Action

This publication aims to increase awareness of space sustainability issues and to take stock of the latest available research to inform policy decisions. The contents are organised as follows:

Part 1. State of the art on the economics of space sustainability... so far

- Chapter 1 introduces the concept of space sustainability and provides background for the OECD project on the economics of space sustainability.
- Chapter 2 summarises the key results from the OECD project so far, including the most recent findings from the academic community and the latest policy developments. It provides an overview of the degree and types of collision risk in different orbital regions, of the known value of space infrastructure at risk and of ways to better assess this value. It then discusses available policy options on the table for decision makers, their effectiveness and potential socio-economic effects.

The following chapters result from original work produced in 2022-23 by academic participants. They provide novel approaches and evidence in two principal areas:

Part 2. New evidence on the costs generated by space debris and the value of space infrastructure.

- Chapter 3 authored by Lee et al., explores the value of public earth observation satellites at risk from space debris within the Korean context and uses contingent valuation to assess the potential lost value of Korean earth observation satellites in the low-earth orbit (LEO) due to space debris incidents. The study identifies an aggregated value loss of EUR 369.6 million (USD 388.7 million) over ten years, indicating not only the importance of the societal services provided by these satellites but also broad popular support for space debris mitigation.
- In Chapter 4, Nakama et al. look at the value of space assets in Japan from a critical infrastructure perspective and explore the difficulties faced in substituting them with alternatives if services were to be interrupted. The chapter proposes a simple theoretical production function model to comprehend the macroeconomic benefits of vital space assets from a governmental standpoint.

- In Chapter 5, Catalano and Morretta present new evidence on the benefits accrued by end users of earth observation services and applications through a survey of the end users of these services in Italy. Earth observation contributes to the understanding, analysis and management of different natural and societal aspects of planet Earth, with relevant socio-economic and environmental implications.
- Chapter 6, authored by Paravano et al., explores the value of space infrastructure by asking commercial end users in Europe the extent to which they adopt satellite data for strategic and tactical decision making in selected emerging markets for such data: energy and utilities, transport and logistics; and insurance and finance. The chapter discusses the gap between the perceived and actual utility (enacted value) of satellite data for these users, and how this may affect further uptake.

Part 3. Assessing the effects of policy options for space debris mitigation

- In Chapter 7, Scuderi discusses whether fiscal measures can be viable tools to address the accumulation of space debris and overcome the inherent fragility of non-binding instruments. Leveraging a literature review and past experiences with the adoption or proposed adoption of user fees for launches, the chapter suggests a design for a space debris mitigation tax scheme embedded in a framework of legal and fiscal principles.
- In Chapter 8, Yap and David build three scenarios of how global space governance might evolve by 2030 and explore the role of a voluntary incentive-based industry certification scheme – the Space Sustainability Rating – in each of these scenarios. This is then used to formulate policy recommendations for how this rating system could contribute to earth-space sustainability in the future.

The OECD Space Forum Secretariat would like to thank again all the participants throughout the project, the authors and their institutions for their engagement, which will encourage further original research on the economics of space sustainability by the OECD, partnering space organisations and academia. This new body of evidence will support important decisions needed by policy makers to support a stable and accessible space environment for the benefit of our societies.

References

Adilov, N., P. Alexander and B. Cunningham (2018), "An economic "Kessler Syndrome": A dynamic model of earth orbit debris", *Economics Letters*, Vol. 166, pp. 79-82, https://doi.org/10.1016/j.econlet.2018.02.025. [4]

Anz-Meador, P., J. Opiela and J. Liou (2022), *History of on-orbit satellite fragmentations: 16th edition*, NASA/TP-20220019160, NASA Orbital Debris Program Office, https://orbitaldebris.jsc.nasa.gov/library/hoosf_16e.pdf. [7]

ESA (2024), *Space debris by the numbers*, webpage, https://www.esa.int/Space_Safety/Space_Debris/Space_debris_by_the_numbers. [10]

ESA (2023), *Annual Space Environment Report 2023*, European Space Agency, ESA Space Debris Office, https://www.sdo.esoc.esa.int/environment_report/Space_Environment_Report_latest.pdf. [6]

Kessler, D. and B. Cour-Palais (1978), "Collision frequency of artificial satellites: The creation of a debris belt", *Journal of Geophysical Research*, Vol. 83/A6, p. 2637, https://doi.org/10.1029/JA083iA06p02637. [3]

Liberty, J. (2024), *Researchers release open-source space debris model*, 10 January, https://news.mit.edu/2024/researchers-release-open-source-space-debris-model-0110. [16]

McDowell, J. (2024), *Jonathan's Space Report*, website, https://planet4589.org/space/index.html. [2]

McKnight, D. et al. (2021), "Identifying the 50 statistically-most-concerning derelict objects in LEO", *Acta Astronautica*, Vol. 181, pp. 282-291, https://doi.org/10.1016/j.actaastro.2021.01.021. [9]

NASA (2024), *Monthly total of objects in orbit by object type*, status as of 3 February 2024, data provided by the NASA Orbital Debris Office. [1]

NASA (2022), *NASA Funds Projects to Study Orbital Debris, Space Sustainability*, webpage, US National Aeronautics and Space Administration, https://www.nasa.gov/news-release/nasa-funds-projects-to-study-orbital-debris-space-sustainability/. [15]

OECD (2023), *The Space Economy in Figures: Responding to Global Challenges*, OECD Publishing, Paris, https://doi.org/10.1787/fa5494aa-en. [11]

OECD (2022), *Earth's Orbits at Risk: The Economics of Space Sustainability*, OECD Publishing, Paris, https://doi.org/10.1787/16543990-en. [14]

Rao, A. et al. (2023), *OPUS: An Integrated Assessment Model for Satellites and Orbital Debris*, Papers 2309.10252, arXiv.org, https://ideas.repec.org/p/arx/papers/2309.10252.html. [17]

UN COPUOS (2018), *Guidelines for the Long-term Sustainability of Outer Space*, Committee on the Peaceful Uses of Outer Space, https://www.unoosa.org/res/oosadoc/data/documents/2018/aac_1052018crp/aac_1052018crp_20_0_html/AC105_2018_CRP20E.pdf. [13]

Undseth, M., C. Jolly and M. Olivari (2020), "Space sustainability: The economics of space debris in perspective", *OECD Science, Technology and Industry Policy Papers*, No. 87, OECD Publishing, Paris, https://doi.org/10.1787/a339de43-en. [5]

US Space Force (2024), *Space-track website*, Data accessed 12 January, https://www.space-track.org/#launchData. [8]

Wells, R. (2022), *New NASA-funded Study Hopes to Put Risks of Space Junk on People's Radar*, University of Central Florida, https://www.ucf.edu/news/new-nasa-funded-study-hopes-to-put-risks-of-space-junk-on-peoples-radar/. [18]

Yap, X. and B. Truffer (2022), "Contouring 'earth-space sustainability'", *Environmental Innovation and Societal Transitions*, Vol. 44, pp. 185-193, https://doi.org/10.1016/j.eist.2022.06.004. [12]

2 Informing government action on space debris mitigation

This chapter summarises the results from the OECD project on the economics of space sustainability so far, including the most recent findings from the academic community and the latest policy developments. It provides an overview of the degree and types of collision risk in different orbital regions, of the known value of space infrastructure at risk and of ways to better assess this value. Finally, it then discusses available policy options, their effectiveness and potential socio-economic effects.

Introduction

In the last five years, space sustainability has become a hot topic in the space community and beyond, in conferences and at high-level space policy meetings. In 2023, the G7 leaders' communiqué from the Hiroshima summit included an entire section dedicated to space sustainability (The White House, 2023[1]). The same year, the European Space Agency introduced its Zero Debris Approach, while the US National Aeronautics Administration (NASA) launched the first part of its integrated Space Sustainability Strategy in 2024 (ESA, 2023[2]; NASA, 2024[3]).

Space sustainability covers many different dimensions, several of which will be explored by the OECD in the coming years, but the focus of this publication is on space debris. This chapter summarises the results from the OECD project on the economics of space sustainability so far, including the most recent findings from the academic community and the latest policy developments as of early 2024.

The following questions are explored in more detail in the different sections:

- How does growing traffic in Earth's orbits affect long-term space sustainability?
- Which space activities are the most exposed to debris and collision risk?
- How to assess the value of space infrastructure and the costs of space debris?
- Is compliance with existing debris mitigation measures insufficient to stabilise the orbital environment?
- How to formulate effective policy responses to address space debris issues?
- How to assess the effects of policy options aimed at improving the orbital environment?
- What are the next steps?

How does growing traffic in Earth's orbits affect long-term space sustainability?

Earth's orbits are busier than ever. Orbital regions, such as the low-earth (LEO), medium- (MEO) and geostationary (GEO) orbits, have specific physical attributes that cater to different types of space applications (Table 2.1). Some orbits are used much more intensively than others because of these differences. For instance, a satellite in geostationary orbit rotates at the same speed as Earth, always hovering above the same spot at its allocated longitude over the equator. One satellite in geostationary orbit can cover about one-third of the earth's surface (Peterson, 2003[4]), which makes this orbit ideally suited for telecommunications and certain meteorological observations.

Table 2.1. Selected Earth's orbits and their characteristics

Orbit	Altitudes	Key attributes	Selected applications	Operational satellites as of May 2023
Low-earth orbit (LEO)	180-2 000 km	Lowest latency for communications, high resolution for remote sensing, high revisit frequency. Requires multiple satellites for global coverage.	Earth observation, telecommunications	6 768 (90% of total)
Medium-earth orbit (MEO)	2 000-35 786 km	Broader field of vision than LEO, requiring fewer satellites for global coverage. Also requires less fuel for station-keeping due to less gravitational pull and atmospheric drag than in lower altitudes.	Navigation	143 (2% of total)

Orbit	Altitudes	Key attributes	Selected applications	Operational satellites as of May 2023
Geostationary orbit (GEO)	35 786 km	Broad geographic coverage of single satellites, constant view of the same surface area.	Earth observation (meteorology), telecommunications	590 (8% of total)

Sources: Building on Riebeek (2009[5]), "Catalogue of earth satellite orbits", https://earthobservatory.nasa.gov/features/OrbitsCatalog and UCS (2024[6]), UCS satellite database, update 1 May 2023, https://www.ucsusa.org/resources/satellite-database.

However, reductions in the costs of access to space are profoundly changing the use of the orbital environment. Since the early 2010s, LEO has been the most popular destination for satellites, currently accounting for some 90% of all operational satellites. Within this orbital region, sun-synchronous orbits play an important role, because observations from this orbit are performed with a consistent angle of sunlight on the surface area, making it possible to track changes over time (Riebeek, 2009[5]). This is highly valuable for science, military intelligence and other earth observation applications. According to the Union of Concerned Scientists, more than 1 200 satellites, some 22% of all operational satellites and about 75% of LEO earth observation satellites, are in a sun-synchronous orbit (UCS, 2024[6]). Satellite broadband constellations in LEO now account for most operational satellites, with the biggest constellation consisting of seve ral thousand satellites organised in multiple orbital shells in mostly non-polar orbits at around 550 km altitude (UCS, 2024[6]).

The increased space activity since 2019 creates new challenges when analysing statistics on satellites and space launches. This report uses data from two complementary sources for active satellites: the database of the Union of Concerned Scientists (UCS) (2024[6]) and Jonathan McDowell's Space Report (2024[7]), both reliable resources relying on original and non-classified sources. Of the two sources, the UCS database has more data categories allowing for richer analysis, but updates are less frequent. This can be a challenge with the current accelerating launch frequency (more than 1 500 satellites have been launched yearly since 2020). In this chapter, data on active satellites and orbit occupancy refer to either 2023 or 2024, depending on the subject.

Which space activities are the most exposed to debris and collision risk?

Satellites and orbital debris are unequally distributed across Earth's orbits, leading to high variation in the levels of congestion and risk of collision with debris, as well as in the expected magnitude of the potential economic impact of such events. There are debris in all of Earth's orbits. But most attention is directed to the LEO region because of the recent increase in space traffic, the higher density of debris objects and the overall higher risk and impact of collisions from a debris-creation perspective (objects have high velocity and many have high mass).

LEO has traditionally been used mainly by government and military actors. But miniaturisation, launcher reusability and the relative proximity of LEO orbits to Earth have lowered the costs of access to space in general and increased the number of commercial actors operating in this orbital region since the early 2010s (OECD, 2019[8])). Early commercial applications included earth observations for geospatial and signal intelligence, but the recent considerable upswing in launch activity is mainly associated with the deployment of several "mega constellations" consisting of hundreds or even thousands of satellites for satellite broadband in LEO (see Box 2.1).

Commercial operators are now dominant in LEO, accounting for more than 85% of satellites in 2023 (UCS, 2024[6]). There is a notable concentration of commercial satellites in the 500-600 km and 1 150-1 250 km altitude ranges (Figure 2.1), which are the respective locations of the Starlink and OneWeb mega constellations for satellite broadband. Other commercial activity, earth observation in particular, is generally concentrated in lower-altitude orbits. The only orbital altitudes with a majority of civilian government and defence operators are those between 600-900 km altitude, mainly for earth observation satellites. This includes about 25% of the satellites recorded by the Committee on Earth Observation Satellites, which collect data on Earth's weather and climate (CEOS, 2023[9]). These are also the orbits with the highest debris concentrations (ESA, 2023[10]).

Box 2.1. Mega constellations for satellite broadband

As of early 2024, there were more than 6 000 satellites in low-earth orbits from two mega constellation operators – SpaceX (US) and OneWeb (UK) – but this will drastically change in the coming years. Filings for permits for radio spectrum with the International Telecommunication Union (ITU) between 2017 and 2022 suggest future launches of more than 300 constellations and a million satellites, including the Cinnamon constellation of some 330 000 satellites (Falle et al., 2023[11]). This number of planned satellites is exaggerated by duplicative and speculative filing applications and multiple projects are likely to fail due to technological problems and lack of finance. But it also reflects the growing strategic and economic importance of satellite broadband and the ongoing race between companies and countries to exploit orbital space and radio spectrum. Table 2.2 presents a non-exhaustive list of currently operational and planned constellations, several of which are backed by governments.

Table 2.2. Selected projects for mega constellations

Standing as of February 2024

Constellation (owner)	Country/Organisation	Orbits (km)	Current size	Planned size	First launch (planned)
Starlink (SpaceX)	United States	540-572	4 762	11 908 approved, total filings comprise more than 34 000 satellites	2018
OneWeb (Eutelsat OneWeb)[1]	United Kingdom	1 177-1 221	624	7 088	2019
Yinhe (Galaxy Space)	China	511	7	1 000	2020
Lynk (Lynk Global)	United States	500	4	2 000	2022
Kuiper (Amazon)	United States	590-630	2 (prototypes)	3 232	2023
GuoWang (China SatNet)[1]	China	590-600, 1 145		12 992	(2024)
Hanwha (Hanwha Systems)	Korea	500		2 000	(2024)
IRIS^2 (European Union) [1]	Europe	n.a.		n.a.	(2025)
Lightspeed (Telesat) [2]	Canada	1315-35		198	(2026)
Cinnamon-937 (E-space)	Rwanda, United States/France	550-638		337 323	?

1. Government system, 2. Supported by national governments via loans and/or equity finance.
Notes: n.a.: Not available.
Source: Expanding on McDowell (2024[7]), "Jonathan's Space Report", https://planet4589.org/space/index.html.

Figure 2.1 shows the distribution of manoeuvrable and non-manoeuvrable satellites and different types of debris. Manoeuvrability requires the existence of some kind of propulsion system and an on-board computer and allows the satellite to carry out collision-avoidance manoeuvres or clear the orbit at the end of the mission.

The Inter-Agency Debris Co-Ordination Committee defines space debris as "all manmade objects including fragments and elements thereof, in Earth orbit or re-entering the atmosphere, that are non-functional"

(IADC, 2007[12]). Debris results from routine space operations, accidents, collisions and explosions and have been accumulating since the first orbital launch in 1957. There were more than 640 confirmed so-called "fragmentation events" between the late 1950s and 2022 (ESA, 2023[10]). These events - in addition to the presence of derelict rocket bodies, mission-related debris and spacecraft - have created (as of February 2024) a debris population of more than 18 000 catalogued and tracked objects (NASA, 2024[13]) to which can be added millions more untracked objects of various sizes (ESA, 2023[10]).

Figure 2.1. Satellites are concentrated in a small number of orbits

Distribution of satellites and debris objects across low-earth orbits, data as of 2022

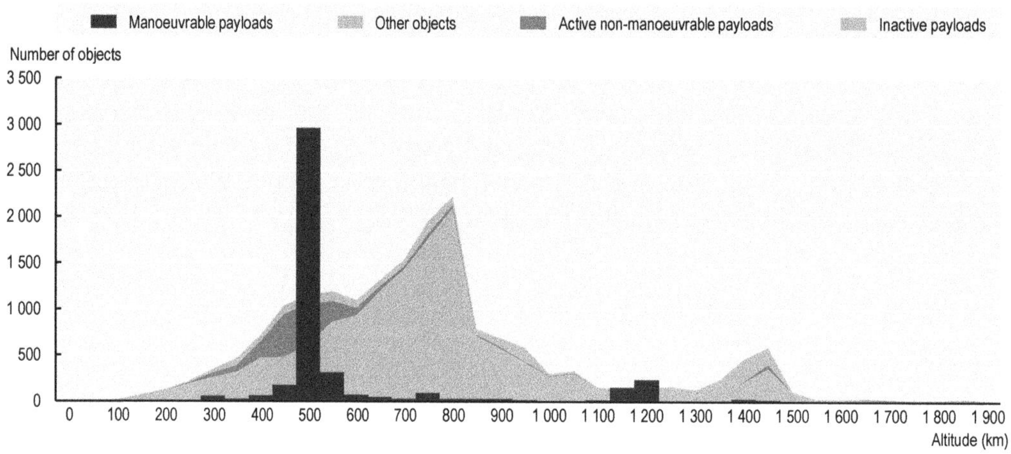

Notes: Payloads refer to space objects (e.g. satellites, space probes) designed to perform a specific function in space, excluding launch functionality. Manoeuvrable payloads typically have an orbit control system (i.e. propulsion system).
Source: ESA (2023[10]), *Annual Space Environment Report 2023*, https://www.sdo.esoc.esa.int/environment_report/Space_Environment_Report_latest.pdf.

In lower orbits below about 650 km altitude, atmospheric drag and other natural phenomena pull debris objects closer to Earth until they mostly burn up upon entering the atmosphere. This process can take days, months or years, depending on the distance to Earth. But in higher LEO orbits, this "natural decay" time is counted in centuries or even thousands of years if above 1 000 km, hence the concentration of objects at these altitudes.

The risk of collision is determined by multiple factors. For example, the density of objects in orbit by both altitude and latitude carries greater risks closer to the poles because of the high number of satellites in sun-synchronous and polar orbits (see Table 2.1). An object's ability or inability to carry out avoidance manoeuvres also determines the risk of collision, making it necessary to distinguish between operational (active) satellites, non-manoeuvrable active satellites and debris objects. Finally, objects' velocity and mass play a role. These latter two factors also affect the number of additional debris objects generated by a collision.

Figure 2.2 shows a 2019 mapping of annual collision risk in LEO, based on modelled accidental close approaches (conjunctions) between active objects; active objects and debris; and between debris objects. Oltrogge and Alfano (2019[14]) estimate the highest accumulated risk at 775 km altitude, with an estimated annual collision rate surpassing 6% and dominated by debris versus debris. The authors note that the analysis covers catalogued objects only (some 4% of the total estimated debris population) and that the actual risk is much higher. Furthermore, this analysis describes the situation at the beginning of the massive deployment of satellite broadband satellites. Between the end of 2019 and 2023, the number of spacecraft tracked by the US Space Force has practically doubled (NASA, 2023[15]).

Figure 2.2. High variation in estimated collision risk in low-earth orbits

Modelled annual collision rates as a function of altitude and types of close approaches, data as of 2019

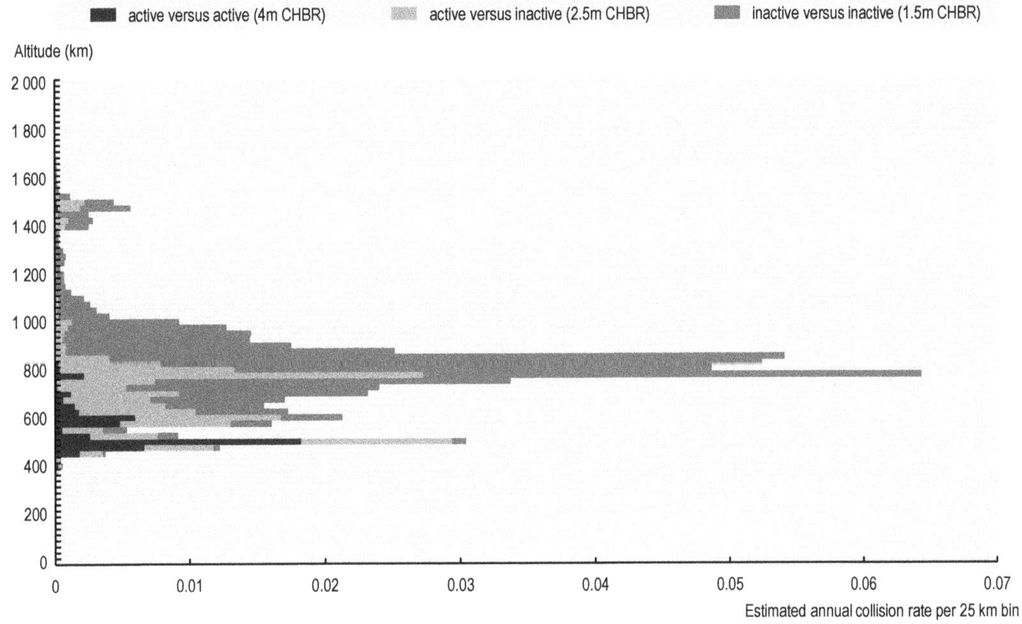

Note: CHBR (combined hard body radius) values are assumed to be 4 metres for non-geostationary (GEO) satellites-on-satellites, 2.5 metres for non-GEO satellites-on-debris and 1.5 metres for non-GEO debris-on-debris.

Source: Oltrogge and Alfano (2019[14]), "The technical challenges of better space situational awareness and space traffic management", *Journal of Space Safety Engineering*, https://doi.org/10.1016/j.jsse.2019.05.004.

Zooming in on high-impact collision risk in LEO (from a debris-generating perspective), McKnight (2021[16]) estimates that the peak risk for future debris generation is situated at 840-975 km and notes that collision risk between active objects in the 500-600 km regions is increasing. This assessment expands on an international effort to statistically identify the most concerning debris objects in LEO which could be good candidates for active debris removal (McKnight et al., 2021[17]).

Researchers at the ESA Space Debris Office have developed a risk metric that combines the probability and severity of an event. This space debris index can be used to compare objects or missions and assess the cumulative risk taken by all objects in space at a given time as well as their behaviour in the future (ESA, 2023[10]; Letizia et al., 2019[18]). Areas with a high risk concentration can be observed at around 850 km of mean altitude and 70-80 degrees inclination (corresponding to a polar orbit). Practically all the risk (97%) is associated with defunct objects, with two-thirds (65%) coming from spent rocket bodies.

Based on the above risk assessments and the database of the Union of Concerned Scientists of operational satellites, some 66% of LEO commercial satellites and 27% of government and military LEO satellites are found in the increasingly congested orbits at 500-600 km altitude. The main risk in these orbits is collisions between active satellites. Only 4% of military LEO satellites and 0.2% of commercial LEO satellites are found in the orbits with peak collision risk, in this case constituted by collisions between debris objects. It is worth noting that the effects of a collision in these orbits can spill over into neighbouring and further afield orbits.

From a traffic management perspective, the 500-600 km orbital region poses considerable co-ordination challenges, with its more than 4 000 satellites and 265 public, private and amateur/university operators from 51 countries. Table 2.3 gives an overview of how the LEO orbits with the highest collision risk exposures are used. Commercial telecommunications dominates in the lower orbits with the highest satellite traffic. Government and military earth observations are more present at higher altitudes, which have the highest debris density including high-risk objects such as multiple derelict rocket bodies (McKnight et al., 2021[17]).

Table 2.3. Operational satellites in orbits at high risk of future debris generation

Data as of 1 May 2023

Mean altitudes (km)	Relative intensity and type of collision risk	Orbit occupancy and composition	Main applications
500-599	Increasing (mainly active versus active satellites, significant presence of non-manoeuvrable satellites)	Total number of satellites: 4 264 Commercial satellite share: 91% Amateur[1] satellite share:2% Number of countries: 56 Number of operators/owners: 304	Commercial telecommunications (Starlink) Commercial earth observation (optical and radar imagery), meteorology, automatic identification system, Internet-of-Things
600-839	High (mixed, both active versus debris and debris versus debris)	Total number of satellites: 553 Commercial satellite share: 33% Amateur satellite share:6% Number of countries: 44 Number of operators/owners: 177	Commercial telecommunications (Iridium, OneWeb) Commercial, government and military earth observation (geospatial and signal intelligence, meteorology, earth science)
840-975	Peak (mainly debris versus debris, including multiple high-mass objects>1 metric tonne)	Total number of satellites: 49 Commercial satellite share: 26% Amateur satellite share:2% Number of countries: 7 Number of operators/owners: 15	Government, military and commercial earth observation (geospatial and signal intelligence, meteorology, earth science)

1. Refers to academic and other "amateur" operators (e.g. amateur radio).
Note: All categories include a small number of dual-use missions (e.g. government-military).
Sources: Based on Oltrogge and Alfano (2019[14]), McKnight (2021[16]) and Union of Concerned Scientists (2024[6]), UCS satellite database, update 1 May 2023, https://www.ucsusa.org/resources/satellite-database.

How to assess the value of space infrastructure and the costs of space debris?

How is society affected by existing space debris and the growing risk of collisions that will generate even more of it? This is the key focus of the OECD project on the economics of space sustainability, which aims to improve decision makers' understanding of the societal value of space infrastructure and the current and future costs imposed by space debris. This evidence is needed to assess the need for debris mitigation and remediation and formulate adequate policy responses.

The negative effects of space debris include costs faced by space operators, such as additional operational costs, loss of spacecraft and foregone opportunities, as well as the costs incurred on society more broadly through a temporary interruption or permanent loss of satellite services due to Kessler's Syndrome (a self-generating chain reaction of collisions between debris objects, see Kessler and Cour-Palais (1978[19])). The total value of the costs of space debris will change according to the level of orbital deterioration.

These two broad categories of negative effects and the different methods used to value their costs monetarily included in this report are presented in Table 2.4. Overall, current operational costs associated with space debris are considered to be "minimal" in the literature. The major share of costs is linked to replacing spacecraft in case of a collision and loss of service revenues. There are furthermore extensive non-market costs, due to the many government and military space missions located in exposed orbital regions.

Table 2.4. Valuation of the costs of space debris

Negative effects		Valuation method	Example
Borne directly by operators	Operational costs (risk assessments, avoidance manoeuvres, etc.)	Labour costs by market value	Colvin, Karcz and Wusk (2023[20])
	Loss of spacecraft	Replacement costs by market value, budgeted cost or insured value	Colvin, Karcz and Wusk (2023[20]), Adilov et al. (2023[21])
	Loss of market satellite services, e.g. telecommunications	Loss of space profits by market value	Rao, Burgess and Kaffine (2020[22])
Borne by public and private operators and/or households	Loss of public satellite services, e.g. data and signals from government missions, such as weather and climate observations, military intelligence and earth science	Stated preference, e.g. willingness-to-pay surveys	Lee et al (Chapter 3 of this report)
		Avoided costs resulting from e.g. improved early warning systems or improved pollution monitoring systems; lives saved; quality-adjusted life years	Eumetsat (2014[23]), Sullivan and Krupnick (2018[24])
		Growth accounting (infers the value of space services from the contribution made to the value of the final product (or service))	Nozawa et al. (2023[25]), Nakama et al. (Chapter 4 of this report),
		Other qualitative and quantitative approaches to indirectly assess the value of space services, such as user surveys, value at risk and value-chain mapping	Catalano and Moretta (Chapter 5 of this report), Vittori et al. (2022[26]),, Sentinel Benefit Studies (EARSC, 2023[27])

Lee, Kim and Hong (2022[28]), in a study conducted during the 2021-22 phase of the OECD project on the economics of space sustainability, provide a comprehensive and useful framework for measuring the costs of space debris. They cover for instance the additional development and operational costs faced by operators due to space debris, such as constellation design, shielding and collision-avoidance manoeuvres; and the direct and indirect costs of interrupted services, loss of research data, etc. This framework importantly incorporates the effects of introducing an additional satellite in the orbital environment, thus increasing the overall collision risk with debris and changing the cost/benefit profile of a mission.

A 2023 NASA cost-benefit analysis for active debris removal (Colvin, Karcz and Wusk, 2023[20]) takes a comprehensive look at the costs of space debris imposed on US operators of different types of missions (ranging from commercial cubesats to government science satellites and large commercial constellations). These costs include the increasing necessity to conduct risk assessments at conjunction (accidental close encounter) warnings, costs generated by avoidance manoeuvres (propellant, labour, temporary loss of services), and the replacement costs and lost services ("operations") in case of a collision. The study finds that the bulk of costs are incurred by collisions (lost vehicle and services), which for most operator categories are caused by small debris objects (1-10 cm). It is worth noting that the study focuses exclusively on the costs potentially incurred by existing space debris, not other active satellites, meaning that the additional traffic management costs in orbits with many active satellites are not included in the calculations.

Following the above, Colvin, Karcz and Wusk (2023[20]) estimate cumulated costs at USD 58 million annually, mainly borne by military and civilian government operators in LEO. The study only counts budgeted operations and programme support costs for these missions, not accounting for other types of "technical, educational, political, and social value" associated with them. This raises a crucial point about the valuation of market and non-market space goods and services (depending on whether or not they are traded in the market), for which market prices do not reflect the full societal value of their use or, as in the case of some public space goods and services, do not exist. These concepts will be further explained in the next paragraphs.

Market goods and services such as satellites, launch services, telecommunications services, etc. are traded in formal markets for prices that are often recorded Assessing the total value of transactions in space market goods and services can be challenging, because of the limited availability of accurate price and quantity statistics, undisclosed transactions and a high level of product customisation in general. Adilov et al. (2023[21]) use available data on insured value to estimate the replacement cost of satellites from collisions with orbital debris. Most of such expected losses were found in LEO, representing some USD 79-102 million annually or 0.16% of the insured value of operational satellites in this orbital region. The study suggests that 70% of losses would occur in orbits at 600-900 km altitude, in line with risk profiles elaborated in the previous section. Rao, Burgess and Kaffine (2020[22]) calculate average annual profits per satellite (USD 2.1 million in 2015), based on estimated revenues from industry-led surveys of establishments in space manufacturing, launch services and multiple "downstream" services, i.e. services that rely on the exploitation of satellite data and signals (see OECD (2022[29]) for space activity definitions and categories).

Non-market goods and services are not traded in markets or do not have an economically significant price – a typical example is public goods provided by the government. In the space economy, such goods are very common. Indeed they are often the key objective of space activities and include for instance military systems; science and exploration missions; meteorology and climate observations; and civilian-military navigation systems, also covering the civilian government and military missions identified by Colvin, Karcz and Wusk above. These activities contribute among other things to improved security, improved public health, and a better managed environment. Focusing on earth observation, Table 2.5 lists some of the most mature applications, most of which come from satellites in sun-synchronous LEO orbits and some that represent the only data source available (OECD, 2023[30]).

Table 2.5. Selected mature earth observation applications and their benefits

Sector	Application	Description
Climate and weather monitoring	Climate monitoring	Space-based observations account for at least half of the essential climate variables that are used to monitor climate change, mainly atmospheric observations but also ocean and land cover characteristics, such as sea surface temperatures, ocean colour, terrestrial vegetation types and ice caps.
	Weather forecasting	The inclusion of space-based observations in numerical weather prediction models allows for more precise and timely forecasts. Satellite observations are particularly important in the southern hemisphere, where *in-situ* observations are sparser than in northern regions. Data denial simulations indicate that withholding satellite observations degrades forecasting skill at day 5 by about two days in the southern hemisphere, compared to 0.5 days in the northern hemisphere (McNally, 2015[31]) Improvements in forecasting skill are associated with considerable cost avoidance and lives saved, see for instance Eumetsat (2014[32]).
Environmental protection	Biodiversity and ecosystem monitoring	Satellite data are essential for detecting and monitoring land cover change (e.g. human conversions of land from a more natural state to a more artificial state that has potentially large implications for ecosystems and biodiversity). While land cover change is a proxy and does not directly measure biodiversity; changes in the spatial structure of natural habitats are considered the best measure currently available to broadly monitor pressures on terrestrial ecosystems and biodiversity (see Hašcic and Mackie (2018[33])).
Disaster management		Satellite imagery contributes to improved disaster prevention planning (land use) and emergency response, by detecting and mapping affected areas and functions. The International Charter for Space and Major Disasters provides satellite imagery and maps free of charge to disaster-affected countries around the world. Initiated in 2000 by the European, Canadian and French space agencies, it was supported by more than 20 organisations in 2023, involving 270 satellites. Since its introduction, the Charter has been activated more than 750 times, by 130 countries (International Charter Space and Major Disasters, 2023[34]).
Food production and security	Crop monitoring	In addition to the benefits of more accurate weather forecasts that are essential for adequately timing planting and harvesting, multi- and hyperspectral imagery can monitor crop vitality and water stress, thus ensuring a more targeted and efficient use of water, pesticides and fertiliser and allowing for higher yields (see for instance the Copernicus Sentinel data benefit studies carried out on farm management in Denmark and Poland (EARSC, 2023[27])).
	Land use management	Compared with other types of data and observations, e.g. land use censuses and aerial surveys, space-based observations offer regularly updated, wide-angle imagery with a growing range of applications following the evolutions in instruments (e.g. hyperspectral imagery) and spatial and temporal resolution.

Sector	Application	Description
		It can be particularly useful in areas where access to field information is limited and smallholder subsistence agriculture dominates (Becker-Reshef et al., 2020[35]).

Source: OECD (2023[36]), *The Space Economy in Figures: Responding to Global Challenges*, https://doi.org/10.1787/fa5494aa-en.

By not accounting for the monetary value of non-market goods and services, one underestimates the full societal value of space-based infrastructure. While not yet very common in the space sector, several initiatives, such as the GEOValue community, the NASA-funded VALUABLES Consortium and the Sentinel Benefits studies funded by the European Space Agency and the European Union, are providing more evidence in this area (GeoValue, 2024[37]; Valuables Consortium, 2024[38]; EARSC, 2023[27]). An international community of practitioners is forming, with the support of the Group on Earth Observations and the OECD Space Forum, which hosted a GEOValue workshop in 2016 together with NASA and the US Geological Survey.

Common methodologies include revealed preference techniques that take advantage of the fact that such goods and services sometimes affect consumer preferences for market products and are therefore implicitly traded in markets; techniques for estimating avoided and replacement costs that indirectly rely on market valuation; stated preference techniques such as willingness-to-pay surveys; estimates of the value of statistical lives saved and/or improved; and growth accounting methods that attempt to estimate the contribution of inputs of space goods and services to the final output of a marketed product.

The value of public earth observation satellites at risk from space debris is studied within the Korean context, in Chapter 3 authored by Lee et al. Using contingent valuation to assess the potential lost value of Korean earth observation satellites in LEO due to space debris incidents, the study identifies an aggregated value loss of EUR 369.6 million (USD 388.7 million) over ten years, indicating not only the importance of the societal services provided by these satellites but also broad popular support for space debris mitigation.

Eumetsat (2014[23]) estimates a minimum of EUR 1.3 billion yearly in avoided costs to property and infrastructure due to improved warning lead times to better prepare for floods, storms and other severe weather phenomena. In North America, a 2018 Resources for the Future study suggests that the information provided by satellite-derived air pollution monitoring systems in the United States could save roughly 2 700 lives annually over and above an alternative scenario where monitoring does not occur. This represents some USD 24.5 billion in avoided social costs, based on a standard value of statistical life (Sullivan and Krupnick, 2018[24]).

It is important to have a thorough understanding of the effects of space services on enabling economic production more broadly. Nozawa et al. (2023[25]) use an economic growth model, augmented with a satellite sector and collision possibility, to model the long-term effects of space debris on global gross domestic product (GDP). The study estimates a 1.95% difference in GDP levels in 2020 between the "business-as-usual" baseline scenario and the most optimistic scenario with a 90% debris removal rate. In Chapter 4, Nakama et al. formulate an aggregate production function to demonstrate the direct and indirect effects of satellite telecommunications and GNSS on society. They explore the link between the penetration and utilisation of space-enabled information and communication services and economic growth in sparsely populated Japanese prefectures with less than 1 million inhabitants.

The total global value of economic activity at risk is estimated to be USD 191 billion with the bulk of the value at risk concentrated in orbits at 500-600 km altitude, by Vittori et al. (2022[26]). They identify economic activities that are fully or partially supported and/or enabled by space-based infrastructure, in a contribution to Phase 1 of the OECD project on the economics of space sustainability. In the second step, they estimate the economic activity at risk from an irreversible deterioration of orbits by combining data on gross value added with estimated dependencies on satellite data and signals and the probability of orbital deterioration.

More qualitative approaches also support this analysis. In Chapter 5, Catalano and Morretta survey Italian (mainly public) end users of earth observation services to better understand these services' penetration in the economy, how they are used and how they contribute to economic performance. A similar survey of Italian firms from Phase 1 of the OECD project found that earth observation services contributed to firms' process and output innovation (e.g. new and improved quality of products and services) and translated into higher turnover and employment (Lupi and Morretta, 2022[39]). This research is supported by numerous case studies on satellite data value chains, such as those conducted within the framework of the Sentinel Benefit Study (EARSC, 2023[27]).

Finally, although it is important not to underestimate the value of space-based infrastructure and services, neither should it be overestimated. In Chapter 6, Paravano et al. study commercial end users in potentially high-value markets such as insurance and finance and energy and utility. They find that these users recognise the potential of satellite data, but face difficulties in realising the expected value over the long term. This could be due to a lack of access to the competencies required to operate specialised technology, interpret satellite data and integrate them into products.

Is compliance with existing debris mitigation measures insufficient to stabilise the orbital environment?

From an economic perspective, Earth's orbital environment is a "common pool resource" (Ostrom, 2009[40]), characterised by a low level of excludability and high subtractability. The use of Earth's orbits by one actor does not prevent others from accessing the same orbits, but the creation of debris could negatively affect future access to space. This is the economic rationale for government intervention in this policy domain.

The first such measures, consisting of voluntary guidelines for debris limitation and mitigation, were introduced at the national level in the 1980s and 1990s. International space debris mitigation measures were first formulated in 2001 and later updated in 2007, with the Space Debris Mitigation Guidelines of the Inter-Agency Debris Coordination Committee (IADC, 2007[12]). These have later been complemented by the Guidelines for the Long-Term Sustainability of Space Activities (UN COPUOS, 2018[41]), and other efforts, e.g. the ISO standard 24113:2023 and International Telecommunications Union recommendation ITU-R S.1003.2 for the geostationary orbit (ITU, 1993[42]).

Countries adapt debris mitigation guidelines to their own national frameworks in different ways (the United Nations Office for Outer Space Affairs provides a non-exhaustive compendium of national provisions) (UNOOSA, 2021[43]). Measures are often voluntary, but in some countries, debris mitigation measures are built into satellite licensing processes (e.g. Canada, France, Korea, United Kingdom, United States). Furthermore, national provisions may be performance-based (e.g. New Zealand) or technology-based (France).

Debris mitigation measures address the most common and harmful sources of debris creation. They focus on several issues: limiting debris during routine operations; minimising the potential for in-orbit break-ups; and conjunction analysis and warning to operators to avoid collisions. They also recommend clearing orbits after the operational end-of-mission within a specific time frame, namely 25 years at the international level (IADC, 2007[12]). However, several organisations are considering shortening it to five years, as is the case for example with the European Space Agency in its Zero Debris Approach (2023[2]).

Studying operator compliance with debris mitigation guidelines since 2000 suggests a positive trend in post-mission disposal both for satellites and rocket bodies. Figure 2.3 breaks down compliance with post-mission disposal guidelines by type of operator: amateur (universities), public (civilian and defence) and commercial actors. Commercial operators have performed significantly better since 2010, mostly because of a surge in commercial activities in orbital regions where satellites decay naturally within the recommended time limit (ESA, 2023[10]). The European Space Agency (ESA) estimates that in 2022, some 55% of satellites and 85% of rocket bodies cleared their orbit 25 years or earlier after their end-of-mission. This is a clear improvement compared with previous years – in 2012, the equivalent figures were 15% for satellites and 10% for rocket bodies – but is still not good enough. Operator compliance would need to approach 100% in order to slow down the ongoing chain reaction of collisions (ESA, 2023[10]).

Figure 2.3. Orbit clearance trends by type of operator and over time

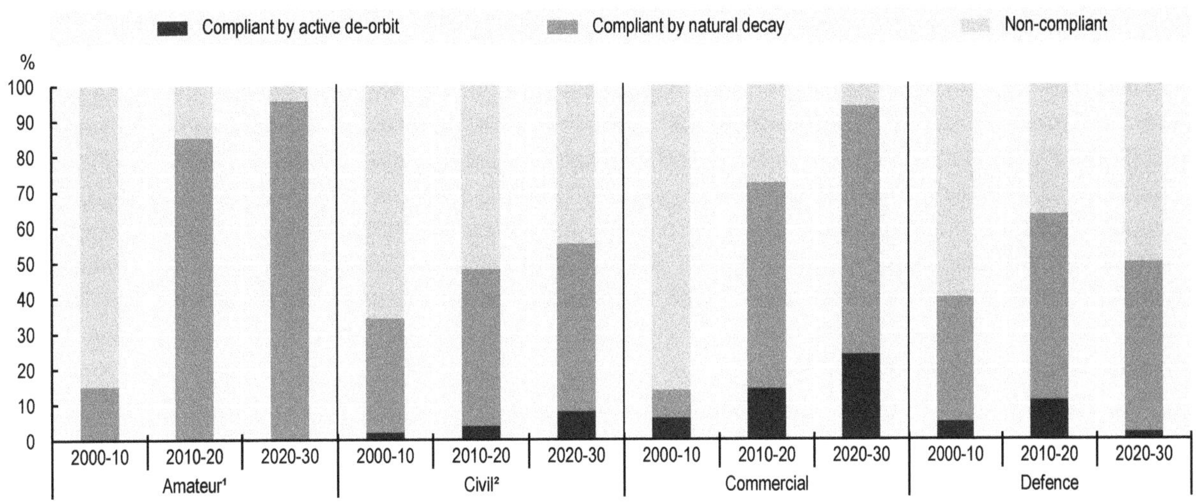

1. Refers to academic and other "amateur" operators (e.g. of amateur radio satellites).2. "Civil" refers to non-military government operators.
Source: ESA (2023[10]), *Annual Space Environment Report 2023*,
https://www.sdo.esoc.esa.int/environment_report/Space_Environment_Report_latest.pdf.

What explains operators' non-compliance? Debris mitigation provisions are generally voluntary, providing few incentives for compliant behaviour. At 650 km altitudes and above, orbit clearance requires dedicated equipment and fuel to actively deorbit the satellite within the stipulated time limit and therefore represents a significant cost to operators. Furthermore, post-mission disposal can also be technologically challenging, with several attempts resulting in failure every year (ESA, 2023[10]). In view of the necessity to clear close to 100% of satellites and rocket bodies from orbits, there is much room for improvement and additional policy efforts. This is the focus of the next section.

How to formulate effective policy responses to address space debris issues?

Governments will need to take a multi-pronged approach to tackle space debris and address changes in the risk landscape. Steps should include reinforcing technological capabilities, reviewing and updating existing policies and, potentially, formulating new policy responses. In parallel, several industry-led initiatives are underway. Table 2.6 presents some of the most common types of policy options for environmental management, including voluntary approaches, command-and-control regulations (e.g. mandatory technological standards) and incentive-based mechanisms (e.g. taxes and subsidies).

Table 2.6. Selected types of environmental policy instruments

Incentive-based measures	Command-and-control regulation	Voluntary approaches
Address the economic incentives of commercial actors and include charges	Direct government regulation accompanied by negative sanctions in	Non-binding approaches to engage stakeholders and build consensus,

Incentive-based measures	Command-and-control regulation	Voluntary approaches
(deposit-refund, taxes and fees), tradeable permits, subsidies and market friction reductions (e.g. liability rules)	the case of non-compliance, e.g. technology and performance standards, emission targets, product bans	e.g. guidelines, industry commitments and environmental labels

Sources: Based on OECD (2024[44]), "Policy Instruments for the Environment Database", https://www.oecd.org/environment/indicators-modelling-outlooks/policy-instruments-for-environment-database/ and Jack, Kousky and Sims (2008[45]), "Designing payments for ecosystem services: Lessons from previous experience with incentive-based mechanisms", https://doi.org/10.1073/pnas.0705503104.

Supporting technological solutions for tracking, mitigation and remediation

First and foremost, technological capabilities need to be strengthened to better assess and manage risks. Potential measures range from improving public and commercial capabilities to detect and track very small orbital objects, to developing more reliable and affordable deorbiting systems for satellites, and maturing capabilities to actively remove specific debris objects (e.g. the high-mass/high-risk objects discussed in previous sections). Improved technological solutions for space situational awareness (SSA) and traffic management are also required, including for example the development of systems to consolidate and share information from multiple sources. Several new initiatives have been launched or are underway. The importance of technological solutions is highlighted for instance in the US National Orbital Debris Implementation Plan (NSTC, 2022[46]).

The orbital environment is monitored by public and private terrestrial and space-based radars and telescopes. In the OECD area, the US Space Force has the strongest public capabilities with more than 170 data-sharing agreements with other countries and private and academic actors in 2023 (US Space Command, 2023[47]). Still, the catalogue covers only a fraction of potentially harmful objects and the extent of information shared remains restricted. This is creating demand for more civil-military joint structures and commercial SSA data and services.

Technical solutions are required for combining different types of data and information and making them available to operators. In the United States, the Office of Space Commerce is developing a Traffic Coordination System for Space (TraCSS) that will provide basic SSA and space traffic co-ordination services to commercial civilian space operators. Contracts have been awarded to commercial firms for providing and testing data products (Office of Space Commerce, 2024[48]). In Europe, the European Union Space Surveillance and Tracking (EU SST) Partnership entered into force in 2022 and consolidates the capabilities of 15 EU member states. It is operated by the European Union Agency for the Space Programme. The United Kingdom will establish a civil-military National Space Operations Centre in 2024 and has announced contracts with several commercial SSA service providers.

From a space traffic management perspective, research is carried out to develop assignment systems in LEO. These are similar to existing slots in the geostationary orbit that are governed internationally by the International Telecommunications Union. Slotting in LEO is complex, as it must allow for "multiple altitudes, eccentricities and overlapping orbits" (Arnas et al., 2021[49]). Arnas et al. (2021[49]) propose a slotting system that preserves a minimum separation distance between satellites.

More progress is also needed on designing more sustainable spacecraft, missions and developing safe and affordable satellite debris removal services. A 2024 NASA study reviewing the costs and benefits of capabilities for mitigating, tracking and remediating orbital debris found that several remediation capabilities (e.g. using lasers to "nudge" large debris off course) compare favourably to capabilities for mitigation and tracking (Locke et al., 2024[50]). Furthermore, the use of lightweight drag devices for deorbit manoeuvres could be particularly cost-efficient (with benefits up to 1 000 times greater than costs), but it was also associated with an increased probability of collision (Locke et al., 2024[50]).

In Europe, ESA has been championing debris-mitigative technologies since 2009. Efforts are directed at research and development (R&D) for environmentally-friendly satellite design, end-of-life technologies, active debris removal and in-orbit servicing. The agency is funding a Swiss-led consortium to actively remove a 112 kg defunct upper-stage rocket currently located in the 664-801 km altitude range, with a planned mission in 2026 (ESA, 2024[51]). Japan's Aerospace Exploration Agency (JAXA) is also supporting commercial active debris solutions. In early 2024 it launched the ADRAS-J satellite to survey a three-tonne Japanese rocket stage through rendezvous and proximity operations. The ultimate aim of the project is to capture and deorbit a large object in the 2025-26 timeframe. Finally, the UK Space Agency has procured active debris removal services for two UK satellites, with the mission planned for 2026 (Astroscale, 2023[52]). Governments are also supporting in-orbit servicing solutions for mission extensions (e.g. the United Kingdom and France and previously the United States). Work is ongoing to normalise in-orbit servicing through industry guidelines (in the consortium for Execution of Rendezvous and Servicing Operations (CONFERS)) and through standards, such as the ISO 24330:2022.

These activities are examples of catalytic procurement, where government actors "kickstart" markets for active debris removal. As discussed in Toussaint and Dumez (2022[53]), these markets suffer from a chicken-and-egg problem and need some kind of public intervention to get started including R&D support, service buys and potentially also government missions to develop and demonstrate technologies. Overall, there is an increased focus on the demand for "green" space technologies, although a consensus on this term's precise meaning does not yet exist (see Box 2.2).

Box 2.2. Understanding "green" space applications and technologies

There is growing use of the term "green" space technologies, but there is no unified understanding of its meaning.

First, it refers to space-based contributions to "green" research, i.e. research that contributes to the green transition such as sustainable energy technologies and food production, circular economy, etc. The Danish Agency for Higher Education and Science defines space-based green research as "a subset of green research conducted in space or based on data and observations from space - either entirely or partly [...]" (Danish Agency for Higher Education and Science, 2022[54]). The same type of observations can be used to support metrics for the emerging fields of "green" finance and investment (see for instance OECD, (2023[36]).

Another meaning of "green" space technologies focuses on the space industry's environmental footprint vis-à-vis terrestrial pollution. For instance, hydrazine is appreciated as a relatively simple and reliable monopropellant for space rockets. It is also highly toxic and is categorised by the European Chemical Agency as a "substance of very high concern", requiring high precaution during storage and use. The industry is searching for less toxic alternatives. Other aspects of this strand of work look at resource depletion, land and water use, carbon emissions and effects on the ozone layer (ESA, 2024[55]).

Finally, the state of the orbital environment adds another dimension to "green" space technologies. This element includes the design of satellites and missions that minimise the chances of accidental explosions and the release of debris. It also includes features that facilitate active removal, such as identifying markers or grappling hooks; in-orbit servicing solutions that extend a satellite's mission life such as refuelling or simple repairs; and, finally, active debris removal services.

Participants in the OECD project on the economics of space sustainability have tried to clarify the concepts of green space technologies and use bibliometrics to provide insights and policy guidance (Dos Santos Paulino and Pulsiri, 2022[56]). The resulting analysis divides green space technology into two domains, space and earth, with the space domain further separated into four types: green energy and propulsion, green material (e.g. nanotube or green-coating materials); green method (e.g. life-cycle assessments); and green service (e.g. in-orbit servicing).

Reinforcing existing policies

Faced with the combined challenges of orbital congestion from active spacecraft and growth in the debris population, debris mitigation policies are evolving. In the United States, the Federal Communications Commission updated its satellite debris mitigation rules in 2020, its first update since 2004. It introduces new disclosure requirements for satellite applicants, for instance to assign numerical values to collision risk and to provide detailed information on the spacecraft's manoeuvrability and trackability. Moreover, in 2022 the Commission voted to reduce the post-mission disposal period for new satellite applications from 25 to 5 years (FCC, 2020[57]; 2022[58]).

In Europe, the European Space Agency has launched a Zero Debris policy aiming for a considerable reduction of debris generation by 2030. The new policy includes updated space debris mitigation requirements for the agency's programmes and projects (ESA, 2023[59]). These provisions also reduce the time limit for post-mission disposal from 25 to 5 years. Furthermore, spacecraft without recurrent manoeuvre capability are proscribed from higher-risk orbital regions (where natural decay durations are much longer). The European Space Agency also tries to "retrofit" older missions to adhere to updated environmental standards. For example, the assisted re-entry of the earth observation satellite Aeolus over the ocean in 2023 was a technological feat because the spacecraft (originally designed in the 1990s and finally launched in 2018) was not designed for such manoeuvres (ESA, 2023[60]). The objective was to reduce the risk of harmful terrestrial debris in case some pieces of the spacecraft did not burn up when re-entering the atmosphere.

Governments are also strengthening oversight and enforcement. In 2019 the New Zealand Space Agency entered a multi-year agreement with commercial space situational awareness service provider LeoLabs for a Space Regulatory and Sustainability Platform, to track New-Zealand licensed satellites. The UK Space Agency and other agencies also purchase commercial services to track satellites under their jurisdiction. In 2023, the US Federal Communications Commission issued its first-ever fine, amounting to USD 150 000, for non-compliance with post-mission disposal rules, when satellite TV provider Dish Network failed to move a geostationary satellite to an assigned "graveyard" orbit due to insufficient fuel (FCC, 2023[61]). The European Commission is drafting a first-ever European space law, where space sustainability is one of the important elements.

Finally, government policy is complemented by several emerging industry-led measures, mainly covering voluntary guidelines and standards as well as information- and data-sharing networks. Organisations such as the Space Data Association, created in 2009, facilitate the sharing of operational data and best practices among satellite operators and work to improve the accuracy and timeliness of collision warning notifications. Other initiatives include the Space Safety Coalition, established in 2019, and the Net Zero Space Initiative, launched in 2021.

Several environmental labels are also emerging. The most mature label is the Space Sustainability Rating (SSR), designed and supported by multiple actors including the World Economic Forum, the European Space Agency and the Space Enabled research group at Massachusetts Institute of Technology and hosted by the Swiss Federal Institute of Technology in Lausanne (EPFL). It provides a composite indicator that aggregates and weights different aspects of mission design and operation and translates ratings into four labels (bronze, silver, gold and platinum) (SSR, 2024[62]). In Chapter 8, Yap and David explore the demand for such labels under different future scenarios. In the United Kingdom, the UK Space Agency supports work to create an earth and space sustainability Kitemark for insurance underwriting and environmental social and governance investment (UKSA, 2023[63]). The Kitemark is a quality and reliability label of the British Standards Institution.

Exploring incentive-based policies

The existing and projected growth in space traffic, the insufficient level of compliance with existing policy frameworks and the current high cost of debris removal and remediation options constitute a considerable challenge for policy makers. Possible solutions that have been proposed include incentive-based policies such as in-orbit third-party liability insurance, marketable permits, regulatory fees, and performance bonds.

For example, the US Federal Communications Commission has expressed an interest in exploring the use of performance bonds to incentivise operators to clear satellites from orbit (FCC, 2020[57]). Such initiatives address two different but interrelated issues: pollution (accidental and intentional space debris creation including non-compliance with post-mission disposal rules) and congestion (orbit occupancy).

Various measures have been proposed to address pollution. First, **in-orbit third-party liability insurance** holds operators responsible for the pollution that they cause while in orbit and is compulsory in some countries such as France, Japan and the United Kingdom. The objective is to incentivise operators to avoid harmful practices in the first place and to ensure that polluters, not taxpayers, cover clean-up costs. The United Kingdom introduced a sliding-scale policy in 2018 aimed at addressing the various levels of severity of space risks by offering the possibility to reduce or even waive insurance requirements for low-orbit/low-risk missions (UK Space Agency, 2018[64]). This is an interesting approach to lowering the barriers to access for more sustainable activities. Critics of in-orbit liability insurance schemes argue that the actual risk of collision is not reflected in insurance pricing and that the insurance market is not set up to tackle an actual claim (Samson, Wolny and Christensen, 2018[65]). Furthermore, there are the problems of insufficient SSA to enable enforcement and the difficulties in attributing actions and debris to specific operators, as well as in determining what constitutes actionable standards of behaviour. Responses to some of these challenges are starting to emerge, as described in the previous sections on industry voluntary standards such as the Space Sustainability Index or the proposed Kitemark for space sustainability.

Then there are **deposit-refund schemes** as proposed for instance by Macauley (2015[66]) which are commonly used in other domains to facilitate waste collection and reduce littering. Operators first pay a tax that is subsequently refunded upon evidence of compliance with a specific action (a space-related example would be the satellite clearing orbit). The performance bonds that interest the US Federal Communications Commission work in a similar fashion in terms of their incentive effect, but they also create tradeable, interest-bearing assets (Adilov, Alexander and Cunningham, 2023[67]). However, great attention would have to be paid to the design and pricing of the measure – experiences from the mining industry in Australia, Canada and the United States show that the level of securities obtained often only partially covers the estimated environmental liabilities – and enforcement can also be a problem (Undseth, Jolly and Olivari, 2020[68]).

Several options are also proposed in the literature for regulating congestion in orbit, notably **launch and satellite taxes** and **cap-and-trade systems**. Examples of such proposals include Adilov, Alexander and Cunningham (2015[69]), Rao, Burgess and Kaffine (2020[70]) and Rouillon (2020[71]). (See also Ateca-Amestoy et al. (2022[72]), which was a contribution to the OECD project on space sustainability in 2021-22). All authors work on the assumption that insufficient government regulation will lead to unsustainable growth in the number of satellites, increasing the collision risk between two active satellites and between active satellites and debris. thereby generating an escalation in economic costs. According to Rao, Burgess and Kaffine (2020[70]), the introduction of orbital-use fees would ensure more efficient use of Earth's orbits and quadruple the long-run value of the space industry by 2040.

Appropriate design will be important for the incentive-based policy options, in terms of the intended objectives (e.g. post-mission disposal or reduced congestion), timing and pricing of the measure. In Chapter 7, Scuderi discusses the design issues of fiscal instruments in greater detail.

How to assess the effects of policy options aimed at improving the orbital environment?

The assessment of policy options needs to be based on their expected effects on the orbital environment and the economy, as well as on their feasibility from a legal and political perspective. So what steps are required for their successful implementation and over which time horizon?

Econometric analysis of policy options for debris mitigation and orbital use is increasingly sophisticated, involving physical-economic models that account for the orbital environment on the one hand and economic behaviour on the other (as applied in for example Rouillon (2020[71]), Rao, Burgess and Kaffine (2020[70]), Rao and Letizia (2021[73]) and Guyot, Rao and Rouillon (2022[74])).

More recently, at the 2023 OECD Space Forum workshop on space sustainability, the Massachusetts Institute of Technology released the beta version of an open-source tool to model the long-term future space environment (MIT Orbital Capacity Assessment Tool - MOCAT) and assess the effects of debris mitigation policy options. The tool provides access to modelling capacities previously reserved for government agencies (Liberty, 2024[75]), as mentioned in Box 1.2. This type of analysis makes it possible to model the relative medium- and long-term effects of policy measures on the orbital environment, albeit under simplified and simulated conditions.

The econometric studies suggest that existing standard-based guidelines on post-mission disposal and satellite/mission design would in some cases be less effective than incentive-based options. Sometimes they may even be counterproductive for stabilising the orbital environment. The following reasons are given:

- Full compliance with existing guidelines may have unintended consequences, such as a higher concentration of objects in lower-altitude orbits with natural debris decay (Rao and Letizia, 2021[73]).
- Furthermore, active debris removal may encourage higher launch activity and therefore more congestion (similar to a rebound effect) (Rao, Burgess and Kaffine, 2020[70]; Rouillon, 2020[71]).
- An imposition of technological standards could lead to economic efficiency losses, for example reducing incentives to innovative (Adilov, Alexander and Cunningham, 2015[69]).
- Explicit taxes that directly target a desired outcome may encourage innovative substitution strategies and also raise revenue (Rao et al., 2023[76]).

This aligns with other environmental research that suggests that incentive-based approaches have proven effective in the regulation of common pool resources such as fish stocks or ground water and in pollution abatement. For example, OECD research on the effects of the European Union cap-and-trade programme to reduce carbon emissions shows that the programme reduced emissions by 10% on average in the 2005-10 period, with no significant impact on the jobs and profits of regulated firms, while simultaneously stimulating "green" innovation to reduce costs (Dechezleprêtre, Nachtigall and Venmans, 2018[77]; Calel and Dechezleprêtre, 2016[78]).

There are, however, several concerns associated with increased stringency of environmental regulation in the space sector, whether such measures are command-and-control or incentive-based.

The first concern is linked to the **competitiveness of the space sector** and the risk of leakage (towards "pollution havens") if policies are not universally applied. The risk of such leakage is affected by the ability of space activity to relocate and the degree of change in the relative costs for operators. Concerning relocation, the number of space launch providers offering launch services to non-domestic clients is growing. There are six economies with demonstrated commercial services to non-domestic clients: the People's Republic of China, India, Europe (in French Guiana), New Zealand, the Russian Federation (through its spaceport in Kazakhstan) and the United States. There are also recently established spaceports in Norway and the United Kingdom and several others currently under development (OECD,

2023[36]), However, the choice of a launch location and licensing organisation is limited by other factors, such as the distance to orbit, launch slot availability and timeliness as well as rockets' flight histories. The limiting factors only apply to purely commercial and civilian missions that are unaffected by trade regulations. Concerning the change in relative costs for operators, these still need to be determined and would largely depend on the type of mission and the nature of the environmental regulation.

The second concern relates to the **technological, legal and geopolitical feasibility** of introducing binding regulations. As above, this varies according to the type of measure, with the enforcement of in-orbit third-party liability rules reliant on precise monitoring capabilities and insurance pricing policies that reflect the collision risk. Neither of these currently exist. Other policy options may be easier to implement at the national level, as illustrated by existing mandatory debris mitigation provisions in several OECD member countries. In the absence of full international consensus, the effects of unilateral action or policy convergence among like-minded countries have been explored in the literature (e.g. in Percy and Landrum (2014[79]) and Jain and Rao (2022[80])). A research project at the University College London, which has participated in the OECD project on the economics of space sustainability (see Box 2.3), is looking at the possibility of introducing space sustainability as a Sustainable Development Goal. This would raise further awareness about the importance of space sustainability at decision maker level and may result in the development of comprehensive metrics to assess country performance and monitor change over time.

Box 2.3. Building metrics for an 18th Sustainable Development Goal for space sustainability

A multi-disciplinary team of students and researchers at University College London in the United Kingdom has explored the use of the framework of the United Nations Sustainable Development Goals (SDGs) to catalyse international discourse, action, and commitment towards maintaining the long-term viability of the near-earth environment.

The essence of effective SDGs lies in their measurability. Hence, the incorporation of straightforward and user-friendly metrics is of utmost importance (Table 2.7). These metrics should enable a comprehensive evaluation of various sustainability facets, ensuring the reliability and accessibility of the requisite data. Furthermore, they should be capable of conveying the issue at hand succinctly to a diverse audience.

Table 2.7. Suggested metrics for an 18th Sustainable Development Goal for space sustainability

Operational resident space objects and launches (annual)	Space debris	Participation of countries in space activities	Internet connectivity
• Total number of launches • Number of satellites that re-entered the atmosphere and burned up, either due to deliberate de-orbiting or natural decay • Number of satellites placed into graveyard orbits • Total number of operational satellites in orbit • Total number of non-operational satellites in orbit • Vis-viva law estimate of operational satellite object energy	• Number of new objects generated annually by launch/deployment (including rocket bodies) • Number of collision events per year: i) spacecraft to spacecraft; ii) spacecraft to debris; iii) debris to debris • Number of explosive or break-up events per year • Number of new debris objects spawned by collisions, explosions, or break-up events • Running total of all debris objects in orbit	• Number of countries benefiting from space technology • Number of countries directly utilising space technology • Number of countries owning and operating space technology • Number of countries running a space/space technology programme	• Percentage of the global population with routine access to the Internet • Number of countries with open access (non-splinternet) to the World Wide Web

Source: Ziebart et al. (2023[81]), "The 18th Set of UN Sustainable Development Goals for Space Sustainability: An initial consideration".

The proposed metrics collectively constitute a global space situational awareness dashboard, serving as a real-time snapshot of the status of the space domain. There are four main categories. Firstly, the category of "operational resident space objects and launches" provides a measure of active engagement in space and allows for an evaluation of the potential impact on the orbital environment. Secondly, "space debris" serves as a crucial indicator of space sustainability, directly impacting the safety and viability of current and future space operations. Thirdly, "participation of countries in space activities" is a valuable proxy for the global democratisation of space access, a critical aspect in achieving the inclusive nature of SDGs. Finally, "internet connectivity" has been included given its growing reliance on space-based infrastructure and its paramount importance for economic activity, societal development, and access to crucial services such as food security information.

Source: Ziebart et al. (2023[81]), "The 18th Set of UN Sustainable Development Goals for Space Sustainability: An initial consideration".

The **broader effects** on the composition and growth of the space innovation ecosystem should also be considered. Do some measures (e.g. launch taxes or caps on the number of satellites in orbit) give undue advantages to incumbents? Are some measures more conducive to promoting innovation? In any case, more stringent environmental regulation in the space sector must not be introduced in isolation but be part of a holistic and mutually reinforcing space policy framework without competing policy goals.

The best policies will most likely include elements of several instrument types, with certain combinations more compatible than others (Gunningham and Sinclair, 2017[82]). Judging by experience in other domains, Gunningham and Sinclair (2017[82]) suggest that voluntarism combines well with command-and-control minimum performance benchmarks, but less well with prescriptive technological standards which give no or little room for manoeuvre. Meanwhile, superimposing command-and-control regulation on incentive-based options that target the same behaviour would limit the opportunity to exploit differences in the marginal cost of abatement between firms.

Similarly, to increase effectiveness, the design and implementation of policy measures would need to be tailored to specific sectoral, national, and international contexts, including different legal frameworks and administrative roles and capabilities.

Next steps

This chapter has summarised key findings on the economics of space sustainability so far, with a focus on space debris issues. The following chapters add to an increasingly well-equipped toolbox for addressing space debris at the government level by providing new evidence on the valuation of space-based infrastructure and policy option assessments.

Future avenues of OECD-led research could involve delving deeper into the effects of different policy options (command-and-control, incentive-based and voluntary) and exploring how specific objectives affect policy design. Other items would include the interaction and effects of policy mixes for space sustainability and how international and domestic administrative and legal arrangements may affect outcomes.

The long-term uses of our space environment are at risk and the OECD work on the economics of space sustainability will continue to support the creation of more evidence to underpin needed corporate and policy decisions at all levels.

References

Adilov, N., P. Alexander and B. Cunningham (2023), "The economics of satellite deorbiting performance bonds", *Economics Letters*, Vol. 228, p. 111150, https://doi.org/10.1016/j.econlet.2023.111150. [67]

Adilov, N., P. Alexander and B. Cunningham (2015), "An Economic Analysis of Earth Orbit Pollution", *Environmental and Resource Economics*, Vol. 60/1, pp. 81-98, https://doi.org/10.1007/s10640-013-9758-4. [69]

Adilov, N. et al. (2023), "An estimate of expected economic losses from satellite collisions with orbital debris", *Journal of Space Safety Engineering*, Vol. 10/1, pp. 66-69, https://doi.org/10.1016/j.jsse.2023.01.002. [21]

Arnas, D. et al. (2021), "Definition of Low Earth Orbit slotting architectures using 2D lattice flower constellations", *Advances in Space Research*, Vol. 67/11, pp. 3696-3711, https://doi.org/10.1016/j.asr.2020.04.021. [49]

Astroscale (2023), *Astroscale on course for first UK national mission to remove space debris*, webpage, https://astroscale.com/astroscale-on-course-for-first-uk-national-mission-to-remove-space-debris/#:~:text=The%20COSMIC%20mission%20%E2%80%93%20Cleaning%20Outer,currently%20orbiting%20Earth%20by%202026. [52]

Ateca-Amestoy, V. et al. (2022), "Estimation of the costs and benefits of debris mitigation", in *Earth's Orbits at Risk: The Economics of Space Sustainability*, OECD Publishing, Paris, https://doi.org/10.1787/b87da674-en. [72]

Becker-Reshef, I. et al. (2020), "Strengthening agricultural decisions in countries at risk of food insecurity: The GEOGLAM Crop Monitor for Early Warning", *Remote Sensing of Environment*, Vol. 237, p. 111553, https://doi.org/10.1016/j.rse.2019.111553. [35]

Calel, R. and A. Dechezleprêtre (2016), "Environmental Policy and Directed Technological Change: Evidence from the European Carbon Market", *Review of Economics and Statistics*, Vol. 98/1, pp. 173-191, https://doi.org/10.1162/rest_a_00470. [78]

CEOS (2023), *CEOS database (October 2023 update)*, Committee on Earth Observation Satellites, https://database.eohandbook.com/. [9]

Colvin, T., J. Karcz and G. Wusk (2023), *Cost and benefit analysis of orbital debris remediation*, NASA Office of Technology, Policy and Strategy, https://www.nasa.gov/wp-content/uploads/2023/03/otps_-_cost_and_benefit_analysis_of_orbital_debris_remediation_-_final.pdf?emrc=507712. [20]

Danish Agency for Higher Education and Science (2022), *Rumbaseret grøn forskning: Bibliometrisk analyse af Danmarks rum-baserede grønne forskning*, https://ufm.dk/publikationer/2022/filer/rumbaseret-gron-forskning-bibliometrisk-analyse-af-danmarks-rumbaserede-gronne-forskning. [54]

Dechezleprêtre, A., D. Nachtigall and F. Venmans (2018), "The joint impact of the European Union emissions trading system on carbon emissions and economic performance", *OECD Economics Department Working Papers*, No. 1515, OECD Publishing, Paris, https://doi.org/10.1787/4819b016-en. [77]

Dos Santos Paulino, V. and N. Pulsiri (2022), “Safeguarding Earth and space’s environment: Issues and trends towards sustainable development”, *International Journal of Technology Management & Sustainable Development*, Vol. 21/3, pp. 353-376, https://doi.org/10.1386/tmsd_00063_1. [56]

EARSC (2023), *Sentinel Benefits Studies (SeBS) portal*, webpage, https://earsc.org/sebs/. [27]

ESA (2024), “clearspace-1”, *ESA website*, webpage, https://www.esa.int/Space_Safety/ClearSpace-1. [51]

ESA (2024), *Ecodesign*, webpage, https://www.esa.int/Space_Safety/Clean_Space/ecodesign. [55]

ESA (2023), *Annual Space Environment Report 2023*, European Space Agency, ESA Space Debris Office, https://www.sdo.esoc.esa.int/environment_report/Space_Environment_Report_latest.pdf. [10]

ESA (2023), *ESA Space Debris Mitigation Requirements*, ESSB-ST-U-007 Issue 1, https://technology.esa.int/upload/media/DGHKMZ_6542582e18e33.pdf. [59]

ESA (2023), *Guiding Aeolus’ safe reentry*, webpage, https://www.esa.int/Applications/Observing_the_Earth/FutureEO/Aeolus/Guiding_Aeolus_safe_reentry. [60]

ESA (2023), *Short introduction to ESA’s Zero Debris Approach*, webpage, https://blogs.esa.int/cleanspace/2023/01/12/short-introduction-to-esas-zero-debris-approach/. [2]

EUMETSAT (2014), *The case for EPS/Metop Second Generation: Cost Benefit Analysis - Full Report*, European Organisation for the Exploitation of Meteorological Satellites, Darmstadt, https://www.wmo.int/pages/prog/sat/meetings/documents/PSTG-3_Doc_11-04_MetOP-SG.pdf (accessed on 5 June 2018). [23]

Eumetsat (2014), *The case for EPS/Metop Second Generation: Cost Benefit Analysis - Full Report*, https://www.wmo.int/pages/prog/sat/meetings/documents/PSTG-3_Doc_11-04_MetOP-SG.pdf (accessed on 5 June 2018). [32]

Falle, A. et al. (2023), “One million (paper) satellites”, *Science*, Vol. 382/6667, pp. 150-152, https://doi.org/10.1126/science.adi4639. [11]

FCC (2023), *FCC takes first space debris enforcement action*, 2 October, https://docs.fcc.gov/public/attachments/DOC-397412A1.pdf. [61]

FCC (2022), *Space Innovation IB Docket No. 22-271 Mitigation of Orbital Debris in the New Space Age IB Docket No. 18-313*, https://docs.fcc.gov/public/attachments/FCC-22-74A1_Rcd.pdf. [58]

FCC (2020), *Orbital Debris in the New Space Age, Report and Order and Further Notice of Proposed Rulemaking*, FCC report FCC-20-54, http://FCC-20-54A1_Rcd.pdf. [57]

GeoValue (2024), *GeoValue Community Portal*, https://geovalue.org/. [37]

Gunningham, N. and D. Sinclair (2017), *Smart regulation*, ANU Press, http://www.jstor.org/stable/j.ctt1q1crtm.16. [82]

Guyot, J., A. Rao and S. Rouillon (2022), *The long-run economics of sustainable orbit use*, BxWP2022-13, Bordeaux School of Economics, https://bordeauxeconomicswp.u-bordeaux.fr/2022/2022-13.pdf. [74]

Haščič, I. and A. Mackie (2018), "Land Cover Change and Conversions: Methodology and Results for OECD and G20 Countries", *OECD Green Growth Papers*, No. 2018/04, OECD Publishing, Paris, https://doi.org/10.1787/72a9e331-en. [33]

IADC (2007), *IADC Space Debris Mitigation Guidelines*, Inter-Agency Space Debris Coordination Committee. [12]

International Charter Space and Major Disasters (2023), *The International Charter Space and Major Disasters website*, https://disasterscharter.org/web/guest/home. [34]

ITU (1993), *Recommendation ITU-R S.1003*, International Telecommunications Union, https://www.itu.int/dms_pubrec/itu-r/rec/s/R-REC-S.1003-0-199304-S!!PDF-E.pdf. [42]

Jack, B., C. Kousky and K. Sims (2008), "Designing payments for ecosystem services: Lessons from previous experience with incentive-based mechanisms", *Proceedings of the National Academy of Sciences*, Vol. 105/28, pp. 9465-9470, https://doi.org/10.1073/pnas.0705503104. [45]

Jain, A. and A. Rao (2022), *International cooperation and competition in orbit-use management*, https://arxiv.org/abs/2205.03926v2. [80]

Kessler, D. and B. Cour-Palais (1978), "Collision frequency of artificial satellites: The creation of a debris belt", *Journal of Geophysical Research*, Vol. 83/A6, p. 2637, https://doi.org/10.1029/JA083iA06p02637. [19]

Lee, C., K. Kim and J. Hong (2022), "An environmental economics framework for measuring the cost of space debris", in *Earth's Orbits at Risk: The Economics of Space Sustainability*, OECD Publishing, Paris, https://doi.org/10.1787/3c45519e-en. [28]

Letizia, F. et al. (2019), "Application of a debris index for global evaluation of mitigation strategies", *Acta Astronautica*, Vol. 161, pp. 348-362, https://doi.org/10.1016/j.actaastro.2019.05.003. [18]

Liberty, J. (2024), *Researchers release open-source space debris model*, 10 January, https://news.mit.edu/2024/researchers-release-open-source-space-debris-model-0110. [75]

Locke, J. et al. (2024), *Cost and Benefit Analysis of Mitigating, Tracking, and Remediating Orbital Debris*, US National Aeronautics and Space Administration, https://www.nasa.gov/wp-content/uploads/2024/05/2024-otps-cba-of-orbital-debris-phase-2-plus-svgs-v3-tjc-tagged.pdf?emrc=224cd2. [50]

Lupi, V. and V. Morretta (2022), "Socio-economic benefits of earth observation: Insights from firms in Italy", in *Earth's Orbits at Risk: The Economics of Space Sustainability*, OECD Publishing, Paris, https://doi.org/10.1787/5982c4af-en. [39]

Macauley, M. (2015), "The economics of space debris: Estimating the costs and benefits of debris mitigation", *Acta Astronautica*, Vol. 115, pp. 160-164, https://doi.org/10.1016/j.actaastro.2015.05.006. [66]

McDowell, J. (2024), *Jonathan's Space Report*, website, https://planet4589.org/space/index.html. [7]

McKnight, D. (2021), *Updating the massive collision monitoring activity - creating a collision risk continuum*, Conference proceedings, ESA Space Debris Office, https://conference.sdo.esoc.esa.int/proceedings/sdc8/paper/22. [16]

McKnight, D. et al. (2021), "Identifying the 50 statistically-most-concerning derelict objects in LEO", *Acta Astronautica*, Vol. 181, pp. 282-291, https://doi.org/10.1016/j.actaastro.2021.01.021. [17]

McNally, A. (2015), *The impact of satellite data on NWP*, Proceeding at the Seminar on Use of Satellite Observations in Numerical Weather Prediction, 8-12 September 2014, https://www.ecmwf.int/en/elibrary/75624-impact-satellite-data-nwp. [31]

NASA (2024), *Monthly total of objects in orbit by object type*, status as of 3 February 2024, data provided by the NASA Orbital Debris Office. [13]

NASA (2024), *NASA's Space Sustainability Strategy*, US National Aeronautics and Space Administration, https://www.nasa.gov/spacesustainability/. [3]

NASA (2023), , *Orbital Debris Quarterly News*, Vol. 27/1, https://orbitaldebris.jsc.nasa.gov/quarterly-news/pdfs/odqnv27i1.pdf. [15]

Nozawa, W. et al. (2023), "To What Extent Will Space Debris Impact the Economy?", *Space Policy*, Vol. 66, p. 101580, https://doi.org/10.1016/j.spacepol.2023.101580. [25]

NSTC (2022), *National Orbital Debris Implementation Plan*, US National Science and Technology Council, https://www.whitehouse.gov/wp-content/uploads/2022/07/07-2022-NATIONAL-ORBITAL-DEBRIS-IMPLEMENTATION-PLAN.pdf. [46]

OECD (2024), *Policy Instruments for the Environment Database*, webpage, https://www.oecd.org/environment/indicators-modelling-outlooks/policy-instruments-for-environment-database/. [44]

OECD (2023), "Space as a provider of critical data and innovative applications", in *The Space Economy in Figures: Responding to Global Challenges*, OECD Publishing, Paris, https://doi.org/10.1787/f2a02d19-en. [30]

OECD (2023), *The Space Economy in Figures: Responding to Global Challenges*, OECD Publishing, Paris, https://doi.org/10.1787/fa5494aa-en. [36]

OECD (2022), *OECD Handbook on Measuring the Space Economy, 2nd Edition*, OECD Publishing, Paris, https://doi.org/10.1787/8bfef437-en. [29]

OECD (2019), "Digital (r)evolution in manufacturing and in the production of space systems", in *The Space Economy in Figures: How Space Contributes to the Global Economy*, OECD Publishing, Paris, https://doi.org/10.1787/bd1505f8-en. [8]

Office of Space Commerce (2024), *Office of Space Commerce places orders for SSA data quality monitoring pathfinder*, webpage, 5 March, https://www.space.commerce.gov/office-of-space-commerce-places-orders-for-ssa-data-quality-monitoring-pathfinder/. [48]

Oltrogge, D. and S. Alfano (2019), "The technical challenges of better Space Situational Awareness and Space Traffic Management", *Journal of Space Safety Engineering*, Vol. 6/2, pp. 72-79, https://doi.org/10.1016/j.jsse.2019.05.004. [14]

Ostrom, E. (2009), “Beyond Markets and States: Polycentric Governance of Complex Economic Systems”, Nobel Prize Lecture, 8 December, Stockholm. [40]

Percy, T. and D. Landrum (2014), “Investigation of national policy shifts to impact orbital debris environments”, *Space Policy*, Vol. 30/1, pp. 23-33, https://doi.org/10.1016/j.spacepol.2014.02.003. [79]

Peterson, K. (2003), “Satellite Communications”, in *Encyclopedia of Physical Science and Technology*, Elsevier, https://doi.org/10.1016/b0-12-227410-5/00673-6. [4]

Rao, A., M. Burgess and D. Kaffine (2020), “Orbital-use fees could more than quadruple the value of the space industry”, *Proceedings of the National Academy of Sciences*, Vol. 117/23, pp. 12756-12762, https://doi.org/10.1073/pnas.1921260117. [70]

Rao, A., M. Burgess and D. Kaffine (2020), *Orbital-use fees could more than quadruple the value of the space industry*, Proceedings of the National Academy of Sciences, https://doi.org/10.1073/pnas.1921260117. [22]

Rao, A. and F. Letizia (2021), *A coupled econometric model of the orbital environment*, ESA Space Debris Office, https://conference.sdo.esoc.esa.int/proceedings/sdc8/paper/206/SDC8-paper206.pdf. [73]

Rao, A. et al. (2023), *OPUS: An integrated assessment model for satellites and orbital debris*, this work was supported by the 2022 NASA ROSES programme, https://arxiv.org/pdf/2309.10252.pdf. [76]

Riebeek, H. (2009), *Catalog of earth satellite orbits*, 4 September, https://earthobservatory.nasa.gov/features/OrbitsCatalog. [5]

Rouillon, S. (2020), “A Physico-Economic Model of Low Earth Orbit Management”, *Environmental and Resource Economics*, Vol. 77/4, pp. 695-723, https://doi.org/10.1007/s10640-020-00515-z. [71]

Samson, V., J. Wolny and I. Christensen (2018), *Can the Space Insurance Industry Help Incentivize the Responsible Use of Space?*, https://swfound.org/media/206275/iac-2018_manuscript_e342.pdf. [65]

SSR (2024), *Space Sustainable Rating website*, https://spacesustainabilityrating.org/. [62]

Sullivan, D. and A. Krupnick (2018), “Using Satellite Data to Fill the Gaps in the US Air Pollution Monitoring Network”, Resources for the Future, Washington, DC, https://www.rff.org/publications/working-papers/using-satellite-data-to-fill-the-gaps-in-the-us-air-pollution-monitoring-network/ (accessed on 21 February 2019). [24]

The White House (2023), *G7 Hiroshima Leaders’ Communiqué*, 20 May, Government of the United States, https://www.whitehouse.gov/briefing-room/statements-releases/2023/05/20/g7-hiroshima-leaders-communique/. [1]

Toussaint, C. and H. Dumez (2022), “On the emergence of an active debris removal market”, in *Earth’s Orbits at Risk: The Economics of Space Sustainability*, OECD Publishing, Paris, https://doi.org/10.1787/fc689ef6-en. [53]

UCS (2024), *UCS satellite database, update 1 May 2023*, Union of Concerned Scientists, https://www.ucsusa.org/resources/satellite-database. [6]

UK Space Agency (2018), *Modern regulation to support UK's growing space sector*, 1 october, webpage, https://www.gov.uk/government/news/modern-regulation-to-support-uks-growing-space-sector. [64]

UKSA (2023), *UK Space Agency launches consultation on variable liability limits for orbital operations*, 14 September, https://www.gov.uk/government/news/uk-space-agency-launches-consultation-on-variable-liability-limits-for-orbital-operations. [63]

UN COPUOS (2018), *Guidelines for the Long-term Sustainability of Space Activities*, UN Committee on the Peaceful Uses of Outer Space, Vienna, http://www.unoosa.org/res/oosadoc/data/documents/2018/aac_1052018crp/aac_1052018crp_20_0_html/AC105_2018_CRP20E.pdf (accessed on 15 March 2019). [41]

Undseth, M., C. Jolly and M. Olivari (2020), "Space sustainability: The economics of space debris in perspective", *OECD Science, Technology and Industry Policy Papers*, No. 87, OECD Publishing, Paris, https://doi.org/10.1787/a339de43-en. [68]

UNOOSA (2021), *Compendium: Space debris mitigation standards adopted by states and international organizations*, United Nations Office of Outer Space Affairs, https://www.unoosa.org/documents/pdf/spacelaw/sd/Space_Debris_Compendium_COPUOS_8_Apr_2021.pdf. [43]

US Space Command (2023), *USSPACECOM and the Qatar Armed Forces sign Space Situational Awareness Data Sharing Agreement*, 31 October, https://www.spacecom.mil/Newsroom/News/Article-Display/Article/3574832/usspacecom-and-the-qatar-armed-forces-sign-space-situational-awareness-data-sha/#:~:text=USSPACECOM%20holds%20more%20than%20170,about%20responsible%20behaviors%20in%20space. [47]

Valuables Consortium (2024), *Valuables Consortium Portal*, Resources for the Future, https://www.rff.org/valuables/. [38]

Vittori, D. et al. (2022), "Identifying the costs caused by an irreversible deterioration of the orbital regimes", in *Earth's Orbits at Risk: The Economics of Space Sustainability*, OECD Publishing, Paris, https://doi.org/10.1787/74213960-en. [26]

Ziebart, M. et al. (2023), *The 18th set of UN Sustainable Development Goals for space sustainability: An initial consideration*, report submitted as part of the OECD project on the economics of space sustainability. [81]

3 Valuing the cost of space debris: the loss of Korean satellites in low-earth orbit

Chanhee Lee, Seoul National University, Korea

Jong Ho Hong, Seoul National University, Korea

Jinyoung Kang, National Research Council for Economics, Humanities, and Social Sciences, Korea

Keewon Kim, Seoul National University, Korea

Habin Kim, Seoul National University, Korea

Heeyoung Seo, Seoul National University, Korea

Space debris presents an increasing challenge to the sustainable use of Earth's orbits, particularly for emerging space nations like Korea. This chapter delves into the often-neglected social value of non-market satellites at risk from space debris within the Korean context and uses contingent valuation to quantify the costs of a space debris incident involving an earth observation satellite. The findings underline the profound significance of these satellites to national welfare and indicate that space debris can lead to substantial social costs.

Introduction

Technological advances and the ongoing expansion of space-faring entities have brought the issue of space debris and the potential for Kessler's syndrome to the fore (Kessler, 1991[1]; Kessler and Cour-Palais, 1978[2]). This trajectory of development and the challenges it brings call for an understanding of the Earth's orbits as a global common-pool resource, (or as an extension of the Earth's ecosystem) and an international conversation on their sustainable management (Lawrence et al., 2022[3]; Morin and Richard, 2021[4]; Newman and Williamson, 2018[5]). Previous dialogues have resulted in several milestones, such as the Inter-Agency Debris Coordination Committee (IADC) Space Debris Mitigation Guidelines (IADC, 2007[6]), and the Guidelines on the Long-term Sustainability of Outer Space Activities (UNOOSA, 2018[7]). Further discussions regarding how best to implement these sustainability practices have also been launched.

An important building block is to clearly understand the costs associated with space debris. Many current business models in the space sector do not incorporate social costs into their decision making processes, resulting in environmental externalities. In economic theory, such externalities can be addressed by introducing an appropriate economic instrument (e.g. a Pigouvian tax) that levies a cost amounting to the environmental damage caused. However, accurately quantifying the costs remains challenging, especially when market prices do not exist or do not fully reflect societal values. Satellites serving public purposes (hereafter "public satellites"), such as climate monitoring, disaster management, and/or national defence, are prime examples. Given that these satellites often have missions tailored to specific national needs, establishing a common measurement for their value becomes even more complex.

However, previous literature has often overlooked public satellites, mainly focusing on commercial satellites (Bongers and Torres, 2023[8]; Rao, Burgess and Kaffine, 2020[9]). This implies that the potential loss faced by countries that predominantly manage public satellites has been largely neglected. Considering that the loss of public satellites affects the broader societal welfare and national interests of a country, the blind spot may be much larger than anticipated. The key contribution of this chapter is to place a spotlight on the lost value of public satellites.

The scope of this study is limited to Korean satellites in low-earth orbit (LEO), where the risks posed by space debris are highest. As all current and planned satellite operations were found to have been assigned earth observation missions, this study specifically quantifies the potential lost value of Korean earth observation satellites in LEO due to space debris incidents. The focus lies on non-market valuation, such as the scientific, governmental, and public benefits provided by the satellites in question. Nonetheless, the results tie back to the global challenge of estimating the cost of space debris, given that the most significant impact of space debris at this time is the destruction and subsequent loss of functionality of satellites.

While the geopolitical context of Korea is distinct, which may amplify public concerns and the sense of loss from critical collision events to a certain extent, the results of the study can provide valuable insight into what is at stake for emerging space players. For instance, the loss of a single satellite can carry considerably more weight for such countries as they run a limited number of satellites. Given such local and global implications, this study can be instrumental in informing policy, directing resources effectively, and strengthening international co-operation to ensure the sustainable use of the Earth's orbits.

In the following section, the research method, including data collection and scenario design, is described. The authors subsequently explain their estimation model, followed by the analysis of results, before discussing the implications and conclusions of the study.

Methodology

Contingent valuation

This study estimates the socio-economic costs arising from the damages caused by space debris using contingent valuation (CV), which elicits willingness-to-pay (WTP) for a contingent commodity based on survey responses. The method holds particular strength in revealing the value of non-market goods and services that are not directly traded in the market and, hence, where traditional market data is sparse. Public satellites fall into this category, as they are predominantly characterised by their public purpose and, thus, the benefits they provide lie largely beyond the realm of market transactions. Another advantage of CV lies in its ability to measure total economic value. This implies that the WTP estimate can serve as a comprehensive assessment of a commodity's value, encompassing both use and non-use values.

Meanwhile, the utmost care must be given in all steps of the process, from defining the contingent commodity to designing and administering the survey, to ensure that the results of the CV study are robust. In accordance with Carson (1998[10]), who underscored the importance of shaping the contingent commodity to hold relevance within the local context, this study chose to estimate the cost of space debris through the value attached to preventing the loss of Korean earth observation satellites in LEO due to space debris incidents. In the scenario, the subject of valuation was materialised into a satellite protection programme. The remaining sections of this chapter elaborate on the subsequent procedures for conducting the survey.

Table 3.1. Survey overview

	Main survey
Population	All households in Korea
Survey period	7-14 August 2023
Sampling method	Quota sampling based on age, region, and gender
Sample size	1 028
Protesters	183 (17.8%)
Survey mode	Web-based survey
Elicitation method	Single-bounded dichotomous choice (SBDC)
Payment vehicle	Increased income tax (entirely allocated to a Satellite Protection Fund)
Time frame of payment	One-time payment
Valued goods	Lost value of Korean earth observation satellites in the low-earth orbit due to space debris incidents
Contingent commodity	Avoiding the loss of satellites due to space debris
Policy options	Satellite protection programme (radar, thruster, shield)
Bid offered	KRW 1 000, 5 000, 10 000, 20 000, 30 000 EUR 0.7, 3.7, 7.4, 14.7, 22.1

Note: 1. EUR 1 = KRW 1 358 (European Central Bank, 2023) 2. Currency conversion is rounded to the first decimal place.

Data collection

The sample consisted of a panel provided by a leading survey agency in Korea. To ensure it accurately represented the general population, the authors adopted quota sampling, based on age, gender, and region.

Due to cost and time constraints, a web-based survey was chosen as the method of data collection (see Table 3.1). A total of 1 032 responses were collected from 7 August to 14 August, but four observations were discarded during the preliminary data cleaning phase: two that indicated they had no annual income, including pensions and unearned income, and two that reported household sizes of 15 or more members. Therefore, the final sample consisted of 1 028 respondents. A comparison of the sample's demographic characteristics with the general population confirmed that the sample was representative in terms of age, gender, and region (see Appendix A).

Survey development and design

Focus groups

The focus groups were carried out in three stages, held on 25 March, 29 April and 24 June, respectively. Each focus group had 5~7 participants, carefully selected to represent diverse backgrounds. The majority had little or no prior knowledge of orbital debris. Given this general lack of familiarity, the first two rounds focused on gauging the average level of interest and knowledge on the topic, as well as identifying key concerns when provided with information on the deteriorating environment in LEO. The second stage concentrated on observing participants' responses to the draft scenario, with particular attention to the issue of credibility. The final stage centred on receiving feedback on the final draft of the survey to ensure that respondents could comprehend all contents clearly.

Pilot survey

The pilot survey was conducted online from 26 July to 27 July, during which 201 responses were collected. The primary purpose was to evaluate the potential response and protest rates, suitable bid levels, and whether any modifications were needed. According to the results, no significant changes were deemed necessary, with a moderate protest rate of 5.5%. In terms of bid levels, respondents were presented with an open-ended question to establish a range of acceptable bid amounts. This process led to the identification of five bid levels, which were determined based on the 15th to 85th percentile range of the responses. These bid levels were set at KRW 1 000 (EUR 0.7), KRW 5 000 (EUR 3.7), KRW 10 000 (EUR 7.4), KRW 20 000 (EUR 14.7), and KRW 30 000 (EUR 22.1). These bid amounts represent incremental increases over the current tax levels that respondents are paying.

Questionnaire

The questionnaire consisted of four sections. The first section was intended to warm up respondents by asking them about their attitudes toward various government policies. The following section presented the scenario with information on the current state of debris in LEO, followed by the dichotomous choice question and debriefing questions to identify protest bidders. The third section asked about attitudes toward science, technology and the environment, as variables potentially correlated with one's response. The final section collected demographic information, including gender, age, parental status, education level, occupation, and religious belief.

A distinctive feature of the survey was that the scenario was presented in three short videos. This approach was considered advisable to facilitate engagement with and understanding of a scenario involving unfamiliar, distant, and complex subject matters (i.e., objects in outer space and new space technology). To ensure that the information was perceived and processed, respondents were not allowed to skip through the video and were required to take a follow-up quiz that recapitulated the most crucial segments. If so desired, they could replay the video.

Scenario

The scenario began by describing the launch plans for Korea within the next three years. As all the country's satellites currently in orbit (i.e., four earth observation satellites) would reach the end of their lifetimes by 2025, they were to be replaced by new ones developed with enhanced skills and technology. In the baseline scenario, however, orbital debris and the likelihood of a critical collision event were expected to increase quickly, to the extent that all the newly launched satellites would lose their functionality within ten years. The implication was a serious threat to national security, broadly defined to encompass disaster and climate change management, public safety, national defence, food security, and land management.

The policy option included measures to predict, prevent and mitigate the impact of space debris incidents. In order to minimise bias, emphasis was put on the fact that the policy would not lead to technological advancement within the country, instead benefitting from products and services already available in the market. In the alternative scenario, in which the policy is adopted, all the newly launched satellites were expected to remain fully functional for the next ten years. The payment vehicle was a one-time tax payment that would be contributed to a national fund designated for the sole purpose of protecting the country's satellites. Bid amounts, determined based on the results of the pilot survey, were randomly assigned from the five options listed above.

In developing the scenario, the authors actively sought advice from experts and scientists in the space sector to ensure that the contents were sound from both scientific and policy perspectives. For further information on the scenario presented to respondents, see Appendix B.

Model estimation

The elicitation method of this study was single-bounded dichotomous choice (SBDC). Given the method, this section first explains the conventional approach of estimating WTP, then describes the baseline model of this study, which better accounts for protest responses (i.e. zero bids motivated by protest behaviour).

Conventional approach

According to the random utility framework and assuming that preferences are linear in income and covariates (Haab and McConnell, 2002[11]; Hanemann, 1984[12]), the respondent i's indirect utility can be expressed as:

$$u_{ij} = \alpha_j X_i + \beta_j y_i + \varepsilon_{ij} \tag{1}$$

where u_{ij} is respondent i's utility with $(j = 1)$ or without $(j = 0)$ the change, X_i is the vector of personal or household characteristics, y_i is income, and ε_{ij} are unobserved preferences. A respondent will accept the bid (i.e. answer 'yes') if they enjoy higher utility in the alternative scenario with the policy, despite the loss of utility from paying the offered bid, t_i. Therefore, the response probability (i.e. the probability of answering 'yes') is:

$$\begin{aligned} \Pr(yes_i) &= \Pr(\alpha_1 X_i + \beta_1 (y_i - t_i) + \varepsilon_{i1} > \alpha_0 X_i + \beta_0 y_i + \varepsilon_{i0}) \\ &= \Pr(\alpha X_i - \beta t_i + \varepsilon_i > 0) \end{aligned} \tag{2}$$

where $\alpha = \alpha_1 - \alpha_0$, $\beta = \beta_1 - \beta_0$, and $\varepsilon_i = \varepsilon_{i1} - \varepsilon_{i0}$.[1] Assuming further that ε_{ij} is independently and identically distributed and follows a standard normal distribution, the response probability can be estimated with the binary probit model as:

$$\Pr(yes_i) = \Pr(\varepsilon_i < \alpha X_i - \beta t_i) = \Phi\left(\frac{\alpha X_i - \beta t_i}{\sigma}\right) \quad (3)$$

where $\Phi(\cdot)$ is a standard normal distribution function, σ is the standard deviation of the error term, and α and β are the parameters of interest.

Given the above, the parameter estimates can be obtained by maximising the following log-likelihood function:

$$\ln L = \sum_{i=1}^{n} Y_i \ln\left[\Phi\left(\frac{\alpha X_i - \beta t_i}{\sigma}\right)\right] + (1 - Y_i)\ln\left[1 - \Phi\left(\frac{\alpha X_i - \beta t_i}{\sigma}\right)\right] \quad (4)$$

where $Y_i = 1$ if respondent i answers 'yes'.

The expected value of WTP for respondent i, which renders them indifferent between the baseline and alternative scenario, can be found by using eq. (1) and conditioning on the parameters as:

$$E_\varepsilon(WTP_i|\alpha, \beta, X_i) = \frac{\alpha/\sigma}{\beta/\sigma} X_i = \frac{\alpha X_i}{\beta}. \quad (5)$$

The mean WTP, $\alpha\bar{X}/\beta$, is an expansion of eq. (5) over the entire sample and can be calculated with the parameter estimates from eq. (4) and confidence intervals following the procedures of Krinsky and Robb (1986[13]).

Sample selection model

The conventional approach, however, may result in an under- or overestimation depending on how protest responses are treated.[2] Including protest bids as 'true zero' WTP valuations risks underestimation, since the true WTP may be positive; on the other hand, excluding protest bids, as suggested by Mitchell and Carson (1989[14]), risks overestimation and the exclusion may introduce selection bias (Strazzera et al., 2003[15]). Therefore, this study adopts a sample selection model, which can produce more reliable WTP estimates. In this model, the respondent's decision can be understood as a joint process, in which they first decide whether to reveal (or state) their WTP, then decide whether to accept the offered bid (Eom and Hong, 2009[16]; Strazzera et al., 2003[15]; Sun, Yuan and Yao, 2016[17]). The former is modelled by the latent variable I_i^*, which is affected by a vector of respondent characteristics, Z_i, while the latter is modelled by the latent variable Y_i^*, which also depends on a vector of respondent characteristics, X_i.

$$I_i^* = Z_i'\gamma + v_i \quad (6)$$

$$Y_i^* = X_i'\beta + \varepsilon_i \quad (7)$$

where v_i and ε_i are error terms.

Whilst neither I_i^* nor Y_i^* are observed, the respective decisions are, thus allowing the joint process to be modelled as Eq. (8). A respondent will reveal their WTP $(I_i = 1)$ if the utility of doing so is greater than or equal to zero $(I_i^* \geq 0)$ and they will accept the bid $(Y_i = 1)$ if their WTP at least amounts to the bid, t_i.

$$\begin{cases} I_i = 1, if\ I_i^* \geq 0 \rightarrow \begin{cases} Y_i = 1, if\ Y_i^* \geq t_i \\ Y_i = 0, if\ Y_i^* < t_i \end{cases} \\ I_i = 0, if\ I_i^* < 0 \end{cases} \tag{8}$$

Accordingly, the likelihood function can be expressed as

$$L = \prod_{I_i=0} P(I_i^* < 0) \cdot \prod_{I_i=1} \left[\prod_{Y_i=1} P(I_i^* \geq 0, Y_i^* \geq t_i) \cdot \prod_{Y_i=0} P(I_i^* \geq 0, Y_i^* < t_i) \right]. \tag{9}$$

Assuming the joint distribution of (v_i, ε_i) follows a bivariate normal distribution with mean zero and the variances of v_i and ε_i are normalised to 1, the log-likelihood is:

$$ln\, L = \sum_{i=1}^{n} (1 - I_i) \ln[1 - \Phi(Z_i'\gamma)] + \sum_{i=1}^{n} Y_i\, I_i \ln\left[\Phi\left(X_i'\beta, Z_i'\gamma, \rho\right)\right] + \sum_{i=1}^{n} (1 - Y_i)\, I_i \ln[\Phi(-X_i'\beta, Z_i'\gamma, -\rho)] \tag{10}$$

where ρ denotes the correlation coefficient between v_i and ε_i (Brouwer and Martín-Ortega, 2012[18]). The mean WTP in the sample selection model is calculated by maximising the above equation, which is comparable to eq. (4) in the conventional approach.

Results

Descriptive statistics

Table 3.2 provides the statistical summary of the survey sample. Beginning with the demographic variables, the average age of respondents hovered around 48 years. Gender representation was balanced, with males and females each making up roughly 50% of the sample. Respondents reported an average annual household income of KRW 56.05 million (EUR 41 274). For education level, where 1 indicates the completion of a 4-year university programme or above and 0 otherwise, 64% of the respondents were found to be highly educated. Finally, the average household size was about three members.

Attitudinal variables were included to capture an individual's awareness, beliefs, and trust in various areas of relevance. 61% indicated prior awareness of the concept of "space debris." Among these informed participants, 71% traced their source to television or newspapers, while 21% referred to YouTube. Environmental attitudes were measured using Dunlap's revised New Ecological Paradigm (NEP) scale, which includes 15 items probing one's ecological worldview (Dunlap et al., 2000[19]). After reverse coding the even-numbered items, so that a higher score represents stronger alignment with the ecological paradigm, and summating the scores of all items, the average score settled at 55 out of 75 points.

The survey also incorporated six items from the "Science and Technology" section of the World Value Survey to assess respondents' perceptions of science and technology (Haerpfer et al., 2022[20]). Using reverse coding to ensure that higher scores indicate more positive views, the average score was observed to be 40 out of 60 points. Lastly, participants were asked to rate their level of trust in government-led policy projects on a 5-point Likert scale, where 1 signifies the least amount of trust and 5, the maximum. The average trust score was 2.7, implying a moderate level of trust in government.

Table 3.2. Summary statistics

Variable category	Variables	Mean	Standard deviation	Min-max
Demographic	Age	47.83	14.54	19 - 79
	Gender (male = 1)	0.50	0.50	0 - 1
	Household income	5 605	4 046	0 – 40 000
	Education level	0.64	0.48	0 - 1
	Household size	3.01	1.31	1 - 9
Attitudinal	Awareness of space debris	0.61	0.49	0 - 1
	Environmental attitude	54.55	7.45	36 - 75
	Attitude toward science	40.09	6.77	17 - 60
	Trust in government	2.69	0.94	1 - 5

N = 1 028. The annual income is displayed in units of KRW 10 000.

Protest response

Among the total of 1 028 respondents, 221 (21.5%) indicated a zero WTP. In order to discern protest bids from true zero bids, the survey included a debriefing question seeking to understand the reasons behind the zero response (Table 3.3). The options were presented randomly, with the exception of "other" which always appeared last, to guard against potential order effects. The results revealed that a significant 82.8% of the zero bids were protest bids, amounting to 17.8% of the entire sample.

Table 3.3. Identification of zero-value bids

		Items	.Frequency	%
True zero willingness-to-pay	1	I cannot afford to pay	23	10.4
	2	Protecting satellites holds no value for me	3	1.4
	3	Our society faces more pressing issues than satellite problems	9	4.1
	4	Other	3	1.4
	Subtotal		38	17.3
Protest bids	5	The survey lacks sufficient information to make a judgement	6	2.7
	6	The government should address the problem with the taxes already collected	95	43.0
	7	Those causing the problems, not the general public, should bear the costs	9	4.1
	8	It's doubtful that funds will be exclusively used for the 'satellite protection programme'	23	10.4
	9	The government plan is not trustworthy	50	22.6
	Subtotal		183	82.8
Total			221	100

To investigate the systemic nature of these protest bids, the authors constructed two probit models, in which the dependent variable is set as 1 for protesters and 0 for those revealing their WTP. Model (1) includes only demographic variables, while model (2) further includes attitudinal variables.

As shown in Table 3.4, in model (1), the results suggest that younger individuals and males are more inclined to submit a protest bid. However, with the introduction of attitudinal variables in model (2), the significance of both the age and gender variables fades. Instead, environmental attitudes, attitudes toward science, and trust in government all surface as statistically significant variables with negative coefficients. This implies that individuals with weaker environmental attitudes, less favourable perceptions of science, and lower trust in government are more likely to give protest responses. Overall, the results indicate that simply removing protesters from the sample may lead to selection bias, since the protests are systematically influenced by certain socio-economic and attitudinal factors.

Table 3.4. Determinants of protest bids

Variable category	Variables	(1)		(2)	
		Coefficient	Standard error	Coefficient	Standard error
Demographic	Age	-0.01**	0.00	-0.00	0.00
	Gender (male = 1)	0.16*	0.09	0.14	0.10
	Household income	-0.00	0.00	0.00	0.00
	Education level	0.06	0.10	0.13	0.10
	Household size	-0.02	0.04	-0.03	0.04
Attitudinal	Awareness of space debris			-0.12	0.10
	Environmental attitude			-0.01**	0.01
	Attitudes toward science			-0.01*	0.01
	Trust in government			-0.42***	0.06
Intercept		-0.60***	0.22	1.62***	0.51
N		1 028		1 028	
Pseudo R^2		0.01		0.08	
Log-likelihood		-476.39		-441.43	

Note: *** p<0.01, ** p<0.05, * p<0.1.

Willingness to pay to avoid the loss of satellites

Three distinct models were used to estimate the WTP for protecting satellites from space debris incidents (Table 3.5). Models (1) and (2) both follow the conventional approach using the binary probit model. However, they differ in that the former includes the entire sample, while the latter excludes the 183 protesters, each with its own shortfalls. In model (1), the mean WTP, estimated as KRW 20 443 (EUR 15.05), risks underestimation since the protesters may genuinely be willing to contribute. Model (2) resulted in a significantly higher mean WTP of KRW 32 755 (EUR 24.12), but risks selection bias by overlooking the systematic occurrence of protesters.

Considering the limitations of both models, the authors turned to model (3), a bivariate sample selection model. In this model, a respondent's decision is understood as a joint process of deciding whether to reveal one's WTP and whether to accept the offered bid. The correlation coefficient, ρ, signifies the potential degree of sample selection and, when positive, implies that eliminating protesters may introduce systematic bias that leads to an overestimation of the mean WTP. With a positive and significant ρ of 0.99, model (3) estimated a mean WTP of KRW 21 171 (EUR 15.59), which was selected as the most representative result in the context of this study.

Across all models, the variables having a statistically significant impact on WTP remained consistent. The bid variable was inversely correlated with WTP at a 0.01 significance level, in accordance with the fundamental notion that higher payments reduce the chances of a 'yes' response. As for the demographic variables, age and household income showed positive coefficients, indicating that older people and those with higher household income are more willing to pay. A notable discovery was the positive correlation between environmental attitudes and WTP. This suggests that individuals with stronger environmental attitudes, or holding attitudes closer to the ecological paradigm, may extend their concerns beyond the boundary of our planet, giving support to the argument that the Earth's orbits constitute an extended ecosystem or, at the least, are a form of common-pool resources (Lawrence et al., 2022[3]; Morin and Richard, 2021[4]). The positive correlation between attitudes toward science and WTP at the 0.01

significance level indicates that the more an individual is interested in science and believes science benefits society, the higher their WTP for satellite protection. The same was found for individuals with higher levels of trust in government.

Table 3.5. Results of parameter estimation

Variable	(1) Full sample		(2) Protesters removed		(3) Sample selection	
	Coefficient	Standard error	Coefficient	Standard error	Coefficient	Standard error
Selection eq.						
Age					0.00	0.00
Gender (male= 1)					-0.17*	0.10
Household income					0.00	0.00
Education level					-0.11	0.10
Household size					0.03	0.37
Awareness of space debris					0.14	0.10
Environmental attitude					0.01*	0.01
Attitude toward science					0.01*	0.01
Trust in government					0.41***	0.06
Constant					-1.45***	0.51
Elicitation eq.						
Bid	-0.00***	0.00	-0.00***	0.00	-0.00***	0.00
Age	0.02***	0.00	0.02***	0.00	0.02***	0.00
Male	-0.03	0.08	0.06	0.10	-0.01	0.08
Household income	0.00**	0.00	0.00**	0.00	0.00**	0.00
Education level	-0.09	0.09	-0.04	0.10	-0.09	0.09
Household size	0.02	0.02	0.00	0.04	0.01	0.03
Awareness of space debris	0.02	0.02	-0.04	0.10	0.02	0.09
Environmental attitude	0.02***	0.02	0.02***	0.01	0.02***	0.01
Attitude toward science	0.03***	0.01	0.03***	0.01	0.03***	0.01
Trust in government	0.36***	0.05	0.23***	0.05	0.35***	0.05
Constant	-3.69***	0.46	-3.13***	0.53	-3.72***	0.45
ρ					0.9999	0.001
N		1 028		845		1 028
Pseudo R2		0.12		0.11		n.a.
Log-likelihood		-623.98		-478.02		-918.99
Mean willingness-to-pay		KRW 20 443 (EUR 15.05)		KRW 32 755 (EUR 24.12)		KRW 21 171 (EUR 15.59)

Notes: *** $p<0.01$, ** $p<0.05$, * $p<0.1$. n.a.: not applicable. In the selection equation, the dependent variable was 1 for true responses (n=845) and 0 for protest responses (n=183). EUR 1 = KRW 1 358 (European Central Bank, 2023).

The aggregated benefit

The aggregated benefit was derived by multiplying the mean WTP by the total population of beneficiaries. Using the estimate from model (3) from Table 3.5 and by conducting 10 000 bootstrapping iterations in accordance with Krinsky and Robb's (1986[13]) simulation method, the aggregate benefit was estimated as KRW 502 billion (EUR 369.6 million). This figure represents the social cost borne by Korean citizens when the country's earth observation satellites are lost for ten years, following a critical collision event with space debris. It is important to note that the estimated lower and upper bounds provided in Table 3.6 are derived from the 95% confidence interval of the Monte Carlo simulation.

Table 3.6. Aggregated benefits

	Lower bound	Mean	Upper bound
Willingness-to-pay	KRW 16 540 (EUR 12.2)	KRW 21 171 (EUR 15.6)	KRW 28 705 (EUR 21.1)
Population (number of households)			23 705 814
Total benefit	KRW 392.1 billion (EUR 288.7 million)	KRW 501.9 billion (EUR 369.6 million)	KRW 680.5 billion (EUR 501.1 million)

1. The population data is drawn from Ministry of Public Administration and Security (2022). 2. EUR 1 = KRW 1 358 (European Central Bank, 2023)

Discussion and conclusions

The looming threat of space debris and its potential implications, especially for emerging space nations, urgently calls for the sustainable use of the Earth's orbits. This, in turn, requires a clear understanding of the costs of space debris and a comprehensive viewpoint that encompasses the diversity of space entities and objects. As one such effort, this study has explored the challenge of estimating the often overlooked social value of non-market satellites at risk due to space debris, focusing on the case of Korea. Given the pivotal roles public satellites serve, such as in the areas of climate monitoring, disaster management and national defence, the potential damage can have deep economic, strategic, and societal impacts.

This study quantifies the cost of space debris incidents involving earth observation satellites, determining a mean WTP of KRW 21 171 (EUR 15.6) per household. This amounts to an aggregated value loss of KRW 501.9 billion (EUR 369.6 million) over a decade for Korean LEO satellites. A key distinction is its singular focus on public satellites, launched for the purpose of serving the larger public interest and increasing the nation's collective welfare. This divergence from commercial considerations inherently led to the adoption of a non-market valuation methodology, another differing aspect. In light of the above, the magnitude of the results can be understood to indicate the profound implications these satellites have for national welfare.

From a policy perspective, these figures not only capture the considerable disutility that can be caused by space debris but also signal a broad social consensus in favour of allocating resources for mitigating the problem. On the economic front, the study provides a tangible monetary assessment using CV, bridging the gap between distant and abstract objects in outer space and people inhabiting Earth. Should this inspire other studies, they will collectively facilitate a better understanding of the economic impacts of space debris and other issues arising in the space environment, enabling policy makers to better prioritise and design interventions, based on empirical evidence rather than mere speculation.

Despite these findings, many paths remain untaken in the field of space sustainability. Further research could explore in more detail the different functions and applications of satellites, as well as the ramifications of their loss. Broadening the scope to other countries could lend comparative insights that can enrich global discussions.

At a time when the race to harness the potential gains from outer space is intensifying, this research offers both a framework for informed policy making and a stepping stone for future academic work. While the study concentrates on Korea, the findings may resonate with newcomers to the space economy and contribute to building a collective understanding of the risks of space debris for the international community, tasked with strengthening co-operation for improved space traffic management and maintaining a sustainable space environment for current and future generations.

References

Bongers, A. and J. Torres (2023), "Orbital debris and the market for satellites", *Ecological Economics*, Vol. 209, p. 107831, https://doi.org/10.1016/j.ecolecon.2023.107831. [8]

Brouwer, R. and J. Martín-Ortega (2012), *Modeling self-censoring of polluter pays protest votes in stated preference research to support resource damage estimations in environmental liability*, Resource and Energy Economics. [18]

Carson, R. (1998), "Valuation of tropical rainforests: philosophical and practical issues in the use of contingent valuation", *Ecological Economics*, Vol. 24/1, pp. 15-29, https://doi.org/10.1016/s0921-8009(97)00584-3. [10]

Dunlap, R. et al. (2000), *Measuring Endorsement of the New Ecological Paradigm: A Revised NEP Scale*, Journal of Social Issues. [19]

Eom, Y. and J. Hong (2009), "Identification and correction of protest responses in the willingness-to-pay estimation for public project feasibility analysis", in *Korean Journal of Public Finance*, (in Korean). [16]

Haab, T. and K. McConnell (2002), *Valuing Environmental and Natural Resources: The Econometrics of Non-Market Valuation*, Edward Elgar Publishing Ltd, https://econpapers.repec.org/RePEc:elg:eebook:2427. [11]

Haerpfer, C. et al. (eds.) (2022), *World Values Survey: Round Seven - Country-Pooled Datafile Version 5.0.*, Madrid, Spain & Vienna, Austria: JD Systems Institute & WVSA Secretariat, https://doi.org/10.14281/18241.20. [20]

Hanemann, W. (1984), "Welfare Evaluations in Contingent Valuation Experiments with Discrete Responses", *American Journal of Agricultural Economics*, Vol. 66/3, pp. 332-341, https://doi.org/10.2307/1240800. [12]

IADC (2007), *IADC Space Debris Mitigation Guidelines*, https://orbitaldebris.jsc.nasa.gov/library/iadc-space-debris-guidelines-revision-2.pdf. [6]

Kessler, D. (1991), "Orbital debris environment for spacecraft in low earth orbit", *Journal of Spacecraft and Rockets*, Vol. 28/3, pp. 347-351, https://doi.org/10.2514/3.26250. [1]

Kessler, D. and B. Cour-Palais (1978), "Collision frequency of artificial satellites: The creation of a debris belt", *Journal of Geophysical Research: Space Physics*, Vol. 83/A6, pp. 2637-2646, https://doi.org/10.1029/ja083ia06p02637. [2]

Krinsky, I. and A. Robb (1986), *On approximating the statistical properties of elasticities*, The Review of Economics and Statistics. [13]

Lawrence, A. et al. (2022), "The case for space environmentalism", *Nature Astronomy*, Vol. 6/4, pp. 428-435, https://doi.org/10.1038/s41550-022-01655-6. [3]

Mitchell, R. and R. Carson (1989), *Using Surveys to Value Public Goods: The Contingent Valuation Method*, RFF Press, New York, https://doi.org/10.4324/9781315060569. [14]

Morin, J. and B. Richard (2021), "Astro-Environmentalism: Towards a Polycentric Governance of Space Debris", *Global Policy*, Vol. 12/4, pp. 568-573, https://doi.org/10.1111/1758-5899.12950. [4]

Newman, C. and M. Williamson (2018), "Space Sustainability: Reframing the Debate", *Space Policy*, Vol. 46, pp. 30-37, https://doi.org/10.1016/j.spacepol.2018.03.001. [5]

Rao, A., M. Burgess and D. Kaffine (2020), "Orbital-use fees could more than quadruple the value of the space industry", *Proceedings of the National Academy of Sciences*, Vol. 117/23, pp. 12756-12762, https://doi.org/10.1073/pnas.1921260117. [9]

Strazzera, E. et al. (2003), "Modelling zero values and protest responses in contingent valuation surveys", *Applied Economics*, Vol. 35/2, pp. 133-138, https://doi.org/10.1080/0003684022000015900. [15]

Sun, C., X. Yuan and X. Yao (2016), "Social acceptance towards the air pollution in China: Evidence from public's willingness to pay for smog mitigation", *Energy Policy*, Vol. 92, pp. 313-324, https://doi.org/10.1016/j.enpol.2016.02.025. [17]

UNOOSA (2018), "Guidelines for the Long-term Sustainability of Outer Space Activities", Conference room paper by the Chair of the Working Group on the Long-term Sustainability of Outer Space Activities, https://www.unoosa.org/res/oosadoc/data/documents/2018/aac_1052018crp/aac_1052018crp_20_0_html/AC105_2018_CRP20E.pdf (accessed on 5 February 2024). [7]

Annex 3.A. Sample representativeness of the survey

Annex Table 3.A.1. Sample representativeness of the survey

Characteristics		Sample (N = 1 028)		Population (Korea)	
		Sample size	Proportion (%)	Population	Proportion (%)
Gender	Male	509	49.5	21 657 711	49.6
	Female	519	50.5	22 037 245	50.4
	Total	**1 028**	**100**	**43 694 956**	**100**
Age	19-29	165	16.1	6 908 937	15.8
	30-39	157	15.3	6 615 511	15.1
	40-49	185	18.0	8 073 117	18.5
	50-59	203	19.8	8 612 064	19.7
	60 and older	318	31.0	13 485 327	30.9
	Total	**1 028**	**100**	**43 694 956**	**100**
Region	Seoul	191	18.6	8 220 164	18.8
	Busan	69	6.7	2 874 159	6.6
	Daegu	49	4.8	2 012 860	4.6
	Incheon	60	5.8	2 514 038	5.8
	Gwangju	29	2.8	1 189 664	2.7
	Daejeon	29	2.8	1 218 773	2.8
	Ulsan	21	2.0	926 012	2.1
	Sejong	10	1.0	292 436	0.7
	Gyeonggi-do	267	26.0	11 355 976	26.0
	Gangwon-do	30	2.9	1 322 365	3.0
	Chungcheongbuk-do	30	2.9	1 354 735	3.1
	Chungcheongnam-do	42	4.1	1 788 033	4.1
	Jeollabuk-do	36	3.5	1 509 155	3.5
	Jeollanam-do	36	3.5	1 557 796	3.6
	Gyeongsangbuk-do	52	5.1	2 237 251	5.1
	Gyeongsangnamdo	65	6.3	2 762 267	6.3
	Jeju-do	12	1.2	559 272	1.3
	Total	**1 028**	**100**	**43 694 956**	**100**

Note: "Population" refers to the count of individuals in South Korea aged 19 or older.
Source: The population data by age was retrieved on Aug 18, 2023, from: Ministry of Public Administration and Security. (2023). Status of Population by Age. https://jumin.mois.go.kr/ageStatMonth.do.

Annex 3.B. Scenario details

Annex Figure 3.B.1. Image of the new satellites to be launched

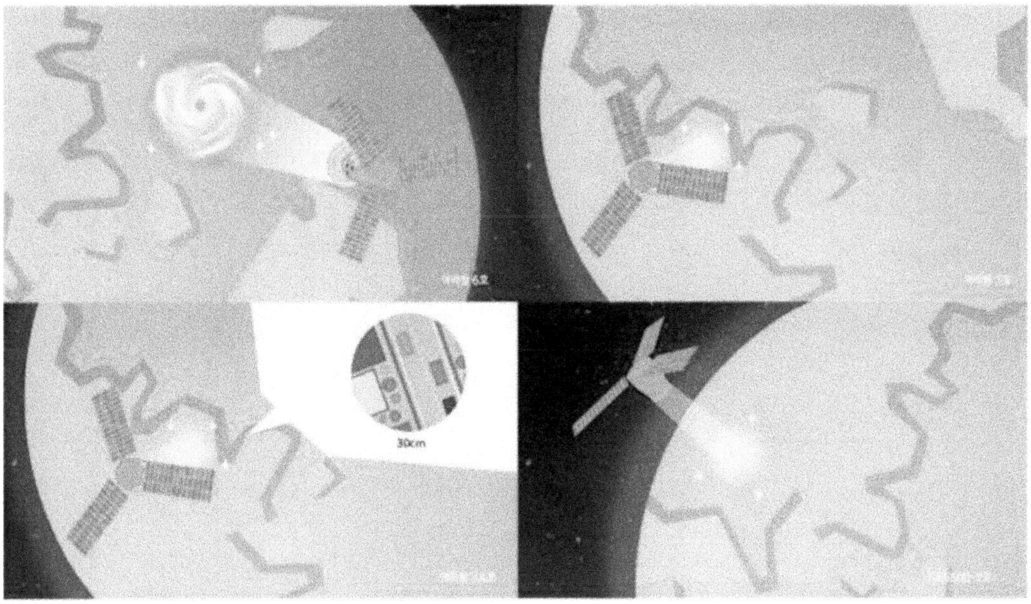

Description: "The development of the new satellites was led by our country using the most advanced technology. KOMPSAT-6 can observe the Earth in any weather condition. KOMPSAT-7 and KOMPSAT-7A can provide 30cm resolution imagery, which matches the best level found across the globe. CAS500-2 is a medium satellite optimised for land management."

Annex Figure 3.B.2. Image of satellite services

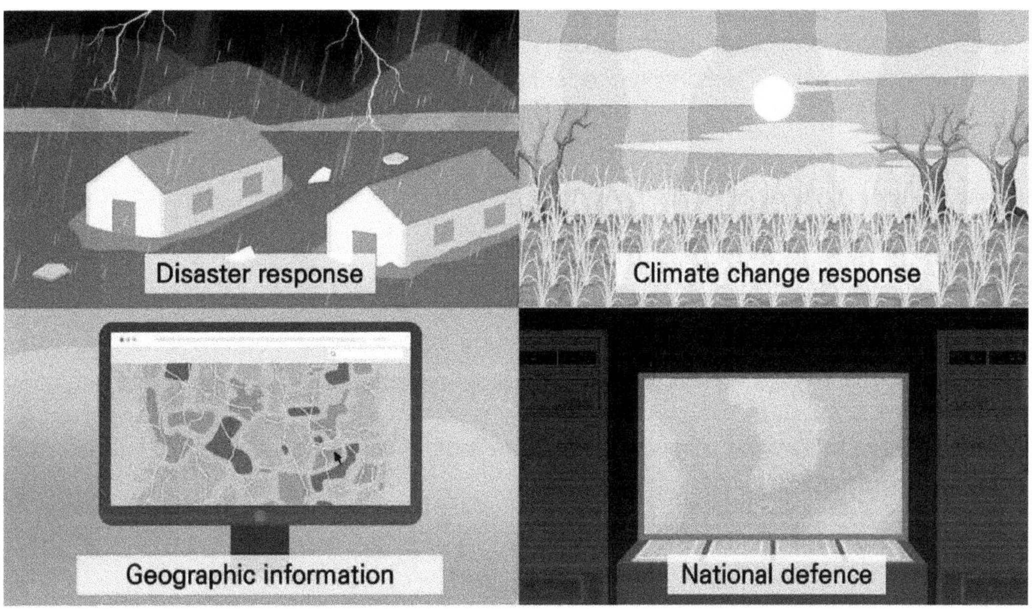

Description: "The satellites hold important missions for the country's management. Firstly, they provide information necessary for disaster response, such as in the case of a typhoon, flood, or landslide. Secondly, they provide information used to respond to severe effects of climate change, such as urban heat islands, the rise of sea surface temperatures, and widespread damage to crops. Thirdly, they provide information crucial for national defence, such as the status of neighbouring countries. Lastly, they provide geographic information for the public."

Annex Figure 3.B.3. Image of the Space Protection Programme

Description: The scientific community suggests three measures to avoid critical collision events with space debris, which together compose the satellite protection programme. The first is prediction. This can be done by subscribing to an existing service that analyses the trajectories of satellites and space debris, using radars in various locations across the globe, and predicts potential collisions. The second is prevention. This can be done by attaching a thruster to satellites, which can effectively prevent collisions by adjusting a satellite's orbit away from approaching space debris. The third is mitigation. This can be done by adding verified shielding, which protects satellites from inevitable collisions. Such shielding technologies have been used by leading space-faring countries and for the International Space Station.

Notes

[1] Note that $\beta_1 y_i - \beta_0 y_i = 0$, under the assumption that the marginal utility of income is constant ($\beta_1 = \beta_0$).

[2] Common motivations for protest responses (or protest bids) are a rejection of the market structure or distrust in the scenario itself.

4 Space assets as critical infrastructure? The socio-economic value of space infrastructure in Japan

Yui Nakama, University of Tokyo, Japan

Quentin Verspieren, University of Tokyo, Japan

Aya Iwamoto, Astroscale, Japan

Very little research has been produced to try to quantify the value of space assets for society and the potential damage that a disruption of space-based services would incur. This chapter explores whether, in a similar manner to other critical infrastructures, space assets hold a significant value in our society due to the difficulties faced in substituting them with alternatives. It further proposes a simple theoretical model to comprehend the macroeconomic benefits of vital space assets from a governmental standpoint.

Introduction

In a modern digitalised society, space-based products and services play a crucial role in social and industrial activities. As the space environment undergoes various transformations, the protection of vital space assets has emerged as an important policy agenda. However, despite this recognition and the general orientation towards greater actions in fields such as space safety and sustainability, space situational awareness or space mission assurance, very little consideration has been put into the quantification of the value of space infrastructure for our societies, and the potential damage that a disruption of space-based services would incur. Considering the strong dependence of other critical infrastructures on space-based services, it is of utmost urgency for governments around the world to understand the socio-economic implications of the possible disruption of specific space assets.

In this study, the authors propose a simple model to evaluate the macroeconomic contribution of space-based services in an advanced spacefaring country like Japan. The ambition of this model is to contribute to evidence-based space policy making by providing quantitative evidence on the value of space infrastructure, which can subsequently be taken into consideration when evaluating the costs and benefits of space mission assurance activities. It also aims, in line with the OECD's project on the economics of space sustainability, to kickstart global reflections on socio-economic valuation models for space infrastructure.

This chapter and its model are based on a detailed case study of the approach of the Government of Japan concerning the protection of vital national space assets. Considering that Japan has been highly active in the fields of space safety, sustainability and security in recent years, the authors discovered, through interviews with government officials, that there was no methodology to either clearly assess the degree of criticality of specific space assets or to quantify the socio-economic impact of a disruption of such assets. The authors therefore decided to investigate other areas of Japanese policy making, especially critical infrastructure protection and telecommunication penetration, to identify elements that could serve to assess the contribution of space-based services to society.

Critical infrastructure in Japan: limited substitutability and high socio-economic impact

The Government of Japan released two different approaches for the protection of its critical infrastructure between 2005 and 2022. First, the "Cybersecurity Policy for Critical Infrastructure Protection", which was revised four times by 2022, placed the emphasis on cyber threats against critical infrastructure sectors and promoting the adoption of strict safeguards by service operators (NISC, 2024[1]). Second, the 2022 Economic Security Promotion Act contained elements on critical infrastructure protection (CIP) and provided a list of "designated social infrastructure services" (特定社会基盤役務) requiring special attention (Cabinet Office, 2022[2])Table 4.1 displays the two lists of critical infrastructure sectors and services in Japan.

Table 4.1. Japan's critical infrastructures in 2022

Critical infrastructure sectors (重要インフラ分野) Cybersecurity Policy for Critical Infrastructure Protection	Designated social infrastructure services (特定社会基盤役務) Economic Security Promotion Act of 2022
Airports	Airports
Aviation services	Aviation
Credit card services	Credit card
Electric power supply services	Electricity
Financial services	Finance

Critical infrastructure sectors (重要インフラ分野) Cybersecurity Policy for Critical Infrastructure Protection	Designated social infrastructure services (特定社会基盤役務) Economic Security Promotion Act of 2022
Gas supply services	Gas
Petroleum industries	Petroleum
Railway services	Railways
Water services	Water supply
Chemical industries	Road cargo
Government administrative services	Ocean cargo
Information and communication services	Communications
Logistics services	Broadcast
Medical services	Post

Note: Similar themes are highlighted in light blue and contrasting themes in dark blue.

The distinctions between these two strategies stem from their distinct objectives: cybersecurity and economic security. However, there are many common topics which have been highlighted in light blue in Table 4.1, as well as a collection of dissimilar themes highlighted in darker blue. According to the National Center of Incident Readiness and Strategy for Cybersecurity (NISC), "critical infrastructures (CI) refers to sectors that comprise the backbone of national life and economic activities formed by businesses providing services that are extremely difficult to be substituted; if the function of the services is suspended or deteriorates, it could have a significant impact on national life and economic activities" (NISC, 2022[3]). The Cabinet Office (CAO) regards "designated social infrastructure services" as "the foundation of people's lives and economic activities and are likely to jeopardise the nation's and citizens' security if their consistent provision is hampered" (Cabinet Office, 2024[4]). Based on these definitions, the government's criteria for its CI can be summarised as limited substitutability and high socio-economic impact.

To identify the methodologies proposed by each of the two CIP approaches for measuring the value of critical national infrastructure as indicated in their definitions, the authors conducted multiple interviews with individuals leading the development of CIP policy in government, industry, and academia. It is pertinent to note that the Government of Japan has no specific economic impact analysis on its CI. This is due to its political decision making process regarding sectors and services considered as "the backbone of national life and economic activities" (NISC, 2022[3]). The officials interviewed by the authors all agreed that the policy documents for CIP are assembled from industry-specific laws relevant to each field, without a thorough evaluation of the socio-economic value of the respective infrastructures at the core of why they should be protected. Beyond Japan, other countries that have also identified space systems as CI or are actively engaged in the protection of space infrastructure, lack economic methodologies and strategies according to the authors' international survey.[1] While the value assessment process based on the definition is still in the early stages of establishment, the CIP itself remains a key indicator of national policy to protect its critical infrastructure.

Space's critical contribution to information and communication services in Japan

Although none of the CIP approaches established by the Government of Japan include space infrastructure, or any part thereof, in their list, space technologies and services are at the foundation of most of the listed sectors and services. In fact, except for three ministries,[2] all ministerial policy papers indicate an active usage of space infrastructure and reliance on it is growing, notably reliance on the "information and communication services" or "communications" sector. Telecommunications from outer space offer wide-area and multi-address capabilities, allowing for simultaneous transmission or communication to a significant number of individuals across a large region from a high altitude location.

The PwC study on the "Dependence of the European Economy on Space Infrastructures" released in 2017 concludes that the telecommunications sector is the least reliant on the space infrastructure due to the high-quality coverage offered by terrestrial communication networks in Europe (PwC, 2017[5]). This dependence, however, largely affects remotely located economic activities such as offshore stations and maritime or rural areas, which account for a lower percentage of the European Union's economy. Despite having a relatively high coverage ratio of terrestrial network services, Japan, being a major maritime power, depends on maritime transportation for 99.7% of its trade volume. Additionally, the island country is confronted with the major challenges of an ageing society and declining birth rates. According to the latest demographic estimates by the Ministry of Internal Affairs and Communication (MIC), the rate of elderly individuals aged 65 and more reached a record high of 29.0%, while the overall population fell by 556 000 from the previous year to 124 947 000, marking the twelfth consecutive year of decline (MIC, 2023[6]). Addressing rural depopulation, which stagnates local economies and widens disparities with urban regions, remains an important and urgent policy agenda in Japan.

It should also be noted that, due to their distance from Earth, space-based telecommunications services are an essential means of communication and information gathering for disaster management, providing administrative support and ensuring the safety of communities. As a disaster-prone country, Japan relies heavily on space infrastructure as the "foundation of people's lives" (Cabinet Office, 2024[4]). Immediately after the significant 7.0-magnitude earthquake during the Great East Japan Earthquake, approximately 340 satellite-based mobile phones were supplied to disaster areas where the transmission line to the communication station had been cut off (MIC, 2011[7]). Around 6 700 NTT Docomo, 3 700 KDDI (au), 3 800 Softbank, and 700 EMOBILE communication stations were offline at that time, and space-based telecommunication equipment played an essential role (MIC, 2011[8]).

Space infrastructure contributing to "information and communications" services

Satellite communications (satcom) and the global navigation satellite systems (GNSS) are central components of space-based information and communication networks. Vittori, et al. (2022[9]) identified the dependency rate of satcom and GNSS on the information and communication industry in Europe as 85% and 15% respectively.

Satcom provides a variety of information and communication services by transmitting and receiving radio telecommunications signals, including voice, data and video, between transmitting sources and receiving stations. The three fundamental operations are communication-by-satellite (point-to-point), broadcasting (point-to-multipoint), and data collection (multipoint-to-point), which are widely recognised as ubiquitous and cost-effective services. Table 4.2 lists eleven Japanese primary satellites in geostationary orbit (GEO),[3] while Table 4.3 shows the other four non-geostationary orbit satellite constellations for telecommunications as of 2022.[4]

Table 4.2. Japan's primary telecommunication geostationary satellites in 2022

Satellite	Owner	Mission	Band	Orbit	Launch date
1. JCSAT-85/Intelsat 15	Sky Perfect JSAT/Intelsat	Data transmission (incl. image, voice)	Ku	GEO 85.15(°E)	December 2009
2. JCSAT-110A	Sky Perfect JSAT	Communication and broadcasting	Ku	GEO 110(°E)	December 2016
3. JCSAT-4B	Sky Perfect JSAT	Communication and broadcasting	Ku	GEO 124(°E)	May 2012
4. JCSAT-3A	Sky Perfect JSAT	Communication and broadcasting	C, Ku	GEO 128(°E)	August 2006
5. JCSAT-5A/N-STAR d	Sky Perfect JSAT/NTT Docomo	Broadcasting	S, C, Ku	GEO 132(°E)	April 2006
6. N-STAR e	NTT Docomo	Broadcasting	S, C	GEO 136(°E)	July 2002
7. SUPERBIRD-C2	Sky Perfect JSAT	Communication and broadcasting	Ku	GEO 144(°E)	August 2008
8. JCSAT-1C	Sky Perfect JSAT	Communication and broadcasting	Ku, Ka	GEO 150(°W)	December 2019

9. JCSAT-2B	Sky Perfect JSAT	Communication and broadcasting	C, Ku	GEO 154(°E)	May 2016
10. SUPERBIRD-B3	Sky Perfect JSAT	Communication and broadcasting	Ku, Ka	GEO 162(°E)	April 2018
11. Horizons-3e	Sky Perfect JSAT/Intelsat	Data transmission (incl. image, voice)	C, Ku	GEO 169(°E)	September 2018

Table 4.3. Primary telecommunication non-geostationary satellites used in Japan in 2022

Satellite	Owner	Mission	Number of satellites	Orbit
1. ORBCOMM	ORBCOMM	Data transmission, positioning	16	825 km
2. Iridium	Iridium	Data transmission (incl. voice), Communication (OpenPort)	66	780 km
3. Globalstar	Globalstar	Data transmission (incl. voice), positioning	24	141 km
4. Starlink	SpaceX	Data transmission	4,053	550 km

GNSS offers global positioning, navigation, and timing (PNT) services through a network of satellites that transmit signals to ground-based receivers, allowing these receivers to determine their precise geographic location, velocity, and time. The most well-known example is the Global Positioning System, which was developed in the 1960s by the United States. The single and critical contribution of GNSS signals and frequencies to the information and communication sector is timing and synchronisation for various wired and wireless network management. Table 4.4 displays the present operating status of the Quasi-Zenith Satellite System, the Japanese GNSS, as of 2023.

Table 4.4. Japan's operational navigation satellites in 2023

Satellite	Services	Positioning signals	PRN	Block type	Launch date
1. QZS02	Satellite positioning, navigation, and timing	L1C/A, L1C, L2C, L5	194	IIQ	June 2017
	Sub-metre level augmentation	L1S	184		
	Positioning technology verification	L5S	184		
	Centimetre level augmentation	L6	194		
2. QZS03	Satellite positioning, navigation, and timing	L1C/A, L1C, L2C, L5	199	IIG	August 2017
	Sub-metre level augmentation	L1S	189		
	Positioning technology verification	L5S	189		
	Positioning technology verification	L1Sb	137		
	Centimetre level augmentation	L6	199		
	Disaster management (Q-ANPI)	Sr/Sf	-		
3. QZS04	Satellite positioning, navigation, and timing	L1C/A, L1C, L2C, L5	195	IIQ	October 2017
	Sub-metre level augmentation	L1S	185		
	Positioning technology verification	L5S	185		
	Centimetre level augmentation	L6	195		
4. QZS1R	Satellite positioning, navigation, and timing	L1C/A, L1C, L2C, L5	196	IIA-Q	October 2021
	Sub-metre level augmentation	L1S	186		
	Positioning technology verification	L5S	186		
	Centimetre level augmentation	L6	196		

The space assets depicted in tables 4.2 to 4.4 can be defined as the core space infrastructure for Japan's information and communications sector. Rather than relying on the operations of individual satellites, they work as an integrated system to enable smooth communication services.

Substitutability: alternative solutions to the space infrastructure?

Telecommunications is a mature industry that is primarily reliant on terrestrial communication networks. Considering one of the requirements for critical infrastructure – limited substitutability – the substitutability of satcom and GNSS in the information and communications industry should be examined.

Although satcom capabilities are often considered complementary to terrestrial telecommunication networks in order to meet the "everything, everywhere, all the time" need, terrestrial networks cannot serve as a true alternative option to satcom in certain critical conditions, such as rural and catastrophe locations where terrestrial radio waves are difficult to receive or lacking. Aerial solutions, such as drones, high-altitude balloons, and airborne platforms equipped with communication features, on the other hand, can be viable alternatives in the short term; nevertheless, these technologies are not yet practical market solutions. As a result, when terrestrial communication networks are unavailable or inoperable, satcom remains the best and only choice, indicating "the backbone of national life and economic activities" (NISC, 2022[3]). Satcom offers various advantages that cannot be easily substituted, such as global coverage that is unconstrained by physical infrastructure, rapid deployment, geographic mobility, and wide-area secure communication.

GNSS has been the sole and significant solution providing accuracy, integrity, coverage, continuity and availability of global time, location, and synchronisation services across a wide range of socio-economic activities. In their comprehensive study on PNT systems published in 2023, Critchley-Marrows and Verspieren identified that, for most decision makers and government officials, GNSS serves as the primary source for PNT, which is "either referred to as an enabler of critical infrastructures or as a critical infrastructure in itself" (Critchley-Marrows and Verspieren, 2023[10]). While there are a few alternatives to GNSS timing and synchronisation functions, the options are typically limited to a specific type of application or a specific group of users, with limited spatial coverage. One of the main alternatives is Network Time Protocol, which uses synchronised clocks within a network for relatively exact timing and synchronisation. However, the network-based network systems are constrained by internet availability as well as hardware requirements such as high-performance clock sources for accuracy. As a result, GNSS, as a satellite-based system independent of network infrastructure, is far more competitive.

Socio-economic impact: the value of space infrastructure in Japan

Following the evaluation of the substitutability of space-based products and services in the information and communication sector, this section qualitatively analyses the other requirements for critical infrastructure – a high socio-economic impact. Space-based global connectivity improves and expands high-speed information sharing and access to services, overcoming geographical limitations even in distant or challenging-to-reach regions where terrestrial infrastructure is unreachable. The Government of Japan promotes the use of space communications infrastructure through two primary initiatives: regional revitalisation and disaster management.

In most cases, the difficulties in building terrestrial networks stem from technical, geographical, and economic barriers. Remote locations, far from metropolitan areas, necessitate large increases in infrastructure deployment and maintenance expenses and effort. Geographical complexity, such as hilly regions, woods, deserts, or areas with many lakes, can further hamper the construction of terrestrial networks. Operating ground-based networks can also be challenging in areas prone to severe weather or natural disasters. Furthermore, low population density places may not have enough information and communication demand to justify the cost-effectiveness of setting up terrestrial systems.

Overcoming these challenges, satellite-based networks can provide high-quality connections to large remote areas while being economical. CAO released the "Vision for a Digital Garden City Nation" in 2022 to build digital infrastructure stretching to every corner of the ageing and depopulating country (Cabinet Office, 2022[11]). In the medium and long term, the strategy focuses on digital transformation, aiming for regional revitalisation using information and communication technology (ICT), including space infrastructure. Building robust and frequent satellite communication links largely contributes to local economic growth by facilitating many different aspects such as the expansion of telework environments.

Geographically, Japan is particularly vulnerable to natural disasters, experiencing countless earthquakes, typhoons, floodings, and volcanic eruptions. Every year, many people are reported as missing or dead as a result of these inevitably difficult situations. In times of natural hazards, the infrastructure of terrestrial communication and power networks is often disrupted or destroyed. On the other hand, space-based systems, with their independent communication pathway, can provide fundamental and dependable communication platforms for all risk management processes, including prevention and mitigation, prompt emergency response, and recovery.

During the 2011 Great East Japan Earthquake and tsunami, space-based information and communication technologies played three critical roles: administrative assistance, information gathering, and safety confirmation. Satellites assisted public authorities in successfully disseminating essential damage status information, safety instructions, and evacuation notifications to impacted populations, saving lives and lowering casualties. Besides responding to the government's safety alerts, the affected people themselves utilised space infrastructure for enhanced situational awareness, in order to make informed choices by collecting and analysing data on weather patterns, water levels, seismic activity, and other crucial factors. Additionally, space-based communication services enabled safety assurance via phone calls and emails. Disaster response communication systems including satellite networks reduced uncertainty, allowing for speedy and safe disaster relief actions. The Government of Japan strongly recognises the critical need to strengthen its resilient, safe and secure information and communication platforms utilising space-based systems for safe and reliable emergency response (Cabinet Secretariat, 2021[12]).

Modelling the socio-economic benefits of space infrastructure for information and communication

Setting out a macroeconomic theoretical model based on the aggregate function, this part provides a quantitative assessment of the socio-economic value of space infrastructure in the information and communication sector, which is critical to national life and economic activities in Japan. The socio-economic impact, as a premise, refers to the direct or indirect effects of certain activities or technologies on the economy, social or cultural practices, livelihoods, and so forth. Since the implications cannot be quantified in terms of market size or development expenses, macroeconomic approaches concentrating on socio-economic performance in the relevant regions are applied. To understand how decision makers understand the value of satcom and GNSS, the authors adapted an existing model developed by the Government of Japan in the early 2000s to assess the significance of infrastructure in the information and communication field.

Introducing the space-based ubiquitous index

The ubiquitous index is a progress indicator towards the ubiquitous network, defined as an environment allowing access at any time, from any location, by any device, and by anybody. This indicator has been used by the MIC to measure the progress of the national ubiquitous network and its impact on regional economic growth, which was encouraged by the 2004 ICT plan "u-Japan Policy" (MIC, 2007[13]). By selecting the variables relevant to space-enabled applications, the general ubiquitous index can be translated into a space-based ubiquitous index, hence providing a simplified model to quantify the socio-economic effects of the spread and use of the space infrastructure. This can be done by following three main steps:

1. The space infrastructure index is assessed through four technological domains: personal computers (PC), internet, broadband, and mobile communication, and two macro areas: telework and multi-use of software, all of which are supported by satcom and GNSS. The index reflects the penetration and utilisation of space-enabled information and communication services.
2. Based on the space infrastructure index, the space-based ubiquitous index is calculated as the average of the six elements by prefecture, demonstrating both the social effects (changes in lifestyle, community, etc.) and the economic effects (changes in the economy, including businesses and individuals).
3. The correlation between the space-based ubiquitous index and the economic growth of a region is evaluated. In contrast to PwC's dependence characterisation model, which measures the severity of dependence primarily on the scale of the economic activity using reasonable hypotheses, the authors' modelling approach takes a broader perspective and is grounded in transparent government databases (PwC, 2017[5]).

The penetration rate of space infrastructure is measured by four technological sectors: PC, internet, broadband and mobile communication devices. Satcom and GNSS have a substantial impact on these modern information and communication systems in various ways, as discussed in previous sections. The combination of space infrastructure and major communication devices allows wide-area coverage, emergency connectivity, mobility, rapid deployment, and digital divide reduction. An overview of the activities conducted within each technological sector is presented below.

- **PCs** are primarily used for information processing, storage, and programme execution, while satellites serve as infrastructure to facilitate data transmission and internet connectivity. The PC household penetration rate is calculated using data from the "Q1 Ownership Status of Information Communication Equipment" on the "Communication Usage Trend Survey (households)" for each year between 1996 and 2022 with a database by prefecture from 2010 (MIC, 2022[14]).
- While PCs assist with individual information processing as one of the computer devices**, the internet** refers to the worldwide network that links computers and servers in different locations, enabling information sharing. Satellites can deliver wireless internet signals blasted down from a satellite circling the Earth, in addition to adding to internet connectivity and mobility. The internet population penetration rate is estimated using data from the "Q1(1) Internet usage experience in the last year (excluding non-responders)" on the "Communication Usage Trend Survey (household members)" for each year from 1997 through 2022 with a database by prefecture starting in 2010 (MIC, 2022[15]). The current definition of "internet users" includes citizens aged 6 and over who use the internet for any purpose, not just for personal use, regardless of device or location.
- **Broadband** encompasses high-speed, high-bandwidth communication technologies or network connections that allow the rapid and efficient transmission of large amounts of digital resources. Broadband subscribers are measured in the "Q2 Connection lines of households using the internet at home" in the "Communication Usage Trend Survey (households)" for each year from 2002 through 2022 with a prefecture-specific database beginning in 2010 (MIC, 2022[14]).
- **Mobile communication** refers to the technology of exchanging data and information that enables users to communicate in various situations, including everyday life, business, and emergencies, independent of their location. Mobile communication subscribers are counted in the "Q1 Ownership Status of Information Communication Equipment' on the 'Communication Usage Trend Survey (households)" for each year between 2006 and 2022, with a prefecture-specific database from 2010. Mobile devices include mobile phones, smartphones, personal handyphone system (PHS) devices and personal digital assistants (PDAs), and the statistics display the percentage of households that own at least one of these devices (MIC, 2022[14]).

The utilisation rate of space infrastructure is evaluated in two macro areas: telework and multi-use of software. The MIC also adopts the "information distribution census" or the "information distribution index" indicating the volume of information distributed and consumed domestically, as the ubiquitous index variables (MIC, 2008[16]). However, owing to the rapid advancement of ICT in recent years, information sources have become more diverse, extending beyond the conventional analogue paradigm. As a result of the uncertainty surrounding its validity, the survey on information distribution was discontinued in 2009 (MIC, 2009[17]). Therefore, this study's model does not adopt the index. An overview of the activities conducted within each of the macro areas is presented below.

- **Telework** is the practice of working from a location other than the conventional office setting. Instead of commuting to a physical office, employees have the option to work remotely utilising ICT outlined in the penetration rate of the space infrastructure. Telework implementation rates in businesses are aggregated in "Q4 Telework Introduction Status" on the "Communication Usage Trend Survey (companies)" for each year between 2000 and 2022 with an eleven-regions-specific database introduced in 2010 (MIC, 2022[18]).
- **Multi-use software** facilitates access by numerous media sources after secondary usage while preserving the same content, demonstrating the diversity of information distribution channels. The market share of multi-use software can be found in the "Survey of the Current State of Media and Software Development and Dissemination" for each year spanning from 2001 to 2021 (MIC, 2022[19]).

Based on these six indicators, Figure 4.1 represents the penetration rates of space infrastructure (Panel A) and the utilisation rates (Panel B) between 1996 and 2022. The penetration rates experienced a significant increase by 2003, followed by a remarkable surge in utilisation, particularly in teleworking, in the aftermath of the 2020 pandemic.

Figure 4.1. Measures for space infrastructure penetration and utilisation in Japan

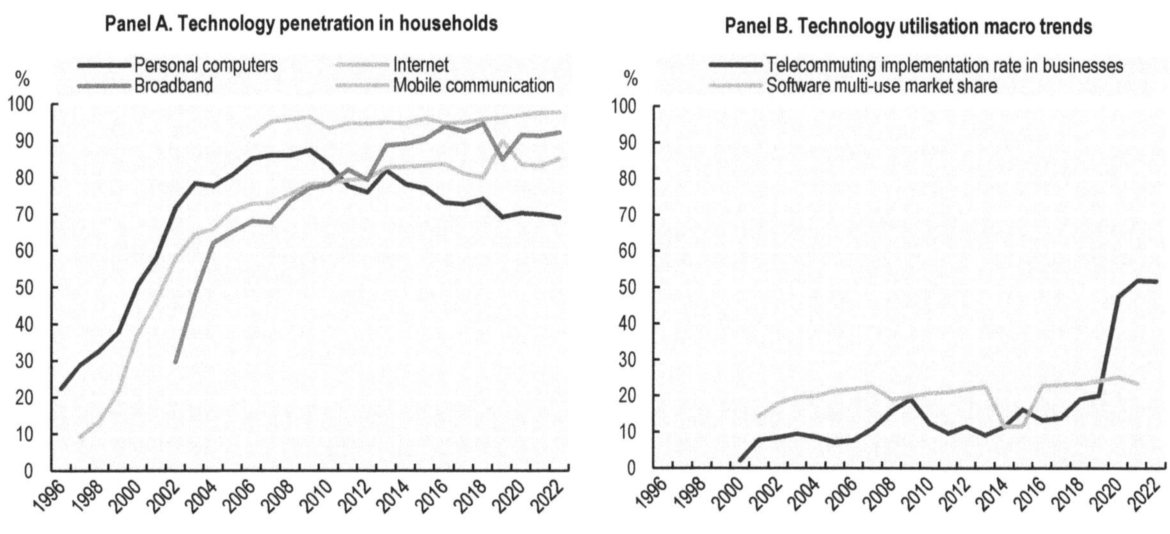

Source: Authors' compilation of survey data from Japan's MICs.

The space-based ubiquitous index is derived by taking the average of the six space infrastructure indicators for every prefecture in Japan. Due to the unavailability of prefecture data, telework implementation rates rely on regional data, while multi-use software market shares refer to nationwide data. Figure 4.2 demonstrates the evolution of the space-based ubiquitous index in Japan's 47 prefectures between 2010 and 2021.

Figure 4.2. The evolution of Japan's space-based ubiquitous index over time

Maximum, median and minimum values for Japan's 47 prefectures

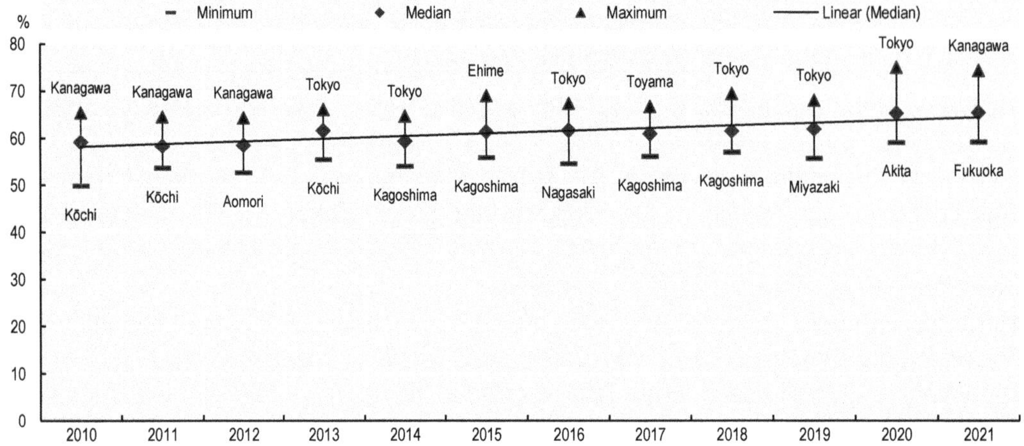

Notes: The space-based ubiquitous index is calculated as the average by prefecture of six indicators (household penetration of PC, internet, broadband and mobile communication; the share of business firms implementing telework; and the market share of multi-use software). Due to the unavailability of granular data, telework implementation rates rely on regional data, while multi-use software market shares refer to nationwide data.
Source: Authors' calculations based on survey data from Japan's Ministry of Internal Affairs and Communications.

Value of space-enabled activities

It is additionally critical to quantify the extent to which the technological progress in information and communications, including space applications, benefits regional society and the economy. In line with the government's vision of creating a Digital Garden City Nation in rural areas, the relationships between the advancement of ICT and regional revitalisation are presented in Figure 4.3 (Cabinet Office, 2022[11]).

The six case studies demonstrate a strong correlation between the space-based ubiquitous index and the real gross domestic product (GDP) growth rate in Japanese prefectures with the smallest populations below one million people (MIC, 2020[20]). The real GDP by prefecture is based on the 2005 chain price for the 2010 value and the 2015 chain price for 2011-2019 values from the database of prefectural accounts by CAO (Cabinet Office, 2014[21]). The surges in the space-based ubiquitous index coincide with a rise in GDP, indicating a mean correlation of 0.52. The most notable correlation stands at 0.82 observed in Yamanashi prefecture.

As a starting point for estimating the value of space-enabled activities, the socio-economic impacts should be clearly defined. Social impacts are the effects of a particular action or event on individuals, communities, and society as a whole, such as changes in public health, education, community cohesion, lifestyle, cultural practices, and overall quality of life. Economic impacts, on the other hand, are the consequences of actions, events, policies, or technology on the economy, including businesses and individuals. These outcomes can have an impact on economic growth, employment, as indicated by GDP, employment rates, consumer spending and so on. In many cases, the social and economic impacts are interconnected.

Figure 4.3. Space-enabled society in selected sparsely populated prefectures in Japan

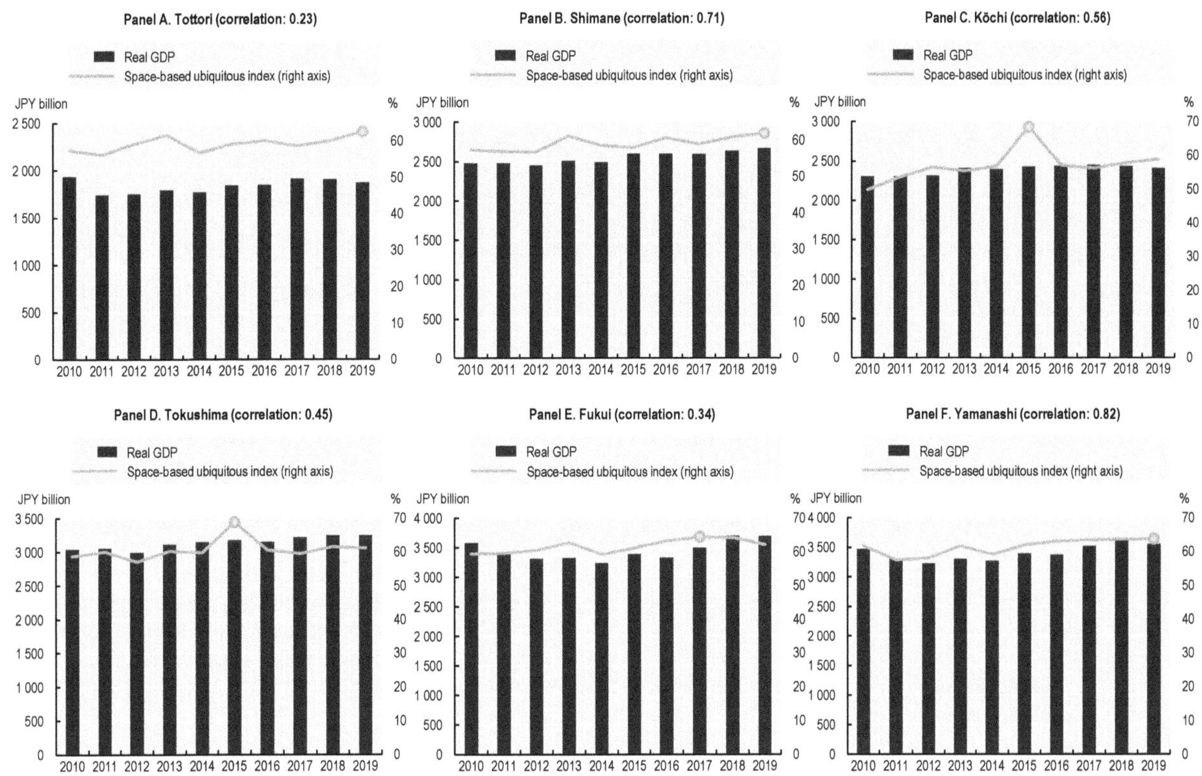

Notes: GDP: Gross domestic product. The space-based ubiquitous index is calculated as the average by prefecture of six indicators (household penetration of personal computers, internet, broadband and mobile communication; the share of business firms implementing telework; and the market share of multi-use software). Due to data unavailability, telework implementation rates rely on regional data, while multi-use software market shares refer to nationwide data.
Source: Authors' calculations based on survey data from Japan's Ministry of Internal Affairs and Communications.

To estimate the socio-economic impacts of space infrastructure, the model applies the aggregate production function which explains how the total real GDP is affected by available inputs in the economy. The following factors influence aggregate output: production function, technological capabilities, total amount of capital stocks, and total workforce. The key concept is that economic growth increases when aggregate production increases as a result of technological, human capital, knowledge, and social infrastructure changes. Based on the calculated space-based ubiquitous index in previous parts, which reflects not only the amount of information capital but also the implications of ICT utilisation, the macroeconomic model demonstrates direct and indirect impacts both on society and the economy. Based on Ministry of Internal Affairs and Communications (2008[16]), the authors estimate the following equation:

Estimate equation:

$$ln\left(\frac{Y}{L}\right) = ln\,A + \alpha' \cdot ln\frac{Kall}{L} + \beta \cdot ln(K \cdot Us) \cdot S$$

$$*With\ A>0,\ \alpha'>0,\ \beta>0,\ Us>0,\ S>0$$

When calculating the socio-economic impacts by prefecture, a dummy variable for each region is added.

$$ln\left(\frac{Y}{L}\right) = ln\,A + \alpha' \cdot ln\frac{Kall}{L} + \beta \cdot ln(K \cdot Us) \cdot S + \delta Dummy$$

$$*With\ \delta Dummy = \sum_{\iota=1}^{47} \beta\iota \cdot dp\iota$$

Table 4.5. Variables for estimating the socio-economic impact of space infrastructure

Variables	Description	Database
Y	Aggregate output is defined as an economy's total productivity, or gross domestic product (GDP). GDP represents the sum of value added by all its producers. This study employs real GDP, an inflation-adjusted measure.	National Accounts of Japan or Prefectural Accounts, Cabinet Office
A	A denotes the technological factor measuring the economy's overall productivity, called Total Factor Productivity (TFP).	-
Kall	Capital stock is the total quantity of non-human capital input into the economy. The amount encompasses physical and financial assets developed and employed by businesses or governments in the production process, such as buildings, plants, machinery, equipment, and ownership interests. *Estimate equation:* $K\tau^i = I\tau^i + (I-d_1{}^i)I^i\tau_{-1} + (1-d_2{}^i)I^i\tau_{-2} + \ldots + (1-dsi^i)I^i\tau\text{-}si$ τ: point of time, dj: cumulative depreciation rate at time j, * j$\in \{1, 2, \ldots, s\}$ $I\tau$: capital investment at time j, s: service life $K\tau = K\tau^1 + K\tau^2 + K\tau^3$	Gross Capital Stock of Private Enterprises, Cabinet Office
Ki	Telecommunication capital stock is measured in the perpetual inventory method: $Kt = It + (1-d)Kt\text{-}1$ I: flow investment, d: depreciation rate, t: year	ICT Economic Analysis Survey, Ministry of Internal Affairs and Communication and/or Estimation of Information Capital Stock by Prefecture, InfoCom Research, Inc.
L	Labour input = Number of employees in the entire economy × Total hours worked in the entire economy	Labour Force Survey, Ministry of Internal Affairs and Communication and/or Prefectural Accounts, Cabinet Office and/or Monthly Labor Survey, Ministry of Health, Labour and Welfare
Us	Space-based ubiquitous index	calculated
S	Space infrastructure's contribution to the space-based ubiquitous index	Not currently available

Source: Adapted from MIC (2008[16]), "ビキタス化による地域経済成長に関する調査報告 [Research Report on Regional Economic Growth as a Result of the Progress of Ubiquitous Networks]", https://www.soumu.go.jp/johotsusintokei/linkdata/other033_200803_hokoku.pdf.

Figure 4.4. Illustration of the model's economic implications

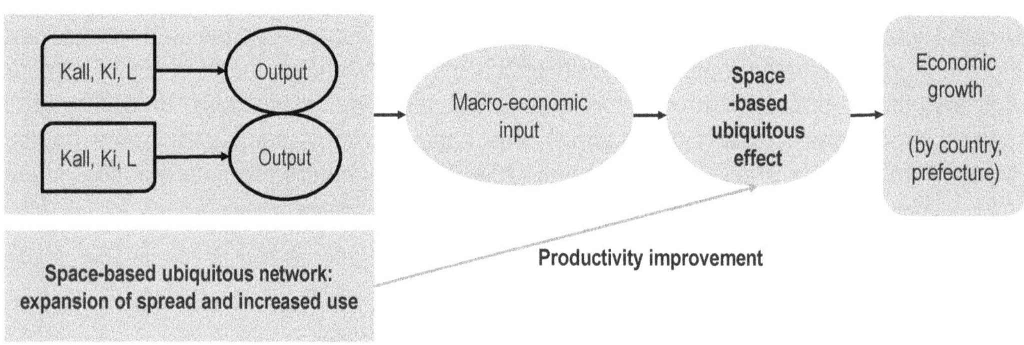

Notes: Kall refers to Capital stock; Ki refers to telecommunication capital stock; and L refers to Labour input. See Table 4.5 for further information.
Source: Adapted from MIC (2008[16]), "ビキタス化による地域経済成長に関する調査報告 [Research Report on Regional Economic Growth as a Result of the Progress of Ubiquitous Networks]", https://www.soumu.go.jp/johotsusintokei/linkdata/other033_200803_hokoku.pdf.

Figure 4.4 illustrates the economic implications of the model. Reflecting the effects of a space-based ubiquitous network, the model represents the productivity enhancement brought by space infrastructure.

As the model measures the value across time on real GDP, it is applicable even in unusual situations such as natural disasters.

Contributions from space infrastructure

S denotes the pure benefits of space infrastructure. To narrow the contribution from space infrastructure in the space-based ubiquitous index, the proportion of satcom and GNSS involved in each of the six indicators must be identified. In other words, the positive socio-economic impacts from other information and communication products and services that do not have access to space systems need to be excluded. The current absence of precise databases on *S*, such as the number of mobile satellite communication subscribers and the household members' ratio of satellite utilisation in internet and broadband communication, poses a challenge to the proposed model. However, the contribution from space infrastructure to the information and communication industry has been increasing in Japan, as evidenced by Figure 4.5 illustrating the rapid growth in the number of radio stations for mobile satellite services between 2004 and 2015.

Figure 4.5. Number of radio stations for mobile satellite services

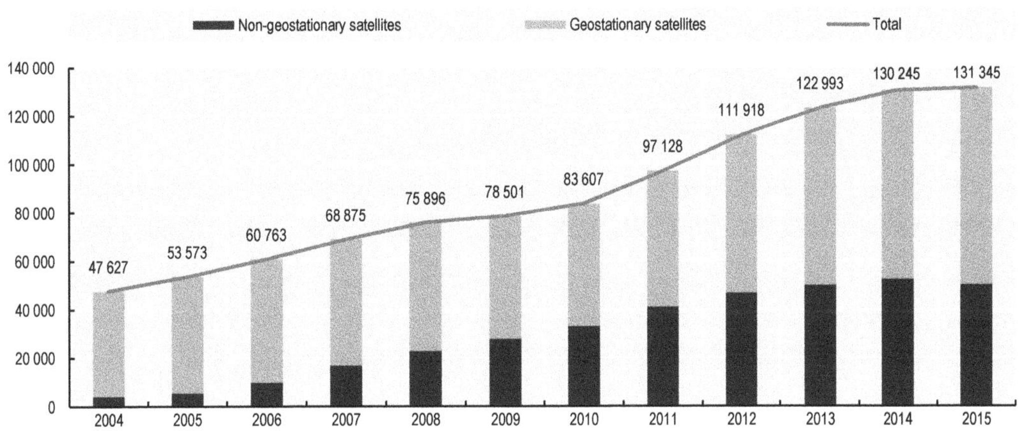

Source: MIC (2016[22]), "平成28年度　情報通信白書 [FY 2016 Information and Communications White Paper]", https://www.soumu.go.jp/johotsusintokei/whitepaper/ja/h28/pdf/n5300000.pdf.

Discussion and conclusions

Space infrastructure has become an integral part of our daily lives. This chapter provides a macroeconomic framework to quantify the socio-economic impact of space infrastructure in the information and communication sector. The rational sector selection is based on a review of official policy documents as well as the key criteria to CIP: limited substitutability and exceptionally high socio-economic impact. In Japan, an isolated, ageing, depopulating and disaster-prone country, space assets in the information and communication industry can be considered as vital infrastructure to maintain national life and economic activities.

To understand the government's perspectives on critical infrastructure, the model applies the MIC's approach to evaluate the significance of general ICT based on the aggregate production function. The space-based ubiquitous index, which is measured by six technological sectors and two macro areas to which satcom and GNSS contribute, indicates the socio-economic impacts of space-enabled information and communication services on the model. The simplified equation, which is applicable to various use cases such as broadcasting and other countries, demonstrates the correlation between the deployment of space infrastructure and economic growth based on clear and unified government databases. The main challenge to the modelling is however the lack of precise data on the pure benefits of satcom and GNSS in the sector.

As the reliance on space-based products and services has grown, so have the risks to space assets. This economic study gives essential evidence-based arguments for international policy discussions on space safety and sustainability. Additionally, the case study in Japan provides an interesting ilustration of how one of the major spacefaring countries may develop a policy framework for the protection of its critical space infrastructure.

References

Cabinet Office (2024), "経済施策を一体的に講ずることによる安全保障の確保の推進に関する法律, [Act on the Promotion of Security Assurance through the Integrated Implementation of Economic Measures]", e-gov Japan, Government of Japan, https://elaws.egov.go.jp/document?lawid=504AC0000000043_20250616_504AC0000000068 (accessed on 11 January 2024). [4]

Cabinet Office (2022), "デジタル田園都市国家構想基本方針 [Vision for a Digital Garden City Nation]'", Government of Japan, www.cas.go.jp/jp/seisaku/digital_denen/pdf/20220607_honbun.pdf. [11]

Cabinet Office (2022), "経済安全保障推進法の概要 [Overview of the Economic Security Promotion Act]", Government of Japan, www.cao.go.jp/keizai_anzen_hosho/doc/gaiyo.pdf. [2]

Cabinet Office (2014), "県民経済計算（平成13年度 - 平成26年度)(1993SNA,平成17年基準計数) [Prefectural Accounts (2001-2014) (1993SNA/2005 base figures)]", Government of Japan, www.esri.cao.go.jp/jp/sna/data/data_list/kenmin/files/contents/main_h26.html. [21]

Cabinet Secretariat (2021), "Action Plan of the Growth Strategy", provisional translation, Government of Japan, www.cas.go.jp/jp/seisaku/seicho/pdf/ap2021en.pdf. [12]

Critchley-Marrows, J. and Q. Verspieren (2023), "Ensuring PNT Resilience: A Global Review of Navigation Policies and Roadmaps", Science, Technology and Innovation Governance (STIG) Reports, University of Tokyo, https://stig.pp.u-tokyo.ac.jp/stig/wp-content/uploads/2023/07/Resilient_PNT_Policy_Report_FINAL_ONLINE.pdf (accessed on 11 January 2024). [10]

MIC (2023), *Population estimates*, Government of Japan, Ministry of Internal Affairs and Communication, www.stat.go.jp/data/jinsui/2022np/index.html. [6]

MIC (2022), "'メディア・ソフトの制作及び流通の実態に関する調査 [Survey of the Current State of Media and Software Development and Dissemination]", Ministry of Internal Affairs and Communications, Government of Japan, www.soumu.go.jp/iicp/research/media_soft.html. [19]

MIC (2022), "Communications Usage Trend Survey 1966-2022 (Households)", Ministry of Internal Affairs and Communications, Government of Japan, www.soumu.go.jp/johotsusintokei/statistics/statistics05b1.html. [14]

MIC (2022), “Communications Usage Trend Survey 2010-2022 (Companies)”, Ministry of Internal Affairs and Communications, Government of Japan, www.soumu.go.jp/johotsusintokei/statistics/statistics05b2.html. [18]

MIC (2022), “Communications Usage Trend Survey 2010-2022 (Household Members)”, Ministry of Internal Affairs and Communications, Government of Japan, www.soumu.go.jp/johotsusintokei/statistics/statistics05b1.html. [15]

MIC (2020), “2020 Population Census”, e-stat Japan, Ministry of Internal Affairs and Communications, Government of Japan, www.e-stat.go.jp/en/stat-search/files?page=1&layout=datalist&toukei=00200521&tstat=000001136464&cycle=0&tclass1=000001136466&tclass2val=0 (accessed on 12 January 2024). [20]

MIC (2016), *平成28年度　情報通信白書 [FY 2016 Information and Communications White Paper]*, Ministry of Internal Affairs and Communications, Government of Japan, www.soumu.go.jp/johotsusintokei/whitepaper/ja/h28/pdf/n5300000.pdf. [22]

MIC (2011), “Part 1 Information and Communications in the Aftermath of the Great East Japan Earthquake”*, 2007 WHITE PAPER Information and Communications in Japan'*, Ministry of Internal Affairs and Communications, Government of Japan, www.soumu.go.jp/johotsusintokei/whitepaper/eng/WP2011/part1.pdf. [7]

MIC (2011), “東日本大震災における通信の被災状況、復旧等に関する取組状況 [The state of communications damage caused by the Great East Japan Earthquake, and the state of recovery efforts]”, Ministry of Internal Affairs and Communications, Government of Japan, www.bousai.go.jp/kaigirep/kentokai/kinoukakuho/2/pdf/1.pdf. [8]

MIC (2009), “我が国の情報流通量の指標体系と計量手法に関する報告書 [Report on the index system and measurement method for the volume of information distributed in Japan]”, Ministry of Internal Affairs and Communications, Government of Japan, www.soumu.go.jp/main_content/000030652.pdf. [17]

MIC (2008), “ユビキタス化による地域経済成長に関する調査報告 [Research Report on Regional Economic Growth as a Result of the Progress of Ubiquitous Networks]”, Ministry of Internal Affairs and Communications, Government of Japan, www.soumu.go.jp/johotsusintokei/linkdata/other033_200803_hokoku.pdf (accessed on 12 January 2024). [16]

MIC (2007), “Chapter 1: Progress of Ubiquitous Economy and Global Expansion”, in *FY 2007 Information and Communications White Paper*, Ministry of Internal Affairs and Communications, Government of Japan, www.soumu.go.jp/johotsusintokei/whitepaper/eng/WP2007/chapter-1.pdf. [13]

NISC (2024), *National Center of Incident Readiness and Strategy for Cybersecurity*, www.nisc.go.jp/eng/index.html (accessed on 11 January 2024). [1]

NISC (2022), *The Cybersecurity Policy for Critical Infrastructure Protection*, Cybersecurity Strategic Headquarters. Government of Japan, www.nisc.go.jp/eng/pdf/cip_policy_2022_eng.pdf (accessed on 11 January 2024). [3]

PwC (2017), *Dependence of the European Economy on Space Infrastructures: Potential Impacts of Space Asset Loss*, Publications Office of the European Union, https://doi.org/10.2873/81127 (accessed on 11 January 2024). [5]

Vittori, D. et al. (2022), "Identifying the costs caused by an irreversible deterioration of the orbital regimes", in *Earth's Orbits at Risk: The Economics of Space Sustainability*, OECD Publishing, Paris, https://doi.org/10.1787/74213960-en. [9]

Notes

[1] The authors conducted international research through literature reviews and interviews, mostly in France and the United Kingdom.

[2] The three ministries are as follows: the Ministry of Justice, the Ministry of Finance, and the Ministry of Health, Labour and Welfare in Japan.

[3] A geostationary orbit (GEO) is a circular geosynchronous orbit 35 786 km in altitude above Earth's equator following the direction of Earth's rotation. GEO satellites seem stationary from the ground, and due to their high altitude, three satellites can cover the whole world, excluding the polar regions, which are utilised for fixed and mobile communications.

[4] Non-geostationary orbits (NGSO) generally refer to those that are closer to Earth than GEO, such as a low earth orbit (LEO) below 2 000km. Therefore, non-GEO satellites offer less transmission latency than GEO satellites, have less terminal output, and can be smaller and portable, making them ideal for mobile communications.

5 The socio-economic benefits of earth observation (EO): Insights from the end users of EO services and applications in Italy

Gelsomina Catalano, Csil, Italy

Valentina Morretta, University of Milan, Italy

Earth observation (EO) is a strategic and fast-changing domain of the space economy that increasingly contributes to the understanding, analysis and management of different natural and societal aspects of Earth. A range of socio-economic benefits may derive from the use of EO data. This chapter aims to identify the benefits accrued by end users of EO services and applications, on which there is scarce evidence in the literature. With the objective of filling in this gap, the chapter relies on a survey distributed to the end users of EO services in Italy, a country which is active along the whole value chain of the space economy.

Introduction

Earth Observation (EO) is a strategic and fast-changing domain of the space economy. It consists of collecting chemical, biological and physical data and imagery of planet Earth via remote sensing technologies (GEO, 2020[1]; Onoda and Young, 2017[2]).

In recent years, EO infrastructure, particularly the number of satellites, has rapidly grown (Bryce Space and Technology, 2018[3]). Recent advancements in space manufacturing and digital technologies, in addition to increasingly attractive market opportunities, have fostered the involvement of the private sector along the entire value chain within the "new space" economy paradigm (Weinzierl, 2018[4]). While the public sector still drives the industry, commercially-driven space projects and their economic exploitation for commercial reasons have also become salient. The satellite database of the Union of Concerned Scientists counts more than 1 000 operational earth satellites in orbit (OECD, 2023[5]), allowing observation of phenomena that would otherwise be difficult and expensive to monitor from the ground with the same optimal coverage, accuracy and consistency.

PwC (2019[6]) estimated the global EO economy in 2017 between EUR 9.6 and 9.8 billion, only considering sales of EO satellites (the so-called upstream sector) and EO data acquisition, their processing and transformation into products, services and applications for end users (the downstream sector). However, these numbers capture only a tiny portion of the potential socio-economic impact of EO. For example, in Europe, the European Space Agency (ESA) has invested heavily in developing satellites dedicated to EO, particularly the Sentinels satellites of the Copernicus programme. According to PwC (2019[6]), investments in the European Copernicus programme – which equalled EUR 8.2 billion between 2008 and 2020 - could generate between EUR 16.2 and EUR 21.3 billion in the coming years. This excludes non-monetary benefits and considers the added value created in the upstream industry, the sales of services and applications developed in the downstream sector, and the benefits deriving from the exploitation of these services by the end users in different fields.

EO is increasingly contributing to the understanding, analysis and management of different natural and societal aspects of planet Earth, with relevant socio-economic and environmental implications. A growing variety of innovative services and applications using EO data have risen in prominence across a variety of different sectors, including climate change monitoring, human health prevention, agriculture efficiency, urban planning, ecosystems and civil protection (NEREUS, Commission and ESA, 2018[7]; Daraio et al., 2014[8]; PwC, 2019[6]).

The socio-economic benefits deriving from EO programmes are broad. Different stakeholders along the EO value chain may directly or indirectly take advantage of investments in EO, including firms operating in the industrial and information and communications technology (ICT) sectors, research institutes, scientists, and civil society (Morretta, Vurchio and Carrazza, 2022[9]).

Among European countries, Italy has a long tradition in the space sector. It is one of the few countries to actively operate along the whole EO value chain from the upstream industry (given its predominant role in the manufacturing of cutting-edge satellites) to downstream activities with high-value-added services, mainly developed and managed by small and medium-sized enterprises (Lupi and Morretta, 2022[10]; Ministero delle Impresse e del Made in Italy, 2019[11]). The growing availability of satellite data, together with advancement in ICT technologies – pushed by the development of powerful processors and machine learning – is contributing to the exponential growth of the downstream segment of the value chain (Probst, Pedersen and Dakkak-Arnoux, 2017[12]) and, therefore to the creation of new services and applications in a wide range of fields.

While recent studies have investigated the magnitude and characteristics of the Italian downstream market (e.g. firms that develop EO services and applications for end users) (Lupi and Morretta, 2022[10]), very little is known about the end users of such services and applications. Additionally, an evaluation of the benefits deriving from such services and applications has never been carried out in Italy, except for some very narrow case studies (NEREUS, Commission and ESA, 2018[7]; Sawyer and Khabarov, 2022[13]).

In this chapter, the authors contribute to filling in this gap by focusing exclusively on the benefits accrued by end users of EO services and applications, such as national and local governments, public and private firms and individuals who use these applications or services in a wide range of fields. More specifically, the authors focus on the economic benefits that direct end users gain through the use of such services, such as increased efficacy and efficiency. At the same time, the authors exclude the benefits accrued by other indirect users and society at large. The social and environmental impacts of EO service on these latter categories have the potential to be large but are often left unexpressed and unmeasured and are thus beyond the scope of this study.

From this perspective, the authors aim to answer the following research questions: i) Who are the end users of EO services and applications in the Italian market? ii) What benefits may stem from using such services? iii) What barriers are currently hindering the development of this sector in Italy?

The final use of EO services and data: a brief overview of the literature

Identifying and investigating EO adoption areas is crucial to disentangling who the current and potential end users of EO are, and the economic benefits that they can experience. The existing literature on this topic is rich and allows us to pinpoint the main areas in which EO end users operate beyond military applications. For example, NEREUS et al. (2018[7]) report 99 end users' successful stories, highlighting how EU public administrations (being one of the most representative but not exclusive end users of EO services) are using Copernicus data to improve the quality of life of European citizens. The studies are grouped around several domains, as reported Figure 5.1.

The European Association of Remote Sensing Companies (EARSC) also monitors the new areas of EO implementation in the framework of the Sentinel Economic Benefits Study (SeBS), which provides valuable examples and case studies and seeks to identify and evaluate EO benefits.

Figure 5.1. End users' adoption areas of EO services

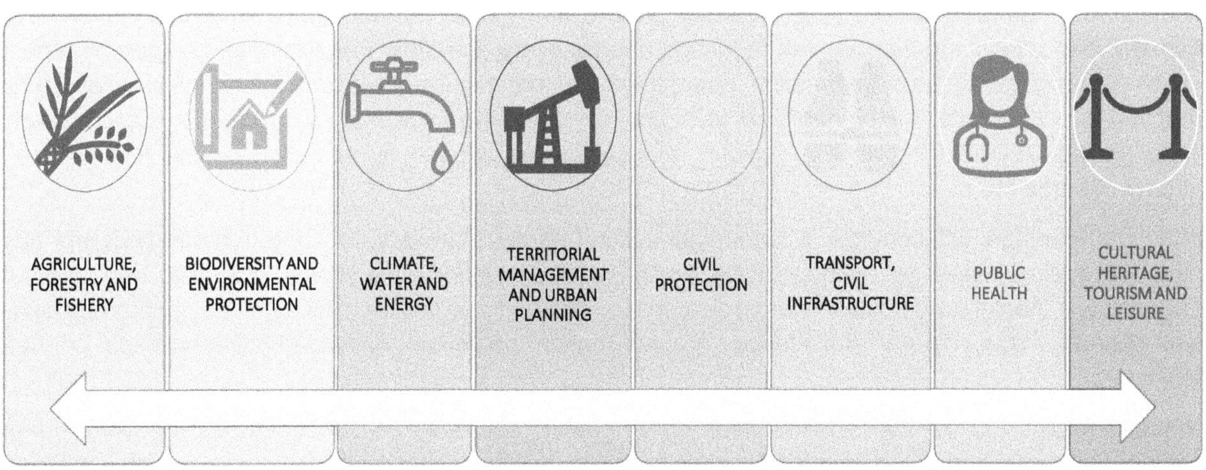

Thanks to the use of EO, direct end users can gain economic benefits when delivering their usual or innovative services to groups of citizens (e.g. in the case of governments) or customers (e.g. in the case of companies). Such benefits typically include saving costs, increasing revenues, gaining efficiency and increasing efficacy and quality. Other types of benefits may be reputational and strategic, among others.

A key example of this can be observed through the use of EO in the agriculture sector. Sawyer, Oligschläger and Oligschläger (2019[14]) present the case of an application using EO data by Belgian potato farmers to obtain information on field management. This application provides farmers with timely information regarding the optimal time to irrigate, plant and fertilise their crops, using satellite imagery of vegetation colour. This was estimated to increase yields by up to 20% and improve the overall quality of the potatoes farmed. The adoption of the app contributed to increasing revenues and income for the farmers and produced indirect economic benefits for the whole potato industry value chain (including agronomists, consultants, processors, distributors, supermarkets) up to the final consumers.

In the realm of forestry and environmental protection, Sawyer, Dubost and Vries (2016[15]) examined the impact of satellite imagery on forest management by the Swedish public administration. In this case, the designed EO service contributed to a decrease in illegal logging and a lack of immediate replanting and pre-commercial thinning. The cost of collecting satellite imageries was EUR 64 000 relative to a benefit of between EUR 16.1 and EUR 21.6 million per annum. Direct economic benefits derived from a decreased cost of physical inspections using aircraft, in addition to the long-term value increase as a result of higher timber quality and production volumes.

Examples of the use of EO services in climate, water and energy are also common. For instance, weather forecast information is increasingly used by decision makers to ensure the safety of the population, protect property, and add value to the economy (EUMETSTAT, 2014[16]). In energy, Leibrand et al. (2019[17]) review how many existing EO applications support rural electrification planning, renewable energy resource assessment, grid operation and reliability, as well as disaster risk reduction in interruption of the service.

In territorial management and urban planning, EO services are increasingly supporting public administrations in building more efficient and resilient urban transport facilities. For example, in Norway, a new service showing ground motion based on EO data contributes to saving costs in the construction and management of road infrastructure (Sawyer, Boyle and Khabarov, 2020[18]). In Italy, a similar service is used by Azienda Nazionale Autonoma delle Strade and produced an economic benefit of between EUR 3.8 and EUR 8.6 million per annum, predominantly influenced by a reduction in construction and monitoring highways, plus other societal and environmental benefits (Sawyer and Khabarov, 2022[13]).

The use of EO in civil protection is also extremely valuable, where advanced EO services have been extensively used to support crisis managers, civil protection authorities, and humanitarian aid actors dealing with natural disasters (e.g. earthquakes and landslides), human-made emergency situations, humanitarian crises and disaster risk reduction and recovery activities. For example, a report by NASA (2013[19]) using the "Value of Information" approach found that the use of EO data during the Eyjafjallajökull eruption in 2010 reduced the probability of an aircraft experiencing a volcanic ash incident by approximately 12%, saving USD 25–72 million in avoided revenue losses caused by unnecessary flight delays and aircraft damage costs.

In cultural heritage, EO contributes to tangible cultural heritage preservation and management and has been increasingly used by agencies such as the United Nations Educational, Scientific and Cultural Organization thanks to ad hoc services dedicated to archaeological site identification and monitoring, land-use change maps, natural subsidence, ground motion detection, bathymetry and climate change indicators.

In public health, EO services provide alerts on air quality, outbreaks of disease carried by water-borne vectors or insects, and assessments of access to health facilities, among other uses. As reported in Florio and Morretta (2021[20]), Dawes et al. (2013[21]) carried out a case study illustrating the benefits of EO data in monitoring air quality in some remote areas of the United States. In monetary terms, their analysis shows that satellites provide timely $PM_{2.5}$ information to 82% of the 18.1 million people currently living in unmonitored areas at no additional cost. In contrast, the purchase, installation, and operation of ground infrastructures would have cost USD 25.9 million and covered only 44% of those unmonitored people in the subsequent five years.

The above are just selected examples. The high quantity of information provided by EO data, coupled with rapid advances in artificial intelligence, has led to a constant increase in the applications and services benefiting from EO data. Its use has been extended to services monitoring oil spills in the Mediterranean Sea, in addition to applications in agri-tech solutions, biodiversity and ecosystems loss; climate services; emergency management; fisheries; infrastructure; insurance; road and automotive sectors; maritime and inland waterways; and urban development. However, the existing literature mainly focuses on identifying and describing successful stories and case studies worldwide, restricting our understanding of the impact of EO services in specific country contexts, and inhibiting the detection of other sectors that could benefit from EO adoption in the future.

Method

Ideally, economic benefits should be appraised by looking at the incremental revenues, added efficacy or efficiency (or other profit margins) of end users delivering a public/private service, using a sample comprised of units using an EO service, and a counterfactual group providing the same service without using EO. However, since this analysis is not specific to a single EO service but rather aims to provide a general overview of the Italian market by looking at different users, services and fields of application, this analysis uses primary data collected through an online survey disseminated with the support of the Italian Space Agency. The survey is based on approximately 30 semi-structured questions to explore i) who are the main end users of the services/applications offered, in which sectors they operate and how they use the service; (ii) to what extent the use of EO services in their field contributes to their economic performance, according to their perceptions; and (iii) what factors may promote or hamper their diffusion among end users. Most questions exploit a Likert scale ranging from 1 to 5.

The survey ran over six months (launched on 30 April 2022 and closed on 30 November 2022) and targeted 3 235 potential users, whose contacts were collected from different sources. A list of potential users of EO services had not previously been built. This study's contribution fills in this gap by having gradually collected contacts from different sources, including interviews with key stakeholders (e.g. speakers at relevant conferences - Prisma, ESA events, etc. COSMO-SkyMED users), Orbis databases (by selecting large companies operating in sectors where, according to the literature, the use of EO is more relevant, such as construction, agriculture, forestry and fishing, transport, mining industries, etc.), firms carrying out precision farming, national, regional and local authorities involved in civil protection, municipal companies involved in the delivery of services of general interests (e.g. water and wastewater supply, sewage collection, etc.). The invitations were sent by email, presenting the reasons and objectives of the survey and indicating the access link to the questionnaire. The survey was conducted with Computer Assisted Web Interviewing methodology and had a dedicated telephone and email assistance service to solicit answers.

Overall, the authors collected information from 106 respondents who use EO services and applications which are either internally developed or purchased by third parties.

Main results

EO users' profiles and their use of EO services and applications

The 106 users of EO services and applications answering the survey are mostly territorial public bodies (31%) or national public bodies (18%), followed by private (14%) and public-owned companies (10%), municipalities (11%), regions (10%), national government (2%) and others (3% e.g. research entities). They are mostly large or medium-sized institutions/companies (49% and 18% respectively), accounting for more than 150 employees. Their headquarters are mostly located in the north and centre of Italy (41% and

36% respectively), with the highest number concentrated in large cities such as Rome and Milan. Over a third (36%) of respondents operate in the public administration and are responsible for managing housing construction and regional planning projects; ensuring environmental protection; carrying out activities of the fire brigade and civil protection; general planning activities; and general statistical services. The sample also includes a high portion of respondents (10%) dealing with professional, scientific and technical activities (including weather forecasting), with the supply of water, sewerage, waste management and remediation activities (12%), as well as working in the agriculture, forestry and fishing sectors (9%).

The majority of respondents (87%) use EO services and applications which rely on data provided by satellites. ESA Sentinels rank first amongst data providers, followed by NASA Landsat and ASI Prisma (Figure 5.2). Over three quarters (80%) of user respondents also declare that EO services and applications that they use take data from drones and/or aerial images. The acquisition of this data mostly occurs directly from public portals and or Italian companies, whilst rarely from foreign companies, universities or other public institutions (Figure 5.3).

Figure 5.2. Most frequently used satellite data providers for EO services/applications

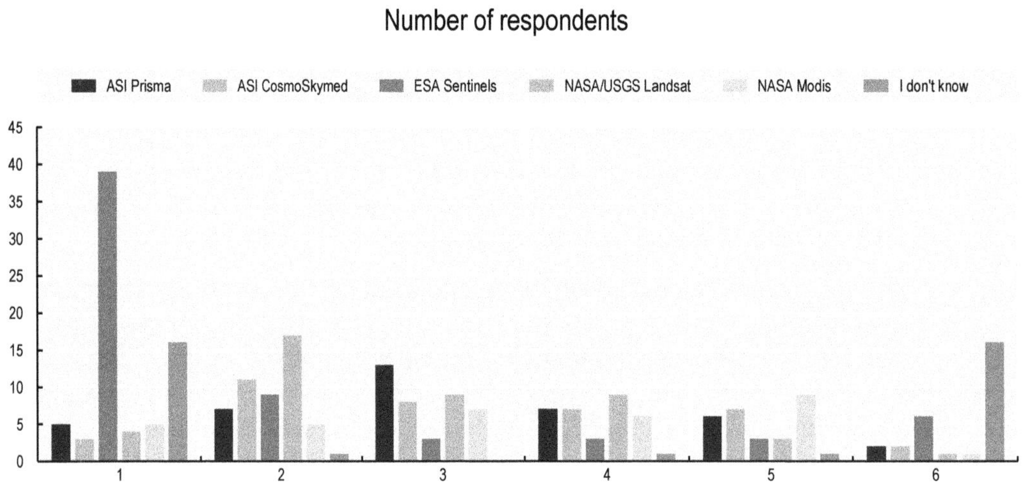

Notes: The frequency scale ranges from 1 (most frequent) to 6 (least frequent). N=106.

Figure 5.3. Main sources of EO services and applications

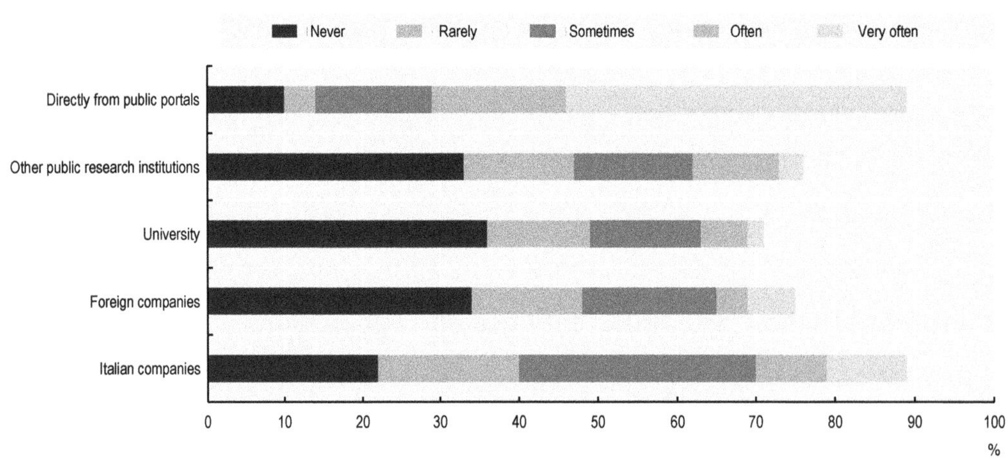

Amongst respondents, there is a significant number (55 out of 106 users) who use EO services and applications which have been internally developed or both internally and externally provided. The most effective channels to obtain knowledge about EO services and applications are through direct contacts (65 respondents), and participation in research programmes/project (55 respondents).

A certain level of experience with the use of these services and applications has been detected among the surveyed respondents (Figure 5.4). The institutions and companies where respondents currently work predominantly started using EO services and applications over the last 10 years (51 respondents, 48%); a significant number of respondents (30, 28%) declared that their institutions started to use these applications and services between 10-20 years ago while a relatively low number of respondents (21, 20%) starting more than 20 years ago.

Figure 5.4. Respondents' years of experience in using EO services/applications

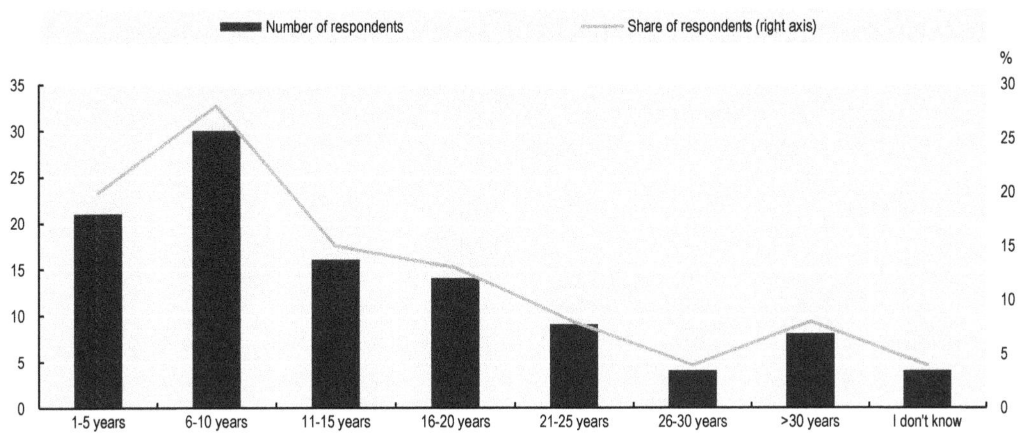

Figure 5.5. The importance of the use of EO services/applications for daily activities

Number and share (%) of respondents

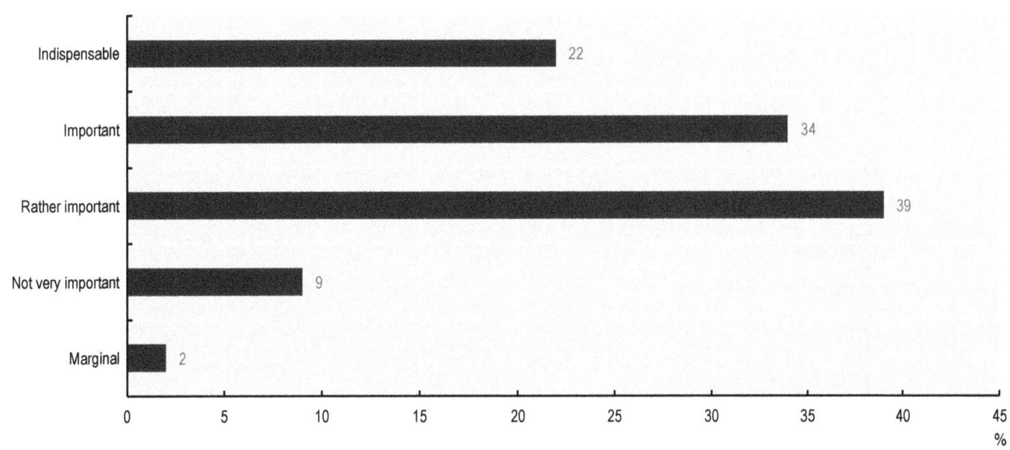

Overall, more than half of the respondents agree that the use of these applications and services is important, or even indispensable, for the daily activities carried out at their institutions/companies (Figure 5.5). The evidence collected confirms that EO data are used for a variety of purposes: detecting inefficiencies in the transport sector and identifying the restoring interventions that are needed; monitoring territories and coastlines to prevent natural risks (e.g. headquarters, flooding, etc.); planning and designing environmental and urban interventions; monitoring specific areas subject to environmental crimes, as well as marine and coastal areas (chlorophyll, turbidity, algal blooms, dispersion of floating waste, etc.); monitoring and classifying land use; providing licences for mining activities; reconstructing glacier perimeters to detect glacial lakes; analysing and monitoring cultivated areas; monitoring weather and supporting flight planning; monitoring water loss and planning restoring interventions; developing cartographic rendering; and assessing the technical feasibility of new infrastructure.

The socio-economic benefits of EO services and applications

The use of EO services and applications has allowed the majority of respondents to improve the quality of the products and services offered (57% of respondents agreed), R&D capabilities (56%), and the efficiency of production processes and/or service provision (51%), as shown in Figure 5.6. The use of these services and applications also contributes to increased collaborations with other subjects (38%) and the development of new services and products (42%), new software and technologies (30%), and new research projects (34%). Conversely, the contribution of EO services and applications was limited in the development of new trademarks and registered patents (52% of respondents disagreed), in entering new markets and industries, and in starting a new business or research and development unit.

Figure 5.6. Miscellaneous benefits from the use of EO services/applications

Share (%) of respondents

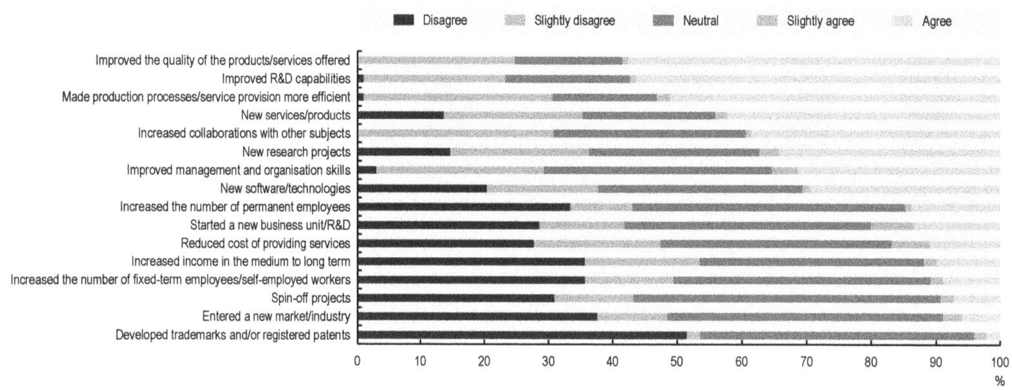

Figure 5.7. EO services and applications' contribution to average increases in revenue

Trend observed between 2019 - 2022, number and share (%) of respondents

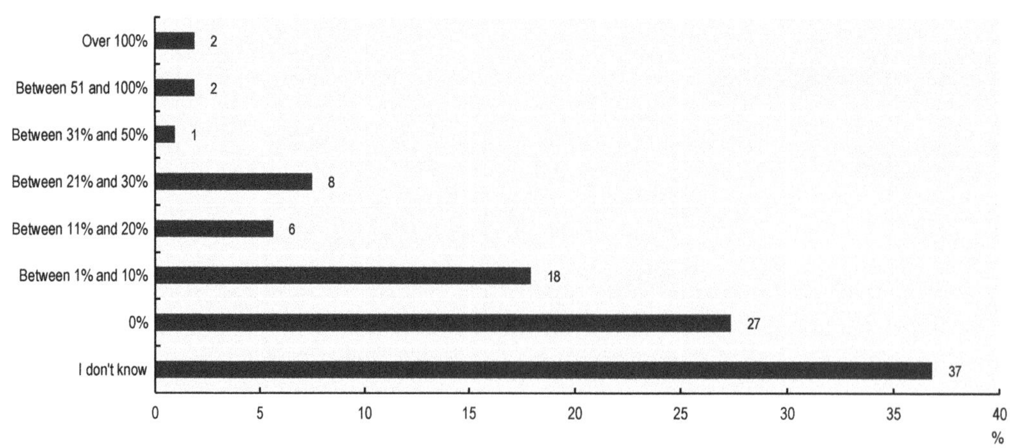

The majority of respondents were not able to answer the questions about how much the use of these services and applications allowed them to increase revenues (37% declared "I don't know") or to reduce production costs (41% declared "I don't know") (Figure 5.7). A significant percentage of respondents suggested that the use of EO services and applications had no effect on either revenues or production costs (27% and 24% respectively). They mostly ascribe this trend to the effects of COVID-19, which slowed down sales and production processes. They would have declared a higher impact considering the trend observed over the last ten years. Nevertheless, it is worth pointing out that 38% of respondents observed a positive effect on revenues, mostly in the range of 1-30%. Additionally, 30% of user respondents reported a reduction in production costs resulting from the use of EO services and applications in the range of 1-30% (Figure 5.8).

Figure 5.8. EO services and applications' contribution to reducing production/provision costs

Trend observed between 2019 - 2022, number and share (%) of respondents

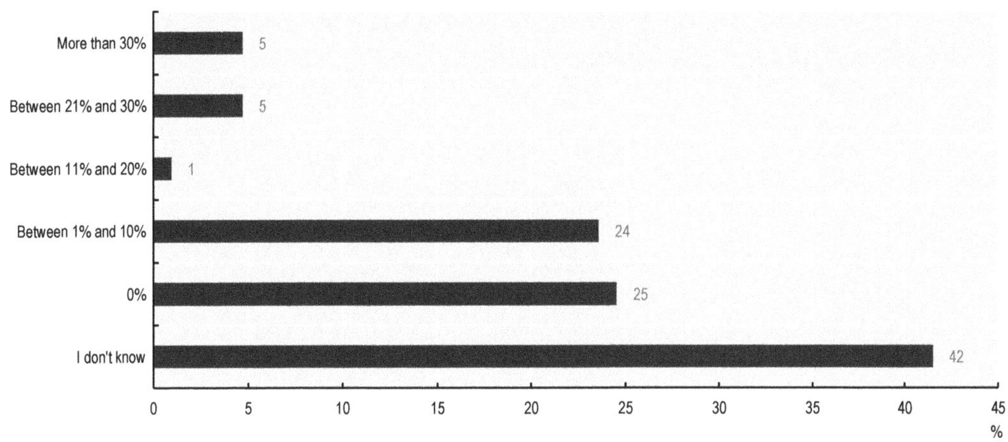

Figure 5.9. Organisations' contribution to Sustainable Development Goals thanks to the use of EO

Number of respondents, multiple answers allowed

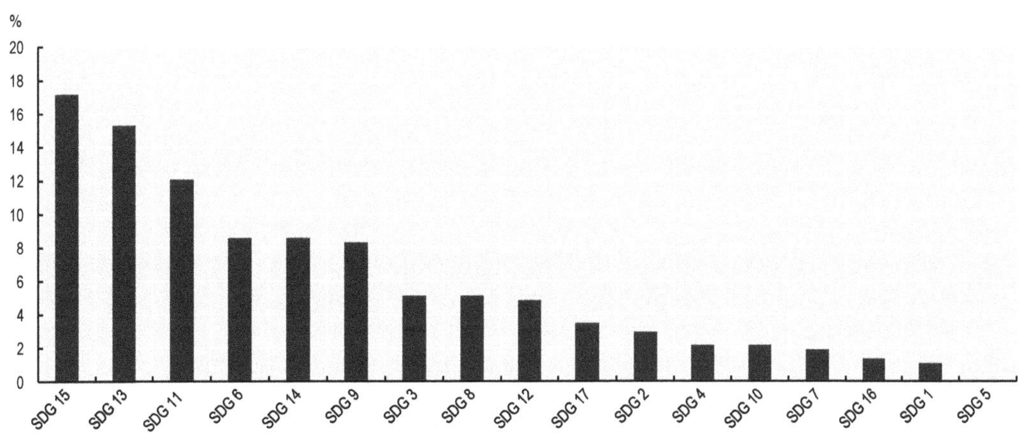

Thanks to the use of EO services and applications, respondents confirmed that they were also contributing to the achievement of Sustainable Development Goals (SDGs), and in particular to SDG 15 (to protect, restore and promote sustainable use of terrestrial ecosystems, sustainably manage forests, combat desertification and halt and reverse land degradation and halt biodiversity loss), SDG 13 (to take urgent action to combat climate change and its impacts), SDG 11 (to make cities and human settlements inclusive, safe, resilient and sustainable), SDG 14 (to conserve and sustainably use the oceans, seas and marine resources for sustainable development), SDG 6 (to ensure availability and sustainable management of water and sanitation for all) and SDG 9 (to build resilient infrastructure, promote inclusive and sustainable industrialisation and foster innovation), as shown in Figure 5.9.

Obstacles to the use of EO services and applications

According to their experience, respondents largely agree that the factors which mostly hamper the diffusion and use of EO services and applications in Italy include: the lack of knowledge of the opportunities deriving from the use (45% of respondents); the lack of a long-term strategic vision (43%); and the lack of personnel with technical skills (see Figure 5.10). Regarding the required expertise (Figure 5.11), the majority of respondents report that they face difficulties in finding and hiring qualified personnel who know how to effectively use EO services and applications (33% of respondents face this issue often, 22% sometimes, and 10% always). To ensure an effective use of these services and applications, they mostly need engineers, computer scientists and geologists. One respondent also mentions agronomists, experts in geographical information systems and data scientists.

Figure 5.10. Main factors hampering the diffusion and use of EO services and applications in Italy

Share(%) of respondents

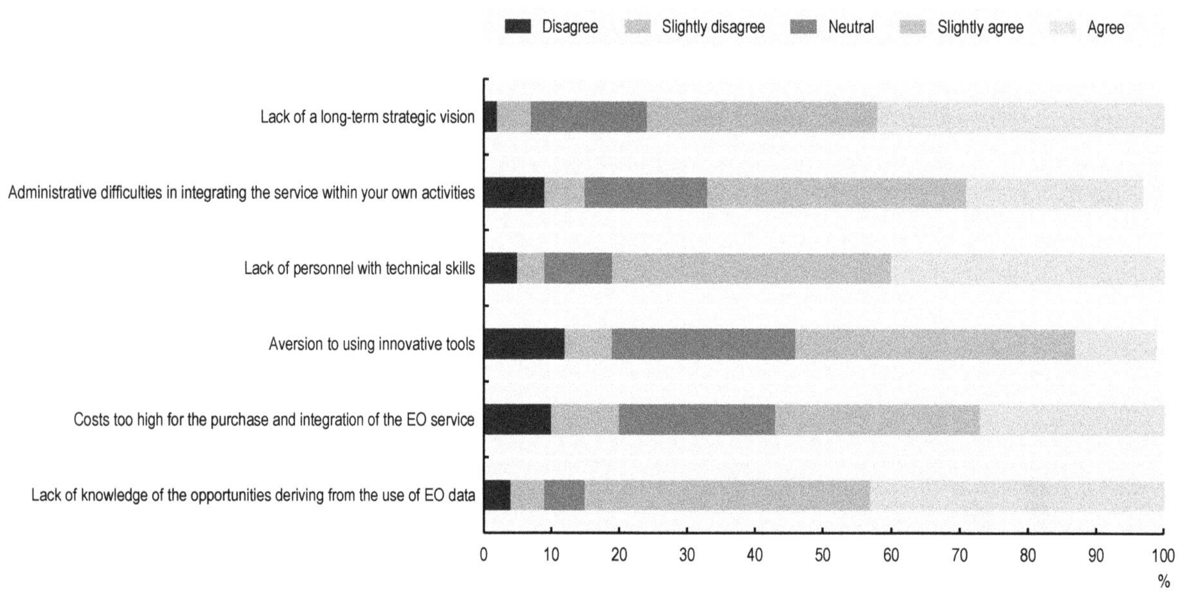

Despite these difficulties, respondents confirm their willingness not only to use existing but also new EO services and applications in the future. Some of them expect that their use will be enhanced for monitoring water service infrastructure, as well as for the prevention of natural disasters (e.g. flooding), supporting the restoration of natural habitats and fostering the development of precision agriculture.

Figure 5.11. Difficulty finding/hiring qualified personnel

Share (%) of respondents

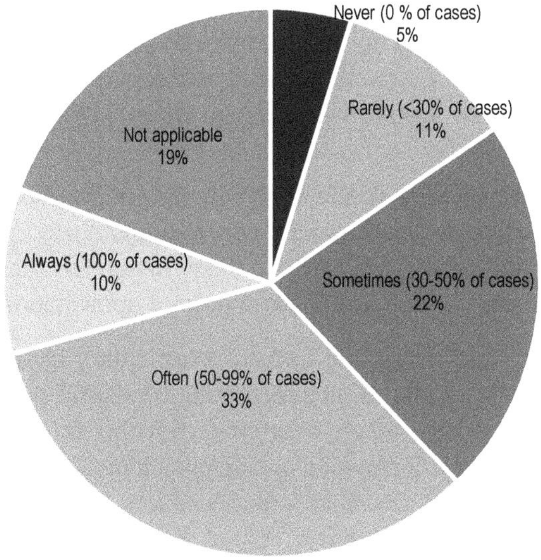

Conclusions and next steps

This chapter contributes to gaps in the existing literature by providing an assessment of the benefits derived from EO services and applications from the perspective of end users. An evaluation of the benefits derived from such services and applications had previously never been carried out, except in the context of narrow case studies, and acts as a fundamental exercise to fully assess the potential impact of EO.

The analysis specifically focuses on the Italian economy, and the results confirm the use of EO services and applications by end users covering a range of purposes. Based on the evidence collected, the authors can draw the following conclusions:

- Survey respondents reporting the use of EO services and applications are mostly territorial public bodies (31%) or national public bodies (18%), followed by private (14%) and public-owned companies (10%), municipalities (11%), regions (10%), national government (2%) and others (3% e.g. research entities). They are mostly large or medium institutions or companies (49% and 18% respectively), accounting for more than 150 employees; their headquarters are mostly located in the north and centre of Italy (41% and 36% respectively), with the highest number concentrated in large cities, such as Rome and Milan.
- The majority of respondents (87%) use EO services and applications which rely on data provided by satellites. ESA Sentinels rank first amongst data providers, followed by NASA Landsat and ASI Prisma. Eighty per cent of respondents also declare that EO services and applications they use take data from drone and/or aerial images. The acquisition of this data mostly occurs directly from public portals and or Italian companies, rather than from foreign companies, universities or other public institutions.
- The results suggest that the use of EO services and applications has allowed the majority of respondents to improve the quality of the products and services offered (57% of respondents agreed), R&D capabilities (56%), and the efficiency of production processes and/or service provision (51%). There is also evidence that the use of these services and applications contributes to increased collaborations with other subjects (38%) and the development of new services and products (42%), new software and technologies (30%), and new research projects (34%).

- Conversely, the contribution of EO services and applications was limited in the development of new trademarks and registered patents (52% of respondents disagreed), in entering new markets and industries (38% disagreed), and in starting a new business or research and development unit (29% disagreed).
- According to their experience, respondents largely agreed that the factors hampering the diffusion and use of EO services and applications in Italy include the lack of knowledge of the opportunities deriving from the use (45%), the lack of a long-term strategic vision (43%), and the lack of personnel with technical skills (41%).
- Regarding expertise, the majority of respondents report that they face difficulties in finding and hiring qualified personnel who know how to effectively use EO services and applications, especially among engineers, computer scientists and geologists. Despite these difficulties, user respondents confirm their willingness to use both existing and new EO services and applications in the future.

The authors are aware that their results would need additional and complementary analysis to produce more robust findings. They can consequently be considered as simulations of what-if scenarios trying to assess the potentialities of earth observation for the Italian economy. Beyond providing preliminary predictions of the benefits accruing to end users from EO services and applications, this exercise points to some methodological findings which can be taken into account for future research and replications in other countries.

- Having a large, comprehensive database of potential users of EO services and applications is a crucial starting point for this type of analysis. This would require some time to be built. From the authors' experience, both desk research (e.g. on public authorities portals, speakers at relevant conferences, etc.), as well as consultations with sectoral stakeholders (e.g. firms belonging to relevant sectors), and national public agencies are relevant sources which can be used for this purpose.
- A concise and efficient questionnaire, including mostly closed questions, should be drafted and fine-tuned before the launch of the survey based on tests with 4-5 selected stakeholders.
- The questionnaire should be uploaded on a web platform (e.g. SurveyMonkey) which is easily accessible to respondents.
- A management survey plan should be adopted to solicit answers. The plan should define the timing and approach to send reminders, either by email or phone calls. Also, it should detail the allocation of resources (e.g. time of the staff involved) to carry out this activity.
- If needed, the evidence collected through the survey may be complemented with in-depth interviews with selected stakeholders. This complementary evidence may help in the interpretation of results.

References

Bryce Space and Technology (2018), "State of the satellite industry report", Report commissioned by the Satellite Industry Association (SIA), www.satelliteconfers.org/wp-content/uploads/2018/12/Therese-Jones-Satellite-Industry-Association-.pdf. [3]

Daraio, M. et al. (2014), "Cosmo-SkyMed Data Utilization and Applications", Proceedings of the International Astronautical Congress, IAC 4. [8]

Dawes, S. et al. (2013), "Socioeconomic Benefits of Adding NASA Satellite Data to AirNow", *NASA*, NASA, www.ctg.albany.edu/media/pubs/pdfs/sti_finalreport.pdf. [21]

EUMETSTAT (2014), "The Case for EPS/Metop", www.eumetsat.int/media/16881 (accessed on 9 January 2024). [16]

Florio, M. and V. Morretta (2021), "Earth Observation and Economic Studies: A Cross-fertilization Perspective", *Space Policy*, Vol. 57, p. 101429, https://doi.org/10.1016/j.spacepol.2021.101429. [20]

GEO (2020), "What is earth observation?", website, Group on Earth Observation, www.earthobservations.org/g_faq.html. [1]

Leibrand, A. et al. (2019), "Using Earth Observations to Help Developing Countries Improve Access to Reliable, Sustainable, and Modern Energy", *Frontiers in Environmental Science*, Vol. 7, https://doi.org/10.3389/fenvs.2019.00123. [17]

Lupi, V. and V. Morretta (2022), "Socio-economic benefits of earth observation: insights from firms in Italy", in *Earth's Orbits at Risk The Economics of Space Sustainability*, OECD Publishing. [10]

Ministero delle Impresse e del Made in Italy (2019), "PMI innovative", www.mimit.gov.it/it/impresa/piccole-e-medie-imprese/pmi-innovative (accessed on 9 January 2024). [11]

Morretta, V., D. Vurchio and S. Carrazza (2022), "The socio-economic value of scientific publications: The case of Earth Observation satellites", *Technological Forecasting and Social Change*, Vol. 180, p. 121730, https://doi.org/10.1016/j.techfore.2022.121730. [9]

NASA (2013), "Measuring Socioeconomic Impacts of Earth Observations: A Primer", NASA, https://newspaceeconomy.ca/wp-content/uploads/2023/04/socioeconomicimpactsprimer.pdf (accessed on 9 January 2024). [19]

NEREUS, E. Commission and ESA (2018), "The Ever Growing Use of Copernicus Across Europe's Regions: A Selection of 99 User Stories by Local and Regional Authorities", www.copernicus.eu/sites/default/files/2018-10/copernicus4regions.pdf. [7]

OECD (2023), *The Space Economy in Figures: Responding to Global Challenges*, OECD Publishing, Paris, https://doi.org/10.1787/fa5494aa-en. [5]

Onoda, M. and O. Young (2017), *Satellite Earth Observations and Their Impact on Society and Policy*, Springer Nature, https://link.springer.com/book/10.1007/978-981-10-3713-9. [2]

Probst, L., B. Pedersen and L. Dakkak-Arnoux (2017), "Big Data in Earth Observation", *Eur*, European Commission, https://ec.europa.eu/growth/tools-databases/dem/monitor/sites/default/files/DTM_Big%20Data%20in%20Earth%20Observation%20v1.pdf. [12]

PwC (2019), "Copernicus market report: February 2019", Report commissioned by the European Commission, www.copernicus.eu/sites/default/files/PwC_Copernicus_Market_Report_2019.pdf. [6]

Sawyer, G., D. Boyle and N. Khabarov (2020), "Ground Motion Monitoring in Norway Sentinels Benefits Study (SeBS)", EARSC, https://earsc.org/sebs/wp-content/uploads/2020/07/Ground-Movement-Monitoring-in-Norway-final.pdf. [18]

Sawyer, G., A. Dubost and M. Vries (2016), "Copernicus sentinels' products economic value: a case study of forest management in Sweden. Sentinels Benefits Study (SeBS)", EARSC, https://earsc.org/sebs/wp-content/uploads/2019/03/Forest-Management-in-Sweden.pdf. [15]

Sawyer, G. and N. Khabarov (2022), "Highways management in Italy Sentinels Benefits Study (SeBS)", EARSC, https://earsc.org/sebs/wp-content/uploads/2022/05/Road-Infrastructure-monitoring-in-Italy-final.pdf. [13]

Sawyer, G., C. Oligschläger and N. Oligschläger (2019), "A Case Study: Growing Potatoes in Belgium, European Association of Remote Sensing Companies, Sentinels Benefits Study (SeBS)", EARSC, https://earsc.org/sebs/wp-content/uploads/2019/08/1_full-report-Growing-Potatoes-in-Belgium.pdf. [14]

Weinzierl, M. (2018), *Space, the final economic frontier*, Journal of Economic Perspectives. [4]

6 Value mechanisms of satellite infrastructure in the "new space" economy

Alessandro Paravano, Polytechnic University of Milan, Italy

Giorgio Locatelli, Polytechnic University of Milan, Italy

Paolo Trucco, Polytechnic University of Milan, Italy

New industrial dynamics are disrupting the space sector. Satellite infrastructure must be valuable for a wider set of end users, asking for economic returns and social and environmental benefits. This chapter aims to unveil the end users' value perception of satellite infrastructure in the "new space" economy ecosystem. The authors contextualise their findings using value theory.

Introduction

New industrial dynamics are disrupting the space sector. New players are increasingly interested in developing next-generation space infrastructure and services, bringing together experiences from industries such as finance, technology and others. Space projects should create value for a broader range of end users, requiring economic returns and long-term social and environmental advantages.

In the traditional space economy, space businesses (both upstream and downstream, as described in Figure 6.1) seek to create satellite constellations and design a satellite-based solution that is commissioned and paid for in advance by the client, who is often a space agency. In the “new space” economy, market liberalisation and access to satellite data have altered space organisations' value proposition to end users. Free access to space infrastructure, like global navigation satellite systems (GNSS), has accelerated the development of new products, services, enterprises and industries. For example, end users such as Uber, Ofo, and Deliveroo would not have been able to grow to such into such large enterprises without capitalising on the mobility provided by satellite navigation data. End users can additionally profit from satellite data to start new businesses. However, the complex uncertainties regarding the medium-to-long-term development of such businesses may restrict potential value enactment.

Furthermore, the variety of applications of space technologies in upstream and downstream sectors makes it difficult to identify end users, their needs and effective engagement techniques. Assessing the value created, distributed and captured by satellite infrastructure is challenging due to the wide variety of end users, potential conflict between stakeholders and lack of short-term benefits associated with space activities in terms of their market value. Consequently, this research aims to unveil end users' value perception of satellite infrastructure in the “new space” economy ecosystem. Thus, this study seeks to determine how end users perceive the value of satellite infrastructure in the “new space” economy ecosystem.

Background

The “new space” economy ecosystem

The “new space” economy is defined as "the full range of activities and the use of resources that create value and benefits to human beings in the course of exploring, researching, understanding, managing and utilising space" (OECD, 2019[1]). It is a transitioning innovation ecosystem where stakeholders belonging to space and non-space sectors are increasingly working together to develop next-generation space programmes and satellite infrastructure (Paikowsky, 2017[2]). The authors define "satellite infrastructure" as public and private satellite infrastructure that generates data and satellite-based applications for end users. This study, alongside previous research, focuses on end users' value perception of such infrastructure (Paravano, Locatelli and Trucco, 2023[3]). End users are companies and institutions in demand of new applications and services deriving from the combined use of space and digital technologies. In particular, the authors focus on the earth observation and satellite navigation segments. Figure 6.1 summarises the value streams and segments in the “new space” economy ecosystem in a comprehensive value chain. The segments of analysis considered by this study are highlighted in light blue.

Figure 6.1. The "new space" economy value chain

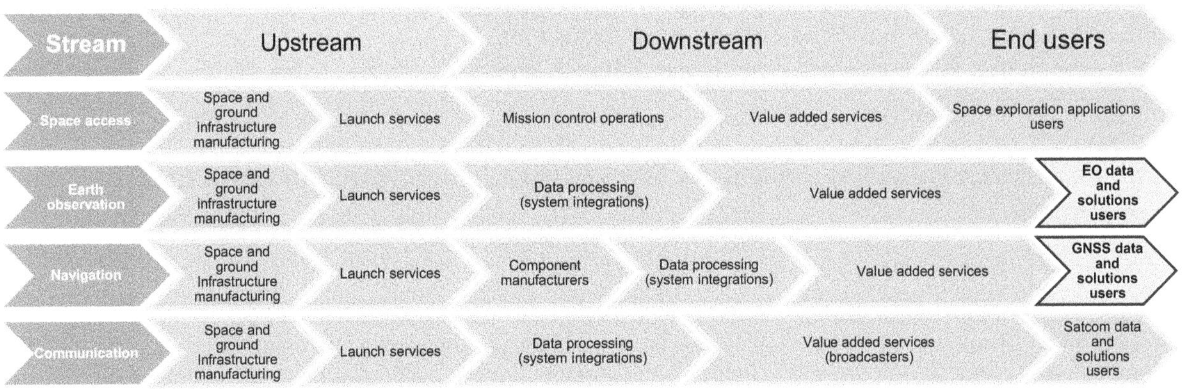

Notes: EO=earth observation, GNSS=global navigation satellite system, Satcom=satellite communications. The highlighted light blue segments are those considered in this study.
Source: Space Economy Observatory website (2020[4]), https://www.osservatori.net/it/eventi/on-demand/convegni/space-economy-la-nuova-frontiera-dellinnovazi.

Value perception and mechanisms in innovation ecosystems

Upstream, downstream, and end-user stakeholders in the "new space" ecosystem create, distribute and capture value by designing, developing, operating and decommissioning satellite infrastructure. This section provides the reader with a comprehensive understanding of the conceptualisation of value mechanisms in the innovation ecosystems literature, grounding the basis for the discussion.

In innovation ecosystems and general management literature, the concept of value is widely discussed. In line with Gil and Fu (2022[5]), the authors define value as "the sum of the economic benefits and wider social gains to be accrued from a new large-scale technology development minus the capital costs to be incurred". This definition of value presents three characteristics that are fundamental for this field of research. First, value is multi-dimensional and is characterised by both tangible and intangible elements (i.e. revenue and knowledge respectively). Triple-bottom-line accounting (Elkington, 1994[6]) is a common framework for conceptualising sustainability in this regard by incorporating economic, social, and environmental issues, and has been widely used in public planning and decision making (Wilhelm et al., 2015[7]; Martinsuo, Vuorinen and Killen, 2019[8]). Second, this definition of value considers change over time. Each project creates both short and long-term benefits, and consequently, satellite infrastructure may yield numerous advantages even decades after completion (Turner and Zolin, 2012[9]). Therefore, examining the expected long-term value is fundamental during the project's design phase (Liu et al., 2022[10]). Third, this definition of value is subjective and different stakeholders have different value perceptions (McGahan, 2020[11]). Satellite infrastructure (e.g. crop monitoring) can be evaluated as valuable if it fulfils the implicit or explicit needs of the individual or organisation demanding it (e.g. providing the means to monitor the crop field with a given revisit time and resolution) (Porter and Kramer, 2011[12]). Thus, any business strategy must consider environmental and social value if stakeholders expect it (Freudenreich, Lüdeke-Freund and Schaltegger, 2019[13]).

Understanding the nature of value mechanisms at the individual or organisational level requires making the fundamental premise that value is subjective. Value mechanisms are the processes that explain how value is created, distributed, and captured by the ecosystem (Lepak, Smith and Taylor, 2007[14]; Laursen and Svejvig, 2016[15]; Della Corte and Del Gaudio, 2014[16]). Scholars distinguish between value creation, distribution, and capture mechanisms (Lepak, Smith and Taylor, 2007[14]; Bowman and Ambrosini, 2000[17]; Laursen and Svejvig, 2016[15]; Zott and Amit, 2010[18]). Value creation involves co-producing offerings (i.e., products, services, and information relationships) in a mutually beneficial seller-buyer relationship (Normann and Ramírez, 1993[19]). Value distribution refers to transferring the value from the seller to the user (Bacq and Aguilera, 2021[20]). Value capture involves securing profits from value creation and distributing those profits among participating actors such as providers, end users and partners (Lepak, Smith and Taylor, 2007[14]). Value capture transcends monetary value and contractual obligations and entails actions that let suppliers and customers choose how to divide the extra value produced (Lepak, Smith and Taylor, 2007[14]).

Value perception is paving the way for next-generation satellite infrastructure development

Taking stock from the previous sections, it appears clear that satellite infrastructure stakeholders create, distribute and capture value by aligning reciprocal goals and creating a clear strategic vision of the project's outcome (Ang, Sankaran and Killen, 2016[21]). Stakeholders should depict the value of multidimensionality, dynamicity and subjectivity in designing the next generation of satellite infrastructure. In this regard, project value mechanisms have been approached from outcome-based and system lifecycle-based perspectives. From the outcome-based perspective, a project only adds value to the primary stakeholders (Edkins et al., 2013[22]). The targeted outcomes are designed on the financial worth of the stakeholders' engaged and short-term project success criteria, like adhering to schedule, budget and scope constraints. With the idea that the project must generate value for the project's sponsor, the outcome-based view highlights the sponsor's involvement (Eweje, Turner and Müller, 2012[23]). On the other hand, the system lifecycle perspective offers a more comprehensive value conceptualisation by examining the project value creation, distribution, and capture not only during the project but also during the operations phase, after it has finished (Artto, Ahola and Vartiainen, 2016[24]),. Value in this context covers both tangible and intangible values for secondary stakeholders and economic value for the primary stakeholders (Pollack et al., 2018[25]). This research adopts a system-thinking approach to assess the value mechanisms within a satellite infrastructure lifecycle, considering both primary and secondary stakeholders and their value perceptions. Figure 6.2 depicts the shifting paradigm from an outcome-based perspective toward a system lifecycle perspective in value mechanisms investigation.

Figure 6.2. Shifting from an outcome-based perspective to a system lifecycle perspective in value mechanisms investigation

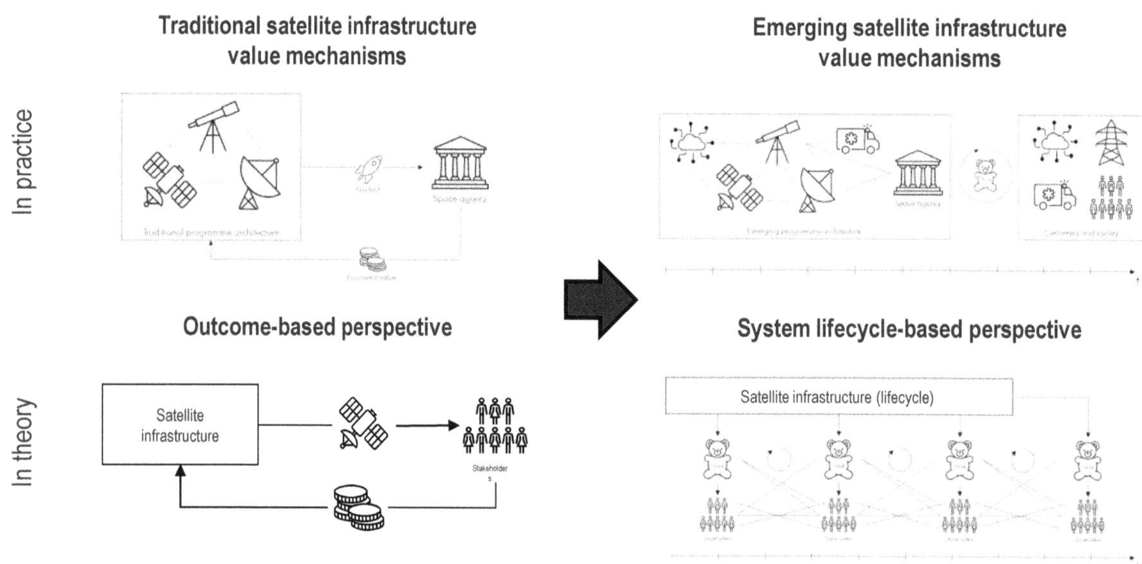

Methodology

Research design

The research design is composed of four steps. First, the authors review the extant body of knowledge of value in innovation ecosystems (including the body of knowledge from other sectors and areas of the economy), identifying the value dimensions. Second, the authors perform a series of interviews with managers belonging to end-user organisations of the "new space" ecosystem. Third, the authors perform a content analysis of the data by looking at value dimensions and their perceptions. Finally, the authors discuss and compare the value perception to assess the value expected and enacted of the selected satellite infrastructure.

The empirical context of the research is the European "new space" economy ecosystem. The unit of analysis is the value perception of end-user stakeholders. The level of the analysis is the satellite infrastructure projects developed in the European "new space" economy ecosystem.

Theoretical lens

The authors identified value theory (Hart, 1971[26]) as the theory with the most explanatory power for the phenomenon under examination. This research leverages two key elements of value theory: i) "expected value" and ii) "enacted value" (Bowman and Ambrosini, 2000[17]). Expected value is the value a subject expects to gain from an object. Value arises in a relation between the object (e.g., satellite data) and the expected value of a subject (e.g., the expected value of a farmer in using satellite data to monitor s crop field) (Hart, 1971[26]). End users interested in adopting satellite data in their decision making consider expected value. Enacted value is the value a subject may (or may not) capture in employing the object (Bowman and Ambrosini, 2000[17]). For example, a farmer adopting satellite data to monitor a crop field may reduce operational costs and increase productivity, enacting the expected value provided by satellite data.

Data collection

The study's analysis is based on two kinds of data. The authors began with open interviews (Aguinis and Solarino, 2019[27]), and subsequently acquired internal records, publicly available data and continuing interaction for triangulation. Interviews can bring essential experts' ideas closer to practice while identifying various problem-solving methods (Flick, 2009[28]), and the interviewer can ask clarifying questions (Saunders, Lewis and Thornhill, 2009[29]). These two data-gathering procedures are standard and acceptable for qualitative research, ensuring the depth of the findings and the aim of triangulation (Jick, 1979[30]).

The authors employed three sequential sampling strategies: one for the end-user sector sampling (i.e., insurance and finance, energy and utility, transportation and logistics), one for organisation sampling and one for manager sampling.

Following the principles outlined by Eisenhardt (1989[31]), the authors chose three distinct end-user sectors from within the European "space economy" ecosystem: insurance and finance, energy and utility and transportation and logistics. Three primary criteria guided this selection. Firstly, the authors emphasised diversity, as these sectors exhibit varying maturity levels in utilising satellite data and satellite-based solutions. Specifically, the transportation and logistics sector demonstrates a high level of maturity, with all end-user companies leveraging satellite data to optimise their logistical operations. The energy and utility sector possesses a moderate level of maturity, with a growing number of companies employing satellite data for infrastructure monitoring, albeit not universally. Conversely, the insurance and finance sector displays a lower maturity level, with only a handful of companies integrating satellite data into their operations. Incorporating these varying maturity levels contributes to the potential applicability of the findings to sectors sharing similar attributes. Secondly, the authors considered the significance of adopting EO and GNSS satellite data and satellite-based solutions, which yielded EUR 94 billion in global revenues in 2021. This figure is projected to surge to EUR 171 billion by 2031 (EUSPA, 2022[32]). Lastly, the authors emphasised data accessibility, as the authors gained direct access to company managers, and these organisations have published a wealth of secondary data pertinent to the research objectives. In summation, these three sectors are poised to be the forefront contenders in adopting satellite data and satellite-based solutions within their operations, imparting significant contributions to the growth of the European space economy ecosystem (OECD, 2022[33]).

To ensure the sample's representativeness, firms were picked using a theoretical sampling procedure, and end-user organisations from the sectors identified in the previous step were included. Interviewing end users allowed the authors to learn about their value perceptions and how they capture that value. Purposive sampling was used to choose managers based on job content and managers' direct connections with space projects and companies (Patton, 2014[34]; Palinkas, 2014[35]).

The authors interviewed 29 managers, each with an average of 15 years of experience. The interviews lasted 58 minutes on average. All talks took place online, and all interviewees and organisations were kept anonymous (Saunders, Kitzinger and Kitzinger, 2014[36]). In adherence to the principles of qualitative research, the authors carefully identify specific sectors, organisations, and managerial participants to attain theoretical saturation (Saunders et al., 2017[37]). The profiles of the interviewees are summarised in Table 6.1.

The authors leveraged the deep knowledge of two of the three authors with the empirical context, conducting open interviews initiated by the question, "how do you perceive the value of satellite-based data and/or infrastructure in your business?". The discussion was an open interview to access the respondent's point of view (Bryman, Alan; Bell, 2011). To triangulate the data, the authors looked for additional material from secondary sources (Jick, 1979[30]). For instance, the authors acquired relevant information on a project if an interviewee mentioned it. Secondary data consisted of information from public and private organisations, such as project reports, presentations, website news, company reports, in-depth plans, and newspaper articles that deal with finished or ongoing projects based on adopting satellite-based solutions in the end users' industry. The data acquired was quantitative and qualitative (Harris, 2001[38]).

Table 6.1. Profiles of interviewees

#	Industry	Job role	Experience
Int 1	Insurance and finance	Data scientist	12 years
Int 2	Insurance and finance	Head of portfolio management	14 years
Int 3	Energy and utilities	Head of assets co-ordination	18 years
Int 4	Energy and utilities	Innovation and partnerships manager	22 years
Int 5	Transportation and logistics	Head of technical department	10 years
Int 6	Insurance and finance	Head of space	25 years
Int 7	Energy and utilities	Head of venture building and scouting	12 years
Int 8	Transportation and logistics	Head of marketing, communication and strategic business	28 years
Int 9	Energy and utilities	Geodynamics dept. Engineer	11 years
Int 10	Insurance and finance	Leading expert space insurance underwriting	24 years
Int 11	Energy and utilities	Head of innovation	18 years
Int 12	Energy and utilities	Head of open innovation	14 years
Int 13	Insurance and finance	Head of innovation	13 years
Int 14	Energy and utilities	Head of innovation	14 years
Int 15	Insurance and finance	Head of business development	13 years
Int 16	Insurance and finance	President	31 years
Int 17	Insurance and finance	Senior project manager	11 years
Int 18	Transportation and logistics	Account manager	12 years
Int 19	Energy and utilities	Senior manager	14 years

#	Industry	Job role	Experience
Int 20	Energy and utilities	Head of digital services	19 years
Int 21	Insurance and finance	Data scientist	13 years
Int 22	Transportation and logistics	Head of innovation	14 years
Int 23	Transportation and logistics	Data scientist	8 years
Int 24	Energy and utilities	Data scientist	12 years
Int 25	Insurance and finance	Business development vice president	15 years
Int 26	Transportation and logistics	Senior manager	12 years
Int 27	Insurance and finance	Head of venture building and scouting	16 years
Int 28	Transportation and logistics	Innovation manager	13 years
Int 29	Transportation and logistics	Head of data analytics	16 years

Data analysis

The authors used an abductive coding method to analyse their data using Atlas.ti software and the guidelines of Hsieh and Shannon (2005[39]). The authors created a framework (Figure 6.3) using existing knowledge and populated it with information about the expected and enacted values of satellite data adoption in decision making, as reported by interviewees. The authors discussed and finalised the coding, thoroughly examining and summarising the transcribed information in the framework (Figures 6.4 and 6.5) (Harris, 2001[38]; Hsieh and Shannon, 2005[39]). The authors also applied value theory (Hart, 1971[26]) in the analysis.

Figure 6.3. Framework of analysis

Strategic decisions			
Tactical decisions			
	Activities	**Services**	**Products**

Source: Paravano, Locatelli and Trucco (2023[3]), "What is value in the New Space Economy? The end-users' perspective on satellite data and solutions", *Acta Astronautica*, https://doi.org/10.1016/j.actaastro.2023.05.001.

The framework differentiates between strategic and tactical decisions. Strategic decisions have a medium-long time horizon, require a large investment of resources, have a cross-functional impact on the organisation and are often irreversible. Tactical decisions have a short time horizon, require limited resources, have a vertical impact on the organisation and are often reversible. End users make strategic and tactical decisions in three main areas: activities, services and products. Activities are internal processes necessary for delivering services and products. Services are the application of competencies to benefit one another. Products are tangible goods sold to satisfy needs. The data is analysed by evaluating the expected and enacted value using a three-dimensional scale, ranging from "low" to "high". The authors also qualitatively compare the expected and enacted value of satellite data adoption. Sectors where the enacted value is equal to or greater than the expected value are in light blue italics, and those where it is less than the expected value are in darker and bold blue (Figures 6.4 and 6.5).

Findings

The expected value of incorporating satellite data into decision making processes varies among sectors: energy and utilities, insurance and finance and transportation and logistics. These sectors expect substantial value in their activities, services and products, as shown in Figure 6.4. Specifically, energy and utilities hold high hopes for strategic activity-related decisions, while insurance and finance place strong value expectations on strategic and tactical decision making for their offerings. In contrast, transportation and logistics emphasise tactical decision making regarding their operations. Subsequent analysis of the practical benefits of using satellite data indicates that various end users are utilising this data to refine their activities, services and products at both tactical and strategic levels.

Figure 6.4. End users' expected value from the adoption of satellite data in decision making

	Activities	Services	Products
Strategic decisions	Energy and utilities ●●● Transport and logistics ●○○ Insurance and finance ●●○	Energy and utilities ●●○ Transport and logistics ●○○ Insurance and finance ●●○	Energy and utilities ●●○ Transport and logistics ●○○ Insurance and finance ●●●
Tactical decisions	Energy and utilities ●●○ Transport and logistics ●●● Insurance and finance ●○○	Energy and utilities ●●○ Transport and logistics ●○○ Insurance and finance ●●○	Energy and utilities ●●● Transport and logistics ●○○ Insurance and finance ●●●

○○○ = low expected value | ●●● = high expected value

However, as shown in Figure 6.5, adoption levels differ across sectors, and the emphasis remains largely on tactical decisions for improving activities. Notably, energy and utilities and insurance and finance experience a shortfall in enacted value compared to their expected value (in bold), particularly concerning strategic decisions about services and products. Findings show that the enacted value of satellite data in making tactical decisions regarding the activities is more or equal to the expected value for all the end users (in light blue).

The enacted value of satellite infrastructure for tactical decisions

The general inclination among end users is to incorporate satellite data primarily in tactical decision making processes, yielding enacted value that exceeds initial expectations. Adopting satellite data is particularly favoured for low-risk, short-term investments, with end users adept at gauging the expected value and exploiting the practical benefits in decision making. As an energy sector participant aptly states, "space is very far from our daily base. We start to explore the value of satellite data for our activities, looking for efficiency improvement that requires small and low-risk investments." The emphasis is placed on enhancing the efficiency of business activities rather than the quality of services and products delivered. For instance, an energy industry expert emphasises the value of earth observation imagery in infrastructure monitoring, noting that "the cost-saving is easy to calculate."

Figure 6.5. End users' level of adoption of satellite data in decision making

	Activities	Services	Products
Strategic decisions	**Energy and utilities ●●○** *Transport and logistics ●●○* **Insurance and finance ●○○**	**Energy and utilities ●○○** *Transport and logistics ●●○* **Insurance and finance ●○○**	**Energy and utilities ○○○** *Transport and logistics ●○○* **Insurance and finance ○○○**
Tactical decisions	*Energy and utilities ●●●* *Transport and logistics ●●●* *Insurance and finance ●●○*	*Energy and utilities ●●○* *Transport and logistics ●●○* **Insurance and finance ●○○**	**Energy and utilities ●○○** *Transport and logistics ●●○* **Insurance and finance ●○○**

○○○ = low adoption | ●●● = high adoption
Light blue if enacted value ≥ expected value
Bold if enacted value < expected value

Source: Paravano, Locatelli and Trucco (2023[3]), "What is value in the New Space Economy? The end-users' perspective on satellite data and solutions", *Acta Astronautica*, https://doi.org/10.1016/j.actaastro.2023.05.001.

Managers appreciate the real-time information provided by satellite positioning data, particularly in transportation and logistics, with one participant stating, "satellite data improves efficiency." Adopting satellite data is regarded to be a means to experiment and innovate internally before introducing new services or products. A participant from the insurance sector articulates this strategic approach: "We prefer first to experience and learn from the benefits of satellites internally. The easy way is to experiment with the adoption of satellite imagery to increase the efficiency of our internal processes before selling a new satellite-based service or product."

However, while satellite data proves valuable in improving activities and services, there is a disparity in its adoption for product-related decisions. End users in the energy and utilities and insurance and finance sectors have high value expectations for tactical product decisions but often find the enacted value lacking. Challenges arise due to the need for specialised competencies in interpreting and integrating satellite data into product design, as another energy sector participant highlighted: "I think we lack the competencies to leverage satellite data to develop our product and meet the expected value."

Additionally, end-user managers express scepticism when available solutions don't align with their product development needs and expectations, with an insurance industry manager stating, "earth observation offers many smart solutions for whom we are unwilling to pay. Why do I have to invest in satellite information when they do not answer my needs, or I can use other sources that provide less expensive solutions?"

The missed enacted value of satellite infrastructure for strategic decisions

Despite the expected value, the adoption of satellite data in strategic decisions remains limited among managers. End users predominantly integrate satellite data into strategic decisions concerning their activities rather than their services or products. Whilst recognising the potential long-term value, managers currently struggle to translate this into enacted value due to the perceived risks and complexities. The uncertainty surrounding the cost-benefit ratio deters them from deeming satellite data suitable for foundational strategic choices. As articulated by an energy sector participant, "satellites will revolutionise our decision making, but nowadays, I can't build my business on information when I don't understand where it comes from. Besides, satellite data requires huge resources and competencies."

In the context of activities, managers underscore the strategic significance of satellite data for tasks like infrastructure planning and climate change mitigation. These insights are especially vital for industries like energy, where "modelling and predicting climate evolution are very important." Whilst end users invest significantly in satellite data to predict environmental changes, realising the expected value is lagging, particularly in the insurance sector. This delay is attributed to the complexity of strategic decisions that require diverse data sources and integration capabilities, areas where end users are currently lacking.

Regarding services, satellite data hold relatively low enacted value, particularly in the insurance sector, due to the centrality of intangible assets. Insurers increasingly leverage satellite data to enhance services and make informed investment decisions in specific markets, such as insuring agriculture in developing countries. Yet, a lack of clarity surrounding the long-term value of satellite data hampers its practical application, leaving end users hesitant to invest significantly in strategic service-related choices.

The value expected for adopting satellite data in strategic product decisions is high among managers. However, these aspirations contrast with their current usage practices. Managers express dissatisfaction with the mismatch between the potential of satellite data and their actual ability to address specific needs. For instance, one energy sector manager states, "providers offer very interesting tools that lack in answering our real needs." Internal approval processes and the perceived risk hinder the adoption process for such data in strategic decisions. Managers' risk aversion and the current immaturity of satellite data and applications contribute to a hesitancy to fully embrace satellite data for product-related strategic choices.

In essence, whilst the potential value of satellite data in strategic decision making is recognised and expected to be transformative, challenges related to perceived risk, reliability and alignment with specific needs are hampering their practical adoption and enactment. As one participant aptly puts it, "We can't bet in our business, we see the potential value of satellite data in our business, but nowadays, it is still too risky and not mature enough."

Discussion

End users predominantly favour adopting satellite data for tactical rather than strategic decisions due to lower resource requirements and associated risks. This approach allows for a more accurate assessment of expected value before implementation, resulting in relatively attainable enacted value in tactical contexts (Eweje, Turner and Müller, 2012[23]). There are notable obstacles to adopting satellite data in strategic decision making. Firstly, end users often perceive promising satellite data and space technologies as distant from their core operations, lacking a comprehensive understanding of the space ecosystem. The perceived resource gap between expected and enacted value impedes adoption (Bacq and Aguilera, 2021[20]). Secondly, managers recognise the potential of satellite data but believe it necessitates radical organisational transformation rather than incremental change, further complicated by existing resource dependencies (Grant, 1991[40])). Lastly, assessing the expected value of satellite solutions requires specialised knowledge, and the lack thereof leads to over-optimism. While transportation and logistics have gained competencies in enacting the value of satellite infrastructure, many end users lack the instruments to evaluate long-term value accurately, leading them to prefer tactical adoption due to lower resource demands and reversibility (Freudenreich, Lüdeke-Freund and Schaltegger, 2019[13]).

End users hold positive expectations regarding the value of satellite data, recognising its novelty and appropriateness for tactical and strategic decisions concerning their activities, services and products. The momentum of the "new space" economy, marked by new technologies, funding opportunities and policies, fuels these value expectations. However, enacting the expected value proves challenging for several reasons. Firstly, adoption hinges on organisational structures and transaction costs between satellite data providers and end users (Martinsuo, Vuorinen and Killen, 2019[8]). High transaction costs contribute to a considerable gap between expected and enacted value (Gil and Fu, 2022[5]). Lowering satellite data management costs characteristic of the "new space" economy could facilitate adoption by minimising transaction costs. To this end, data providers could collaborate with end users to find solutions that reduce such costs and enhance strategic adoption. Second, end users regret limited adoption due to resource and competency constraints (Liu et al., 2022[10]). Data providers should prioritise equipping end users with the necessary resources and competencies, fostering the enactment of expected value. Lastly, while end users perceive the expected value of satellite data, they lack a clear roadmap for enacting the value of satellite infrastructure. This is partly due to the mismatch between solutions offered by satellite data providers and end-user needs. Direct engagement between providers and end users can enhance providers' understanding of end users' needs (Lehtinen, Aaltonen and Rajala, 2019[41]), leading to tailored solutions that properly activate expected value.

Conclusions and recommendations

This study sheds light on the end users' value perception of satellite infrastructure in the "new space" economy ecosystem. In summary, providers, users and policy makers should consider the following key takeaways to enact the value of satellite infrastructure. At the moment, end users adopt satellite data for tactical decisions, focusing on activities rather than strategic choices. This approach stems from the lower resource requirements and risks associated with tactical decisions, which allows for better assessment of both expected and enacted value. Particularly, end users in the insurance and finance and energy and utility sectors exhibit high expected value but encounter challenges in enacting it. Moreover, satellite infrastructure services are embraced by end users as complementary resources for decision making but are perceived as distanced from core business operations, and their associated risks inhibit full adoption. Despite recognising the potential of satellite data, end users face difficulties fully enacting the expected value over the long term due to a lack of literacy and competencies.

This research makes three main contributions. First, policy makers can utilise our findings within the European space ecosystem, including the European Commission and space agencies such as the European Space Agency (ESA) and the European Union Agency for the Space Programme (EUSPA). These stakeholders have the opportunity to shape their endeavours to advance satellite data and solutions derived from satellites within the specific sectors that have been examined. The authors show considerable expected value within the energy and utilities and insurance and finance sectors. However, these benefits have not yet been fully realised due to a deficiency in the knowledge and skills of end users. To address this limitation, policy makers have the option to champion novel undertakings or enhance existing ones. This could involve focusing on intermediary entities like, for example, Copernicus Relays, Copernicus Academy and ESA BICs, all while prioritising enhancing end users' proficiency and abilities in this domain.

Second, satellite infrastructure providers are encouraged to collaborate with end users, negotiating solutions that reduce transaction costs and thus promote the adoption of satellite data in strategic decisions concerning services and products. They should shift their focus from offering mere solutions to providing end users with essential resources and competencies, thereby enacting the expected value of end users. Moreover, direct engagement between data providers and end users is pivotal. This engagement can enhance providers' understanding of end users' needs, paving the way for tailored data and solutions that adequately address these requirements and enable the proper enactment of expected value.

Third, end users in the selected sectors may adopt our framework (Figure 6.5) to self-assess the current level of adoption of satellite data in their activities, services and products.

As outlined in the Introduction, this study is exploratory, serving as a foundation for forthcoming qualitative and quantitative research endeavours. Four limitations temper the extent to which our findings can be generalised. Firstly, our analysis centres on three specific sectors: insurance and finance, energy and utility and transportation and logistics. Future investigations might adopt our research protocol and framework to explore additional sectors. Secondly, our interviews were conducted with managers affiliated with European organisations. Future research has the potential to delve into and juxtapose findings from different geographical areas. Thirdly, the authors focused on private commercial organisations adopting satellite infrastructure exclusively for commercial purposes. Subsequent research could enrich the authors' findings by considering defence, public institutions or private companies employing satellites for non-commercial objectives. Lastly, this chapter predominantly reflects the perspective of end-user managers. Subsequent research could build upon this foundation by interviewing managers responsible for providing data and presenting an additional complementary viewpoint.

In conclusion, while the "new space" economy's promise of satellite data presents vast potential, there are challenges to be addressed in aligning this potential with practical value. By focusing on strategic engagement, reduced transaction costs, enhanced competencies and tailored solutions, the journey from expected to enacted value can be navigated more effectively, ensuring the transformative impact of satellite data in decision making processes.

References

Aguinis, H. and A. Solarino (2019), "Transparency and replicability in qualitative research: The case of interviews with elite informants", *Strategic Management Journal*, Vol. 40/8, pp. 1291-1315, https://doi.org/10.1002/smj.3015. [27]

Ang, K., S. Sankaran and C. Killen (2016), "'Value for Whom, by Whom': Investigating Value Constructs in Non-Profit Project Portfolios", *Project Management Research and Practice*, Vol. 3, p. 5038, https://doi.org/10.5130/pmrp.v3i0.5038. [21]

Artto, K., T. Ahola and V. Vartiainen (2016), "From the front end of projects to the back end of operations: Managing projects for value creation throughout the system lifecycle", *International Journal of Project Management*, Vol. 34/2, pp. 258-270, https://doi.org/10.1016/j.ijproman.2015.05.003. [24]

Bacq, S. and R. Aguilera (2021), "Stakeholder Governance for Responsible Innovation: A Theory of Value Creation, Appropriation, and Distribution", *Journal of Management Studies*, Vol. 59/1, pp. 29-60, https://doi.org/10.1111/joms.12746. [20]

Bowman, C. and V. Ambrosini (2000), "Value Creation Versus Value Capture: Towards a Coherent Definition of Value in Strategy", *British Journal of Management*, Vol. 11/1, pp. 1-15, https://doi.org/10.1111/1467-8551.00147. [17]

Della Corte, V. and G. Del Gaudio (2014), "A literature review on value creation and value capturing in strategic management studies", *Corporate Ownership and Control*, Vol. 11/2, pp. 328-346, https://doi.org/10.22495/cocv11i2c3p2. [16]

Edkins, A. et al. (2013), "Exploring the front-end of project management", *Engineering Project Organization Journal*, Vol. 3/2, pp. 71-85, https://doi.org/10.1080/21573727.2013.775942. [22]

Eisenhardt, K. (1989), "Building Theories from Case Study Research", *Academy of Management Review*, Vol. 14/4, pp. 532-550, https://doi.org/10.5465/amr.1989.4308385. [31]

Elkington, J. (1994), "Towards the Sustainable Corporation: Win-Win-Win Business Strategies for Sustainable Development", *California Management Review*, Vol. 36/2, pp. 90-100, https://doi.org/10.2307/41165746. [6]

EUSPA (2022), "EUSPA EO and GNSS Market Report", https://doi.org/10.2878/94903. [32]

Eweje, J., R. Turner and R. Müller (2012), "Maximizing strategic value from megaprojects: The influence of information-feed on decision-making by the project manager", *International Journal of Project Management*, Vol. 30/6, pp. 639-651, https://doi.org/10.1016/j.ijproman.2012.01.004. [23]

Flick, U. (2009), *An Introduction to Qualitative Research*, 4th edition, Sage Publications Ltd, London. [28]

Freudenreich, B., F. Lüdeke-Freund and S. Schaltegger (2019), "A Stakeholder Theory Perspective on Business Models: Value Creation for Sustainability", *Journal of Business Ethics*, Vol. 166/1, pp. 3-18, https://doi.org/10.1007/s10551-019-04112-z. [13]

Gil, N. and Y. Fu (2022), "Megaproject Performance, Value Creation, and Value Distribution: An Organizational Governance Perspective", *Academy of Management Discoveries*, Vol. 8/2, pp. 224-251, https://doi.org/10.5465/amd.2020.0029. [5]

Grant, R. (1991), "The Resource-Based Theory of Competitive Advantage: Implications for Strategy Formulation", *California Management Review*, Vol. 33/3, pp. 114-135, https://doi.org/10.2307/41166664. [40]

Harris, H. (2001), , *Journal of Business Ethics*, Vol. 34/3/4, pp. 191-208, https://doi.org/10.1023/a:1012534014727. [38]

Hart, S. (1971), "Axiology--Theory of Values", *Philosophy and Phenomenological Research*, Vol. 32/1, p. 29, https://doi.org/10.2307/2105883. [26]

Hsieh, H. and S. Shannon (2005), "Three Approaches to Qualitative Content Analysis", *Qualitative Health Research*, Vol. 15/9, pp. 1277-1288, https://doi.org/10.1177/1049732305276687. [39]

Jick, T. (1979), "Mixing Qualitative and Quantitative Methods: Triangulation in Action", *Administrative Science Quarterly*, Vol. 24/4, p. 602, https://doi.org/10.2307/2392366. [30]

Laursen, M. and P. Svejvig (2016), "Taking stock of project value creation: A structured literature review with future directions for research and practice", *International Journal of Project Management*, Vol. 34/4, pp. 736-747, https://doi.org/10.1016/j.ijproman.2015.06.007. [15]

Lehtinen, J., K. Aaltonen and R. Rajala (2019), "Stakeholder management in complex product systems: Practices and rationales for engagement and disengagement", *Industrial Marketing Management*, Vol. 79, pp. 58-70, https://doi.org/10.1016/j.indmarman.2018.08.011. [41]

Lepak, D., K. Smith and M. Taylor (2007), "Introduction to Special Topic Forum Value Creation and Value Capture: A Multilevel Perspective", *The Academy of Management Review*, Vol. 32/1, pp. 180-194, https://www.jstor.org/stable/20159287. [14]

Liu, J. et al. (2022), "The coevolution of innovation ecosystems and the strategic growth paths of knowledge-intensive enterprises: The case of China's integrated circuit design industry", *Journal of Business Research*, Vol. 144, pp. 428-439, https://doi.org/10.1016/j.jbusres.2022.02.008. [10]

Martinsuo, M., L. Vuorinen and C. Killen (2019), "Lifecycle-oriented framing of value at the front end of infrastructure projects", *International Journal of Managing Projects in Business*, Vol. 12/3, pp. 617-643, https://doi.org/10.1108/ijmpb-09-2018-0172. [8]

McGahan, A. (2020), "Where Does an Organization's Responsibility End?: Identifying the Boundaries on Stakeholder Claims", *Academy of Management Discoveries*, Vol. 6/1, pp. 8-11, https://doi.org/10.5465/amd.2018.0218. [11]

Normann, R. and R. Ramírez (1993), "From Value Chain to Value Constellation: Designing Interactive Strategy", *Harvard Business Review*, Vol. 71/4, pp. 65-77, https://hbr.org/1993/07/designing-interactive-strategy. [19]

OECD (2022), *OECD Handbook on Measuring the Space Economy*, OECD Publishing, Paris, France, https://doi.org/10.1787/8bfef437-en. [33]

OECD (2019), *The Space Economy in Figures: How Space Contributes to the Global Economy*, OECD Publishing, Paris, https://doi.org/10.1787/c5996201-en. [1]

Paikowsky, D. (2017), "What Is New Space? The Changing Ecosystem of Global Space Activity", *New Space*, Vol. 5/2, pp. 84-88, https://doi.org/10.1089/space.2016.0027. [2]

Palinkas, L. (2014), "Qualitative and Mixed Methods in Mental Health Services and Implementation Research", *Journal of Clinical Child & Adolescent Psychology*, Vol. 43/6, pp. 851-861, https://doi.org/10.1080/15374416.2014.910791. [35]

Paravano, A., G. Locatelli and P. Trucco (2023), "What is value in the New Space Economy? The end-users' perspective on satellite data and solutions", *Acta Astronautica*, Vol. 210, pp. 554-563, https://doi.org/10.1016/j.actaastro.2023.05.001. [3]

Patton, M. (2014), *Qualitative Research & Evaluation Methods: Integrating Theory and Practice*, 4th Edition, Sage Publications Inc., New York. [34]

Pollack, J. et al. (2018), "Classics in megaproject management: A structured analysis of three major works", *International Journal of Project Management*, Vol. 36/2, pp. 372-384, https://doi.org/10.1016/j.ijproman.2017.01.003. [25]

Porter, M. and M. Kramer (2011), "The Big Idea: Creating Shared Value", *Harvard Business Review*, Vol. 89/1-2, pp. 62-77, https://hbr.org/2011/01/the-big-idea-creating-shared-value. [12]

Saunders, B., J. Kitzinger and C. Kitzinger (2014), "Anonymising interview data: challenges and compromise in practice", *Qualitative Research*, Vol. 15/5, pp. 616-632, https://doi.org/10.1177/1468794114550439. [36]

Saunders, B. et al. (2017), "Saturation in qualitative research: exploring its conceptualization and operationalization", *Quality & Quantity*, Vol. 52/4, pp. 1893-1907, https://doi.org/10.1007/s11135-017-0574-8. [37]

Saunders, M., P. Lewis and A. Thornhill (2009), *Research Methods for Business Students*, Pearson Education, New York. [29]

Space Economy Observatory (2020), "Space Economy: La nuova frontiera dell'Innovazione si presenta!", webpage, https://www.osservatori.net/it/eventi/on-demand/convegni/space-economy-la-nuova-frontiera-dellinnovazi. [4]

Turner, R. and R. Zolin (2012), "Forecasting Success on Large Projects: Developing Reliable Scales to Predict Multiple Perspectives by Multiple Stakeholders over Multiple Time Frames", *Project Management Journal*, Vol. 43/5, pp. 87-99, https://doi.org/10.1002/pmj.21289. [9]

Wilhelm, M. et al. (2015), “Sustainability in multi-tier supply chains: Understanding the double agency role of the first-tier supplier”, *Journal of Operations Management*, Vol. 41/1, pp. 42-60, https://doi.org/10.1016/j.jom.2015.11.001. [7]

Zott, C. and R. Amit (2010), “Business Model Design: An Activity System Perspective”, *Long Range Planning*, Vol. 43/2-3, pp. 216-226, https://doi.org/10.1016/j.lrp.2009.07.004. [18]

7 Use of fiscal measures for addressing space debris

Erika Scuderi, Vienna University of Economics and Business, Austria

Research shows that economic interests and technical difficulties often compromise compliance with soft law instruments adopted to mitigate risks from space debris. This chapter addresses the question of whether fiscal measures can be viable tools to address these concerns and overcome the inherent fragility of non-binding instruments. Leveraging a review of the existing literature and past experiences with the adoption (or proposal) of user fees for launches, this chapter suggests the design of a space debris mitigation tax scheme embedded in a framework of legal and fiscal principles.

Introduction

The application of satellite technologies permeates many aspects of our daily lives (e.g., climate monitoring, weather forecasting, satellite navigation, national security, etc.). As our economy increasingly relies on space activities, it is necessary to ensure that outer space remains a safe and clean environment. The OECD has estimated that the number of satellites launched into orbit in 2021 was greater than the sum of satellites launched in the last decade and that even more are expected to be sent to space in the next five years (OECD, 2022[1]). Debris objects risk colliding with active space objects, thus endangering space missions and people. Researchers have attempted to calculate the actual collision risk over time (Bradley and Wein, 2009[2]; Liou and Johnson, 2006[3]). Despite the uncertainties on a precise estimate of the number of potential collisions, the socio-economic impacts of a major space debris accident would be dramatic due to the potential chain reaction of collisions between debris objects – the so-called Kessler's Syndrome (Kessler and Cour-Palais, 1978[4]) – could render some high-value orbits unusable and block access to higher orbits (OECD, 2022[1]; Alfano and Oltrogge, 2018[5]; Oltrogge et al., 2018[6]; Jones and Doostan, 2013[7]; Undseth, 2021[8]; Hoogendoorn, Mooij and Geul, 2018[9]). International organisations and space agencies are working to strengthen debris mitigation guidelines[1] and ensure that post-mission disposal (PMD) and active debris removal (ADR) become cheaper and more effective. However, non-binding instruments do not seem to be sufficient to face the challenge raised by space debris (Tapio and Soucek, 2019[10]). According to the OECD (2022[1]), it is necessary to conduct further research to understand which policy instrument is best suited to internalise the costs of space debris and/or incentivise space actors to follow debris mitigation guidelines. In this context, new "standards and market-based instruments such as taxes or insurance" might play a key role.

Research problems, literature review and research questions

Research problem

The congestion of Earth's orbits is considered a classic example of a tragedy of the commons (Lambach and Wesel, 2021[11]; Salter, 2016[12]) for the resolution of which many proposals relying on advanced technologies have been put forward (Lucas-Rhimbassen, 2019[13]; Mark and Kamath, 2019[14]; Skinner, 2017[15]). Clearly, effective technologies are key, but 'the core of the space debris problem is incentives, not technology' (Rao, Burgess and Kaffine, 2020[16]). Indeed, space operators are faced with the question of whether to launch profitable satellites and increase the risk of collision, or not to launch them and leave the profits to competitors. In other words, operators are incentivised to receive the benefits of public goods and common-pool resources without contributing to the costs (Nordhaus, 2015[17]; Adilov, Alexander and Cunningham, 2022[18]). To face this phenomenon referred to as 'free-riding', scholars have suggested adopting incentive-based policies (Rao, Burgess and Kaffine, 2020[16]). As in the context of climate change discourses, it is possible to identify three different categories of responses to the problems caused by space debris: Prevention, mitigation and remediation (de Moor, 2021[19]). Based on the strategy pursued, different incentive-based measures (among which, tax-based incentives) can be conceived, as shown in Table 7.1.

Table 7.1. Strategy and incentive-based measures

Strategy	Incentive-based measures	Examples
Prevention	Supporting research in more robust and sustainable satellite designs.	• R&D tax incentives for sustainable satellite design
Mitigation	Adopting measures aimed at steering operators' behaviour towards desired actions (e.g., fewer launches, post-mission disposal	• Tax-based measures (e.g., launch taxes, orbit taxes) • Market-based measures (e.g., tradable

Strategy	Incentive-based measures	Examples
	(PMD), active debris removal (ADR)).	permits) • Bonds • Fees
Remediation	Supporting research and execution of ADR activities.	• Rebates/refunds for PMD or ADR • Expenditure-based tax incentives for carrying ADR (e.g., tax credits) • Income-based tax incentives for carrying out ADR (e.g., reduced tax rates or tax exemptions on income earned from carrying out ADR activities)

Research goal and research questions

This contribution leverages the knowledge provided by existing economic, tax and legal literature and takes a further step: It explores the rationale behind introducing a new space debris tax/fee and identifies a framework of principles governing the potential adoption of such a fiscal instrument. It also attempts to answer some debated open issues and highlights remaining concerns. The ultimate goal is to shed some light on the available tax policy designs that could serve the purpose of reducing space debris accumulation while complying with space law principles and safeguarding companies' competitiveness. To achieve these goals, this chapter answers the following research questions:

1. What are the available policy options? What are their essential features and flaws?
2. What can we learn from past experiences?
3. What are the tax and legal principles that shall inform the design of a space debris tax/fee?
4. What considerations shall the policy makers take into account from the points of view of international fairness and tax competition?

A crucial distinction to be made is between price-based policies (such as taxes and fees), and quantity-based policies (such as permits tradable in the market). The former puts a price on goods or services and lets the market regulate the amount of goods and services provided/offered. The latter fixes the maximum quantity of goods and services available and lets the market establish the price. Although both strategies achieve the objective of internalising externalities, generally economists tend to favour taxes (e.g., carbon taxes) over tradable permits (e.g., emission trading certificates) to fight climate change (Rao, Burgess and Kaffine, 2020[16]). Weitzman suggests that when the marginal costs of abatement are steeper than the marginal benefits of abatement, price-based policies shall be preferred over quantity-based ones (Weitzman, 1974[20]). It is not known yet whether this holds true also in the case of orbital pollution. Adilov et al. showed that "there exists a tax schedule that induces firms to choose the optimal level of launches and debris creation" but stressed that this "is distinct from showing that a Pigouvian tax is a superior, or even desirable, means of remediation" (Adilov, Alexander and Cunningham, 2015[21]). This contribution focuses on price-based policies in an attempt to bridge the existing research gap and explore the related legal constraints.

Literature review

Considering the similarities between terrestrial and orbit pollution (Adilov, Alexander and Cunningham, 2022[18])scholars have investigated the potential application of environmental policies to the outer space environment (see Table 7.2). For example, some authors support the adoption of taxes (Scheraga, 1986[22]; Limperis, 1998[23]; Macauley, 2015[24]; Béal, Deschamps and Moulin, 2020[25]; Guyot and Rouillon, 2023[26]; Adilov, Alexander and Cunningham, 2015[21]) or fees (Taylor, 2011[27]; Rao, Burgess and Kaffine, 2020[16]) as remedies for debris pollution. Others privilege tradable permits (Buchs and Bernauer, 2023[28]; Pecujlic and Germann, 2015[29]; Macauley, 2004[30]; Macauley, 1994[31]), bonds (Adilov, Alexander and

Cunningham, 2023[32]), or property rights (Scheraga, 1986[22]; Salter, 2016[12]). Little but important research has been conducted on the potential application of fiscal instruments for the protection of the outer space environment. These studies address the question of the adoption of debris fees/taxes from an economic or legal angle, although with a net predominance of the former. More in detail, scholars' proposals focus on several aspects of tax policy design, with the main differences relating to (i) the taxable event (ii) the taxable moment, and (iii) the use of the revenue collected.

In particular, as far as the taxable event is concerned, scholars suggest linking the tax to:

1. the access to outer space / putting a space object into orbit
2. the potential risk of debris generation or potential harm to others
3. the mere use of the orbit
4. the actual formation of debris.

Since the taxable event is the occurrence giving rise to the tax liability but not necessarily to the actual tax collection, the tax can be collected by the tax authorities at a different moment. Scholars propose that the tax shall be collected either at the moment of the launch, orbital use or debris formation.

Finally, as for the use of the revenue, scholars suggest spending the funds to:

1. invest in R&D
2. carry out ADR operations
3. both support R&D and carry out ADR operations
4. refund space operators (e.g., upon proof of successful PMD or in support of those whose active space objects have been destroyed or damaged by collisions).

Table 7.2. Literature review summary

	Moment of tax collection		
Use of revenue	Launch tax	Orbital use tax	Debris formation tax
R&D activities	2012 Evans et al. 2020 Buchs 2020 Béal et al. 2022 Ateca-Amestoy et al. 2023 Buchs/Bernauer	2017 Garber	1998 Limperis
ADR activities	2012 Akers 2014/2020 Adilov et al. 2020 Béal et al. 2023 Buchs/Bernauer 2023 Bernhard et al.	2017 Garber	1998 Limperis 2023 Bernhard et al.
Refunded	2009 Dunstan 2015 Macauley	2012 Evans	
No use of revenue described	1986 Scheraga 1992 Roberts 2021 Bilaney 2023 Guyot/Rouillon	2020 Rao 2021 Bilaney	2021 Bilaney

Learning from past experiences

The idea of fees imposed on space launches is not new. For example, in 1991, the United States adopted a licence fee and per-launch fees. The rationale for the adoption of such fees was to recover part of the "costs for personnel, contracts, and travel associated with the review of licence applications and issuance and administration of licences" by the Department of Transportation's (DoT) Office of Commercial Space

Transportation (OCST), Licence Program Division (see Proposed Regulations: Commercial Space Transportation; User Fees No. 56 FR 8301 3 (Feb. 28, 1991). Thus, the idea behind them was to recover a portion of the OCST's costs related to government-provided goods and services that confer benefits on identifiable beneficiaries. More in detail, the OCST introduced a flat licence fee of USD 2 500 per licence application (irrespective of the eventual approval or denial), and a renewal fee of USD 2 500 to be paid on or before the completion of the first year from the date in which the licence was issued (see 14 CFR, Part 415.4 Launch Fee, 1991). Additionally, a launch fee structure was introduced for orbital and suborbital launches. Orbital launches were subject to a fee of USD 2.50 per pound of delivery capability of the launch vehicle to low-earth orbit for each orbital launch. Suborbital launches were subject to a fixed per-launch fee of USD 1 000.[2] Pursuant to the National Aeronautics and Space Administration Authorization Act, Fiscal Year 1993 (H.R. 6135, 1992), the DoT repealed these fees with effect of 12 January 1993 (Final Rule. Commercial Space Transportation; Removal of User Fees, Federal Register Vol. 58, No. 7, 1993).

More recently, in 2020, Australia had proposed specific user fees to be paid for domestic launches. In particular, it proposed the adoption of fees in the context of its partial cost recovery scheme under which the government would have charged a fee of approximately USD 189 894 per-launch permit application (Draft cost recovery implementation statement. Fees for activities under the Space (Launches and Returns) Act 2018. 2019-2020). After having been deferred for about two years, the proposal was set aside, and the fees were not introduced. The reason was to provide the industry with certainty and help small and medium-sized enterprises to keep growing.[3]

In both examples, the fees were justified as being charged to recover costs related to the agencies' work on the licence applications and not proper space launch taxes. Also, they were not related to debris mitigation at all. However, some lessons can be derived from their design features, the economic impact analyses and the industry's responses.

First, in both cases, comments on the proposed regulations highlighted competitiveness concerns. In particular, commentators on the 1991 American user fees were concerned that such fees would have adversely affected "the competitive position of the US commercial space transportation industry relative to foreign launch providers" (see Final Rule. Commercial Space Transportation: User Fees No. 56 FR 41062, 19.08.1991). In this respect, some commentators specifically suggested that the U.S. Trade Representatives and the European Space Agency reach an agreement on user fees, thus achieving a level playing field for competitors in the international launch services market before they were unilaterally imposed on American commercial launch providers (Final Rule. Commercial Space Transportation: User Fees No. 56 FR 41062, 19.08.1991). Similarly, the Australian industry representatives described the proposed Australian fee as threatening the competitiveness of the domestic industry and "grossly disproportionate to other like-minded spacefaring nations" (Southern Launch, Submission to the Standing Committee on Industry, Innovation, Science and Resources for the Inquiry into Developing Australia's Space Industry, No. Submission 46, 2021, at 27).

Moreover, the OCST conducted an analysis of the economic impact of the adopted used fees and concluded that, as they were designed, they represented "a very small fraction of the total revenues derived from a launch operation" and were "not expected to have a negative impact on the rate growth of the commercial space launch industry or the financial viability of any of the existing firms in the industry" (see Final Rule. Commercial Space Transportation: User Fees No. 56 FR 41062 3). The office specified that it welcomed efforts to reduce the cost of access to space but that it did not expect the rule to have "a seriously adverse impact on the costs of any individual launcher or on those of the commercial launch industry". ((Final Rule. Commercial Space Transportation: User Fees No. 56 FR 41062 3, at 7). The risk assessments conducted by the Australian Space Agency concluded that there was a risk that the cost recovering fees for overseas payload permits (particularly to small businesses and academic organisations) might have been "a disincentive to space participation" but that such risk was mitigated "through the design of the models" that was related "directly to work undertaken" (Draft cost recovery implementation statement. Fees for activities under the Space (Launches and Returns) Act 2018. 2019-2020 10). In the United States, it was suggested not to use the revenue to recover the costs incurred to grant licences to space companies but to channel it through a trust fund and use it for “some worthy purpose that might benefit the industry” (Memorandum of the Hearing on Fiscal Year 1992 NASA Authorization for Space Transportation. HSY065020, 1991), for example to improve the launch facilities and infrastructure technologies which improve the performance or reduce the cost of commercial launch vehicles (Hall, 1991[33]). Such experiences, along with past literature on the topic, help to understand which concerns the policy maker has to keep in mind when developing a new space debris tax or fee.

Framework of principles and assessment criteria

The purpose of this chapter is to identify the essential elements of the fiscal policy option that appear best suited to serve the purpose of mitigating risks from space debris generation. A robust and implementable policy needs to be embedded into a framework of legal and tax principles deriving from international (public and space) law principles, and principles of taxation, as presented in Table 7.3.

Table 7.3. Framework of principles

Elements of the tax and/or fee	Framework of principles	
	Legal framework	Tax framework
Goal	Freedom of exploration and use No harm principle Due regard principle	Equality
Taxable event / Event giving rise to the right	Freedom of exploration and use No harm principle	Certainty
Tax base	Polluter pays principle	Certainty Efficiency
Tax rate	Polluter pays principle	Certainty Efficiency
Moment of tax collection / Moment of grant	Freedom of exploration and use	Certainty Convenience

To determine which policy option is best suited to serve the purpose of a space debris tax and/or fee, the author has selected some criteria against which tax policy options shall be tested:

1. *Legal implications*: Impacts on space and tax law principles.[4]
2. *Economic implications*:
    a. Private entities’ perspective: Convenience, competitiveness.
    b. States’ perspective: Potential impact on the budget.
3. *Behavioural implications*: Incentive for a behavioural shift towards more environmentally friendly solutions.

As for the economic implications, the moment of tax collection plays a key role as from the tax collector’s point of view it is preferable that it is linked to an event certain and definite. Also, a deferred tax collection can bring the risk of bankruptcy that jeopardises the effective collection of the revenue. The contrary would be true from the taxpayer’s perspective as “immediate” tax collection could put an additional economic burden on the companies’ shoulders, while “deferred” tax collection could give them time to be profitable before paying any taxes/fees. This chapter favours the taxpayers’ interests first, as it relies on the assumption that the tax policy measure to be adopted shall not hinder companies’ competitiveness. Clearly, states can adopt different views and make different political choices or can decide to incentivise competitiveness by using other non-fiscal instruments. From the states’ perspective, solutions that require additional state resources to cover either new expense (e.g. refunds) or a decrease in revenue collected (e.g. tax incentives) shall either address the need for the state to find such resources (e.g. through the increase of other existing sources of revenue or the cut of other expenses) or shall be combined with policies raising new resources (e.g. taxes or fees). Finally, as per the behavioural criterion, tax policy options incentivising behavioural changes towards the implementation of more sustainable and safe spacecraft designs, or the completion of PMD and ADR activities are preferred over options that do not stimulate such positive behavioural effects as the achievement of the primary goal of the measure is subject to a behavioural shift.

Proposal for a space debris mitigation fiscal scheme

The design of policy options analysed in the literature might raise uncertainties regarding their effects on the freedom of access to space, the production of positive behavioural change towards ADR, as well as the risk of tying the moment of taxation to an event that is difficult to ascertain and would make the assessment and collection of the tax unclear. Therefore, it is possible to think of a further variant combining elements of the different proposals, which does not jeopardise the possibility of access to the space and brings the desired behavioural change. The proposal for a Space Debris Mitigation Fiscal Scheme (SDMFS) composed of an orbiting debris tax/fee (ODT) and a tax credit for PMD and ADR is embedded in the framework of principles above identified (see Figure 7.1).

Goal of the measure

In the tax and public policy literature, scholars have long debated the purpose of the tax system. In a fascinating paper, Avi-Yonah has answered the question of what taxes are for (Avi-Yonah, 2006[34]). He describes the three goals of taxation: The need to raise revenue for necessary governmental functions, the redistributive function, and the regulatory function. The design of a tax measure can be tailored in a way that best achieves the objective pursued. Consequently, the design of a space debris tax may vary if the main objective of the measure is raising revenue, redistributing wealth or achieving other regulatory goals (such as mitigating orbit pollution). The author suggests that, among the potential goals of the ODT, the objective shall be (1) the internalisation of negative externalities stemming from commercial space activities through a price (the tax and/or fee) imposed on the polluting event (i.e., putting new satellites in orbit thus increasing the risk of debris formation) – and (2) incentivising the removal of existing debris through the tax credit.[5] Such a fiscal measure would thus have a regulatory purpose. The rationale of the SDMFS lies in the price put on each unit of polluting activity identified in the space objects' launches, being the prerequisite for the formation of debris.

Level of design, implementation, assessment, collection and right to use the revenue

Although the delineation of the ideal level of administration and collection of such a tax is beyond the scope of this research, it is worth mentioning that four main approaches might be envisaged:

1. Design, implementation, assessment, collection and right to use the revenue entirely managed at the international level by a supranational authority.
2. Design, implementation, assessment, collection and right to use the revenue entirely managed at a national level by each state.
3. International agreement on the design of the tax, but domestic implementation, assessment, collection and right to use the revenue.
4. International agreement on the design of the tax, but domestic implementation, assessment and collection. The revenue is transferred to a supranational body.

All these approaches have advantages and drawbacks, as explained below. The first option would entail giving an international tax administration (that at present does not exist) the power to design, implement, assess the tax and collect and use the revenue. Such a solution poses the question of the transfer of tax sovereignty to this authority, the consensus for which, as known, is very difficult to reach. The same would hold true in the case of a European space debris tax (on the difficulties linked to the adoption of a European environmental tax, see Scuderi (2022[35])).

The idea of creating a new international body for the administration of international taxes has already been explored in the literature (Adolph, 2006[36]; Tanzi, 2016[37]; Morin and Richard, 2021[38]). Scholars have discussed the potential need for a regulatory agency to have the duty – more generally – to protect the space environment, manage potential conflicts, and safeguard the interests of developing countries (Adolph, 2006[36]; Jakhu, Nyampong and Tommaso Sgobba, 2017[39]; Bernhard, 2023[40]), or called for a global tax authority to administer general global tax issues (Tanzi, 2016[37]). In the space debris context, given the global reach of the problem, global actions seem to be best suited to tackle the problem effectively, while unilateral actions might not be sufficient in the long run (Salter, 2016[12]; Morin and Richard, 2021[38]). In their analysis of the potential use of tax policies to govern global commons, Morin and Richard (2021[38]) highlighted that the absence of a global government having both the legitimacy and the necessary authority to levy taxes represents the main obstacle for debris mitigation. In fact, building on the work conducted by Ostrom (1990[41]), they concluded that a purely global tax might not be necessary to tackle the problem of space debris and that solutions could be based on the existing polycentric nature of space governance. On the other hand, Jakhu (2017[39]) proposed the establishment of an international regulatory regime and an international organisation to undertake ADR and on-orbit servicing activities. They suggest that state parties may be required under such agreement to collect a domestic 'space-garbage-collection' tax on the final users of space-based commercial services in their jurisdictions, to be imposed as a fee for the issuance of a launch licence by a national regulatory entity of a state party (Jakhu, Nyampong and Tommaso Sgobba, 2017[39]). Hobe envisages a legal regime that poses the responsibility to pay a fee to an international fund upon the launch of each space object (Hobe, 2023[42]).

The second solution would be easier to implement, at least in principle. It would entail keeping the design, implementation, assessment, collection and right to use the revenue at the domestic level, hence not requiring any transfer of sovereignty and setting aside the difficulties of finding international consensus. However, due to the global scope of the externality associated with space debris, unilateral action by individual spacefaring nations might not be the most efficient solution. Unilateral actions could lead to different tax policies having diverse scopes, requirements, and levels of taxation. The inhomogeneity stemming from such different domestic solutions would increase the level of complexity and uncertainty, and the possible different tax rates (as well as the possibility for certain states not to introduce any tax) would add a new element of tax unfairness and potentiality tax competition.

The third solution would leave only the design of the tax policy in the hands of an international organisation, with the actual implementation, collection and right to use the revenue at the national level. This option combines the advantage of co-operating at the international level for the design of the tax measure (which would eliminate the problems arising from the potentially different tax models) and the advantage of not transferring tax competencies to a supranational organisation (which could render the adoption of the tax much easier and quicker). This solution shares these features with the fourth one. The only difference is the destination of the revenue. In the third option, countries retain the revenue collected and might decide whether to earmark it based on their domestic policies and goals.

A different approach is suggested by the fourth option, where an international body is responsible for the design of the tax to be implemented and collected at the national level; the international body is then funded by states in order for it to undertake ADR services.

In the context of other areas of environmental policy, empirical studies show that a co-ordinated tax for many countries would lead to substantial cost-savings for taxpayers and tax administrations and would lead to CO_2 emissions reductions at a lower rate and smaller costs (Barker, 1999[43]; Conrad and Schmidt, 1998[44]). Assuming that this holds true also in the area of debris mitigation, an international agreement on the critical elements of the tax could be of utmost necessity.

The proposed SDMFS endorses solution number 3, by virtue of which the essential elements of the tax policy are agreed at the international level, so as to avoid great differences in terms of if and how the policy is realised. The actual implementation, assessment and collection of the tax is left to states. The revenue collected is suggested to be kept by the states and used for achieving the goals of the SDMFS in order to create an additional incentive for states to co-operate in developing such a solution. This solution could be implementable in a relatively short term, considering that it does entail the establishment of a new international organisation or the identification of which among the existing international organisations could pool funds and use them to carry out space debris removal activities. Finally, considering that states retain jurisdiction and control over space objects launched from their territories, any removal operation carried out by an international organisation would require the specific prior consent of the state of registration, bringing the necessity to amend the Liability Convention and the Outer Space Treaty to surrender a portion of state jurisdiction relating to the control of space objects for debris removal. The suggested option number 3 would not need such additional efforts (it shall, however, be considered, that organisations such as the European Space Agency might act as the state of registration, raising the question of which body would be entitled to raise and collect the tax).

Taxpayers

Although governmental space activities produce debris, governments are not considered taxpayers for the purposes of the SDMFS. Only private commercial space actors would be subject to the SDMFS. Some space launches can bring into orbit more than one space object, possibly owned by different actors (e.g., space companies, individuals, research institutions, or other entities). In these cases, the tax shall be determined for each space object carried into orbit, as each of them poses a different risk of debris creation. The taxpayers are thus the owners of such space objects. Caution should be paid to cases where the space object has a dual use (governmental and non-governmental). A solution could be to modulate the tax to reflect the ownership share of private entities.

Taxable event and tax base

As already mentioned, the essential elements of the SDMFS shall be agreed upon internationally. In this context, since the main objective of the tax measure is the mitigation of risks arising from debris formation and collisions, the international agreement may stipulate that the taxable event is an expression of the risk posed by the launch of a new satellite that is expressed in the licence application for the launch of the space object.

The same logic applies to the determination of the tax base. The international agreement may stipulate that it is an expression of the risk posed by putting a new satellite into orbit. At the state level, each state could use different parameters to determine this risk (e.g., mass at launch, payload lifting capacity, mission costs), as long as the chosen criterion is an expression of the risk of debris formation. In the literature, it has been suggested to levy the tax as a percentage of the launch costs or the total mission costs for putting the satellite into orbit (Bilaney, 2021[45]). This option might be explored as the launch costs reflect the dimensions and the payload capacity. However, it should be taken into account that a single launch vehicle can carry several space objects owned by different space companies. Therefore, it would be necessary to either determine the tax based on the costs associated with the launch of the vehicle as a whole or to split the calculation based on each payload carried into space.

Tax rate

Optimal tax theory suggests that the tax rate should be high on goods and services with a low price elasticity, and low on goods and services with a high price elasticity. This means that before setting the rate of the tax, it is necessary to determine the level of elasticity of demand and supply of the specific object of taxation, being it the launch of satellites. Even though the calculation leading to the determination of the applicable tax rate is outside the scope of this chapter, it is worth mentioning the outcome of past research on this topic.

In the economic literature, Béal, Deschamps and Moulin (2020[25]) address the question of whether the tax should be linear or nonlinear and conclude that a flat tax is better than a progressive tax. In the context of the SDMFS, setting a flat rate would be a viable solution if the tax base is determined in a way that already expresses the risk of debris formation effectively. Otherwise, a percentage range should be identified, and the tax rate could be lower for launches that pose fewer risks, and higher for launches that pose more risks. As far as the calculation of the tax rate percentage, Rao et al. (2020[16]) suggest adopting an internationally harmonised "orbital-use fee" (OUF) in the form of a Pigouvian tax. They estimate that "the optimal OUF starts at roughly USD 14 900 per satellite-year and escalate at roughly 14% per year [...] to around USD 235 000 per satellite-year in 2040." Based on their model projects, the application of an orbital fee would increase the space industry's net present value from around USD 600 billion under a business-as-usual scenario to around USD 3 trillion, bringing about a more than four-fold increase in the value of the space industry. In contrast, Davis (2021[46]) notes that "the increase in value does not reflect the concentration of that value across space programmes worldwide".

All these factors must be considered when determining the tax rate. The few – but important – economic studies conducted in this area might serve as a basis for further research on the potentially applicable tax rate of the suggested SDMFS. The tax policy makers shall evaluate the flat tax 'fairness' based on several factors, considering the overall goal of the SDMFS. In fact, since the objective of the measure is to mitigate the risks stemming from debris collision, the measure should be designed in a way that reflects such risks. If the taxable base takes this into account, the tax rate does not necessarily need to be proportional to the risk produced. If the taxable base does not reflect the risk, then it would be appropriate to module the tax rates based on the risk brought about by the specific space object launched. Notably, this latter option would be more difficult to govern from an administrative perspective.

Moment of tax collection

When the licence to launch is requested, a liability to pay a tax for the use of the orbit arises. Since obtaining a licence is mandatory for the launch to happen, linking the event giving rise to the obligation to pay the tax/fee to such a moment can ensure a high degree of "certainty" of the measure. A few considerations are necessary in this respect. As history has shown, applying a tax and/or fee at an initial stage might constitute an element of concern for the industry because the additional burden can potentially lead to less competition, less innovation and less growth.

To avoid introducing an obstacle to the free use of space, the actual collection of the tax/fee might either happen through instalments (i.e., the total amount due is set at the moment in which the licence is requested, with payment of the first instalment, but the other instalments are paid periodically), or through a periodic tax (i.e., the amount to be paid is assessed each year based on a re-evaluation of the risk posed by the space object) or simply be deferred to a later moment identifiable in the registration of the object. The first option provides the certainty required by the framework or principles identified since it sets the total amount of tax/fee due at the moment of the licence application. Additionally, it gives the taxpayer a longer time to actually pay the fiscal debt. To face the risk of bankruptcy which would render the collection impossible, interest rates can apply, or the state can require the taxpayer to include the cost of the tax/fee in the insurance coverage. The second option has been suggested in the literature (Buchs, 2020[47]).

Although interesting, it would not give the taxpayer a clear ex ante overview of the tax liability connected to the launch. In addition, it would still be sensitive to the possibility of bankruptcy.

Both downsides can be overcome. The first is a common element of periodic taxes. The second could be minimised through interest rates or insurance policies. The positive side of the periodical tax is that it could better reflect the actual risk of debris formation at every re-evaluation. The third option would link the collection of the tax to the registration of the space object. The issues related to the registration of space objects are well-known in the literature (Jakhu, Jasani and McDowell, 2018[48]). The fact that registration is sometimes delayed or does not occur at all is a factor to be taken into consideration when evaluating this option. However, linking the duty to register the space objects launched from a state with its taxing rights might (perhaps) encourage greater compliance with the Registration Convention. As a final note, if the Registration Convention were amended so as to make the registration mandatory by a certain deadline after the launch, such concerns would disappear.

The use of revenue collected: The tax credit

The SDMFS entails the combination of the ODT with a mechanism that encourages companies to actively remove debris and clean space from their space object once it becomes unusable (Drago, 2019[49]). This might take the form of a refund or a tax incentive to be granted upon proof of PMD or ADR. The great advantage of the use of tax incentives or refunds in mitigation policies is that they provide a direct incentive for taxpayers to act for the removal of space debris. This chapter suggests the potential adoption of a tax credit designed in a way that encourages prompt debris removal. To achieve this goal, the generosity of the credit shall be higher in the first year(s) following the end of the operations or "death" of the space object and shall decrease over time. In other words, the shorter the time between the moment the space object becomes unusable and the moment it is removed, the higher the percentage of the tax credit.[6] If the object is not promptly removed, the taxpayer will still pay the tax, the liability of which arose at the moment of the licence request but might not get part of, or the whole tax credit.

Figure 7.1. Space debris mitigation fiscal scheme

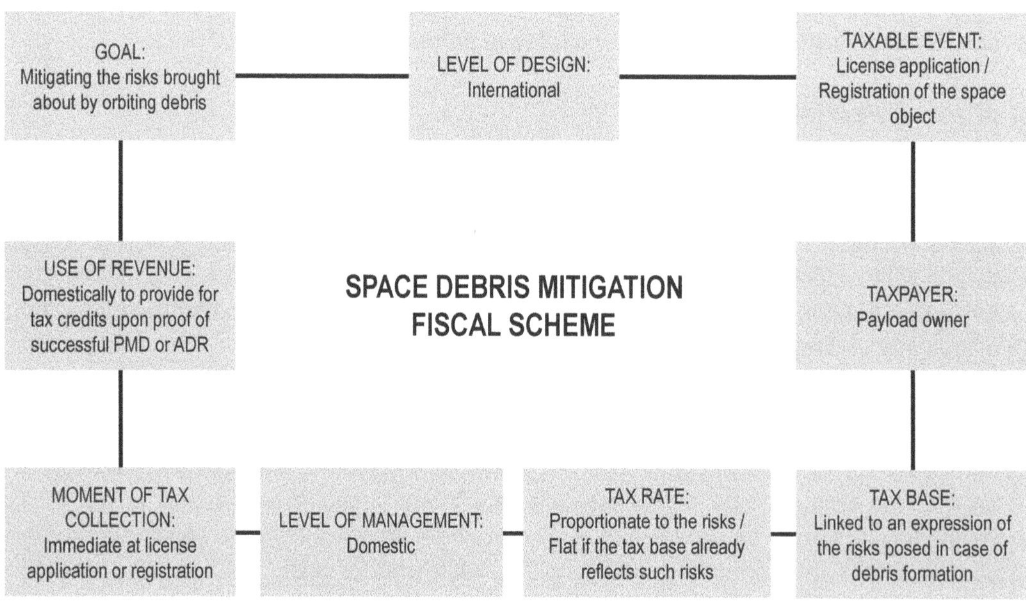

Notes: PMD=post-mission disposal, ADR=Active debris removal.

In order for such a measure to be effective, some conditions must exist. First, ADR technologies shall prove to be effective and reliable. Currently, no ADR mission has ever been carried out. The first launch is scheduled to depart starting the second half of 2026 from Europe's spaceport in French Guiana (Spacewatch Global, 2023[50]). Thus, before implementing a measure that relies on ADR missions, it is necessary to verify that such activities can effectively be carried out. Second, these technologies must be cheap enough to be affordable for space companies, otherwise compromising their ability to get such in-orbit services (Colvin, Karcz and Wusk, 2023[51]; Foust, 2023[52]; Yamamoto and Okamoto, 2017[53]). In addition, further frictions concern the responsibility of the launching state and issues of jurisdiction and control that imply that states must give their consent to ADR if conducted by other companies and/or states.[7] Considering these shortcomings, during the initial phase of the implementation of the SDMFS, the tax credit could be granted following PMD (without considering ADR) or *ex ante* for a higher abatement of research and development costs to stimulate innovation in research for ADR activities or used to directly conduct such ADR activities until the private sector can afford it.

The use of the revenue collected might play an important role in obtaining political approval to raise taxes aimed at financing specific policy goals. In this regard, budget earmarking could be useful. Hypothecation or earmarking links the revenue collected through a tax to a specific expenditure (Burton and Sadiq, 2013[54]; Surrey and McDaniel, 1985[55]; Stewart, 2022[56]; Kotha, 2023[57]). Although green budgeting is the 'least well advanced of ethical or values-based approaches to the budget' (Stewart, 2022[56]) it is considered to have the potential to support governments in a long-term reorientation of tax and expenditure approaches for fiscal sustainability (Stewart, 2022[56]). Earmarking the revenue collected through the tax to expenditures for space cleanup or financing R&D can prove to be a successful policy choice for two main reasons. First, the tax expenditure could directly contribute to the achievement of the objective of the levy if the funds are used to pay for a debris cleanup mission. Second, the tax expenditure can also indirectly contribute to the achievement of the purpose of the levy if the funds are used to finance R&D activities finalised at (i) designing more "environmentally friendly" space objects and (ii) providing cost-effective and cost-efficient ADR mechanisms. If governments decide to adopt new tax incentives, close attention shall be paid to the potential impact of the rules included in the legislations implementing the OECD "Pillar Two" (Scuderi, 2024[58]).

Expected consequences and considerations

Considerations on the level of taxation and the generosity of the tax credit

Based on the above, some considerations on the level of taxation and the generosity of the tax credit are needed. First, the goal of the SDMFS is to mitigate the risks stemming from debris collisions. However, the specific objectives of the two fiscal measures slightly differ from each other, otherwise compromising the overall goal. More in detail, the goal of the ODT is to raise the necessary revenue to fund the tax credit and/or ADR activities. If the goal of such a tax was to bring a behavioural shift toward more environmentally friendly attitudes, its tax rate should be set at a rate high enough to effectively discourage new launches. Notably, higher tax rates decrease the rate of debris creation (Adilov, Alexander and Cunningham, 2020[59]). However, this is not the intention of the author's proposal. The assumption is that launches shall not be discouraged as competitiveness shall not be hindered by the introduction of the new levy. Thus, the tax rate shall be enough high to raise the necessary revenue to achieve the overall goal of the SDMFS but not too high to discourage new launches.

Second, tax policy makers shall carefully consider whether the revenue collected has to be earmarked or not. If earmarked, they shall evaluate for which purpose. On the one hand, a broad and ambitious goal encompassing the provision of a tax incentive and the deployment of ADR would be the gold standard. However, it might risk requiring a too high amount of revenue to cover the costs. This could kill the development of the commercial industry. On the other hand, a too narrow and less ambitious goal encompassing, for example, a minor tax credit for PMD or ADR would not be able to gain traction and bring the behavioural change desired as the incentive coming from the (low) tax credit would not be "worth" the high expenses necessary to conduct PMD or ADR activities.

Potential unfairness in the assignment of taxing rights

Some might argue that if such taxes are paid in the jurisdiction where the launch occurs, the taxing rights would be allocated to a handful of countries having launching capabilities. In the author's view, the assignment of taxing rights to the launching state can be seen as a sort of 'compensation' for its responsibility under the liability convention.[8] In particular, if there is more than one launching state, the state of registration would take precedence and retain taxing rights. Furthermore, the revenue would be used to address a global issue (i.e., space debris) for the benefit of all states. If successful, the SDMFS makes the orbit ready to accommodate other states' satellites, so the collection of revenue from some states right now could be seen as a way of supporting the restoration and preservation of the global commons.

The mentioned approach of hypothecation and/or earmarking could mitigate the concerns surrounding the potential unfairness of the tax and gain political support for its implementation. For the sake of argument, it can also be said that the reason why taxing rights are in the hands of the launching state is because this state is responsible for the damages caused by the objects launched from its territories. This would mean that in case of damage, the launching state can be held responsible. Assigning taxing rights to the launching state can be seen as a sort of 'compensation' for this liability. However, this argument might have a flaw. In fact, according to Article VII OST and Article I of the Liability Convention, the 'launching state' is not only the state from whose territory a space object is launched but also the state (i) that launches, (ii) that procures the launching and (iii) from whose facility a space object is launched. This means that for the same launching from which damage occurs, more than one state can be identified as a launching state based on different grounds, thus being all jointly liable for such damage. Therefore, this being the case, attaching taxing rights only to one of these states could be perceived as unfair. Ways of mitigating such unfairness can be explored.

Tax competition among states and companies

It might be argued that if the tax measure is adopted only by certain countries, it might constitute an incentive for space companies to relocate their launch activities to those countries where the tax/fee is not due. This would introduce a new factor of tax competition. In this respect, it shall be noted that not all launching pads can accommodate every single type of launch. In fact, the choice of the spaceport depends on a number of factors that are unrelated to tax rules (e.g., the type of mission to be carried out, targeted orbit, etc.). This means that – at least at present – there seems to be very little room for tax competition among states. This might change in the future if more spaceports with similar launching capabilities are built in countries that raise such taxes and in countries that do not. The main risk caused by the non-co-ordination of fiscal measures on launches is the disadvantageous position space actors would find themselves in if they can only launch from a given state if that state imposes a levy and other states do not. The additional cost that these actors would have to bear would put them at a competitive economic disadvantage vis-à-vis other space actors abroad, risking threatening their business and slowing down the development of research, innovation, and the space market in general, which, as Weinzierl points out, is made of complementarity and co-ordination between various segments of the sector (Weinzierl, 2018[60]).

Conclusions

This chapter reviewed the existing literature discussing fiscal-based policies for space debris mitigation and tested four different tax policies against specific criteria identified by the author. Some lessons from past experiences remind us of specific concerns that tax policy makers shall address when designing a tax/fee that addresses space launches. Based on this review, the author suggested a framework of principles within which a proposal for a Space Debris Mitigation Scheme is embedded. The proposal envisages the adoption of a tax and/or fee connected to the actual risks stemming from debris formation. By linking the tax/fee to such risks, the domestic tax policy makers have ample room for designing the essential elements of the tax in a way that is compatible with their domestic tax system and constitutional framework, and that is fair and equitable. In the proposal, such tax/fee is complemented by a tax credit granted upon proof of PMD or ADR. Such tax credit shall be designed in a way that encourages prompt disposal and/or removal of the space object once it becomes unusable or debris. Alternative options to the tax credits are also suggested.

Some areas would need further investigation. In particular, research is needed to estimate the elasticity of the demand and supply in the launch industry and the applicable tax rate, or at least its range. Also, the identification of the taxable base needs to be supported by economic studies.

Moreover, the chapter did not discuss the possibility of launching from outer space or the high seas. This aspect shall be evaluated in the design of the measure to include an umbrella clause for situations in which the launch happens from territories in which countries do not have sovereignty. In any case, as a launching state has to be identified for every launch in order to assign jurisdiction, control, liability and responsibility for damages, these situations do not seem at first sight to pose particular issues. Clearly, a deeper investigation is needed to confirm this statement.

From a legal perspective, the modification of the Registration Convention to include a mandatory deadline for the registration of the space objects could ease the connection between the moment of tax collection and such registration.

Additionally, although this proposal advocates for a domestically implemented measure, it does not forget that space debris is a global concern and global actions could be the most desirable outcome. In this respect, further studies on the legal basis for an international action could be conducted. For example, if an international body has to be set up, it would be interesting to explore the possibility of creating coalitions similar to the "Climate Clubs" envisaged by Nordhaus (Nordhaus, 2015[17]), or adopting a rule similar to Article 82 United Nations Convention on the Law of the Sea (Bird and Mintz, 2019[61]; Burch, 2019[62]). Last, but not least, tax policies are only one tool at the disposal of governments to tackle the challenges brought about by space debris. It would be worth exploring the combination of fiscal policies with other market-based instruments, such as a cap-and-trade system similar to the EU Emission Trading System (Bullock and Johanson, 2021[63]; Rao, Burgess and Kaffine, 2020[16]).

References

Adilov, N., P. Alexander and B. Cunningham (2023), "The economics of satellite deorbiting performance bonds", *Economics Letters*, Vol. 228, https://doi.org/10.1016/j.econlet.2023.111150. [32]

Adilov, N., P. Alexander and B. Cunningham (2022), "Understanding the Economics of Orbital Pollution Through the Lens of Terrestrial Climate Change", *Space Policy*, Vol. 59, p. 101471, https://doi.org/10.1016/j.spacepol.2021.101471. [18]

Adilov, N., P. Alexander and B. Cunningham (2020), "The Economics of Orbital Debris Generation, Accumulation, Mitigation and Remediation", *Journal of Space Safety Engineering*, Vol. 7/3, pp. 447-450, https://doi.org/10.1016/j.jsse.2020.07.016. [59]

Adilov, N., P. Alexander and B. Cunningham (2015), "An Economic Analysis of Earth Orbit Pollution", *Environmental and Resource Economics*, Vol. 60/1, pp. 81-98, https://doi.org/10.1007/s10640-013-9758-4. [21]

Adolph, J. (2006), "The Recent Boom in Private Space Development and the Necessity of an International Framework Embracing Private Property Rights to Encourage Investment", *The International Lawyer*, Vol. 40/4, pp. 961-985, www.jstor.org/stable/40708019. [36]

Alfano, S. and D. Oltrogge (2018), "Probability of Collision: Valuation, variability, visualization, and validity", *Acta Astronautica*, Vol. 148, pp. 301-316, https://doi.org/10.1016/j.actaastro.2018.04.023. [5]

Avi-Yonah, R. (2006), "The Three Goals of Taxation", *Tax Law Review*, https://doi.org/10.2139/ssrn.796776. [34]

Barker, T. (1999), "Achieving a 10% Cut in Europe's CO2 Emissions Using Additional Excise Duties: Coordinated, Uncoordinated and Unilateral Action Using the Econometric Model E3ME", *Economic Systems Research*, Vol. 11/4, pp. 401-422, https://doi.org/10.1080/09535319900000029. [43]

Béal, S., M. Deschamps and H. Moulin (2020), "Taxing congestion of the space commons", *Acta Astronautica*, Vol. 177, pp. 313-319, https://doi.org/10.1016/j.actaastro.2020.07.036. [25]

Bernhard, P. (2023), "Large satellite constellations and space debris: Exploratory analysis of strategic management of the space commons", *European Journal of Operational Research*, Vol. 304/3, pp. 1140-1157, https://doi.org/10.1016/j.ejor.2022.04.030. [40]

Bilaney, S. (2021), "A Tax to Ensure Space Sustainability", *Tax Notes International*, www.taxnotes.com/lr/resolve/tax-notes-international/a-tax-to-ensure-space-sustainability/784hw. [45]

Bird, R. and J. Mintz (2019), "Sharing the Wealth: Article 82 of UNCLOS-The First Global Tax?", *British Tax Review* 4, www.sweetandmaxwell.co.uk/Product/Taxation-Law/British-Tax-Review/Journal/30791232. [61]

Bradley, A. and L. Wein (2009), "Space debris: Assessing risk and responsibility", *Advances in Space Research*, Vol. 43/9, pp. 1372-1390, https://doi.org/10.1016/j.asr.2009.02.006. [2]

Buchs, R. (2020), "Pricing space junk: A policy assessment of space debris miitgation and remediation in the new space era", Master's thesis, ETH Zurich, www.research-collection.ethz.ch/bitstream/handle/20.500.11850/481152/RomainBuchs-Masterthesis-Pricingspacejunk.pdf?sequence=1&isAllowed=y. [47]

Buchs, R. and T. Bernauer (2023), "Market-based instruments to incentivize more sustainable practices in outer space", *Current Opinion on Environmental Sustainability*, Vol. 60, https://doi.org/10.1016/j.cosust.2022.101247. [28]

Bullock, C. and R. Johanson (2021), "Policies for Incentivising Orbital Debris Assessment and Remediation", *MIT Science Policy Review*, Vol. 2, pp. 8-14, https://doi.org/10.38105/spr.16gdw8z5d4. [63]

Burch, M. (2019), "Extranational Taxation: Canada and UNCLOS Article 82", *Canadian Tax Journal/Revue fiscale canadienne*, Vol. 67/3, pp. 729-753, https://ssrn.com/abstract=3461831. [62]

Burton, M. and K. Sadiq (2013), *Tax Expenditure Management*, Cambridge University Press. [54]

Colvin, T., J. Karcz and G. Wusk (2023), "Cost and Benefit Analysis of Orbital Debris Remediation", NASA, www.nasa.gov/wp-content/uploads/2023/03/otps_-_cost_and_benefit_analysis_of_orbital_debris_remediation_-_final.pdf. [51]

Conrad, K. and T. Schmidt (1998), "Economic Impacts of an Uncoordinated Versus a Coordinated Carbon Dioxide Policy in the European Union: An Applied General Equilibrium Analysis", *10.1080/09535319808565472*, Vol. 10/2, pp. 161-182, https://doi.org/10.1080/09535319808565472. [44]

Davis, I. (2021), *Orbital Use Fees Stifle Developing Space Programs*, Socio-technical research paper presented to the faculty of the School of Engineering and Applied Sciencde, University of Virginia, https://libraetd.lib.virginia.edu/downloads/br86b4355?filename=Davis_Ian_STS_Research_Paper.pdf. [46]

de Moor, J. (2021), "Postapocalyptic narratives in climate activism: their place and impact in five European cities", *Environmental Politics*, Vol. 31/6, pp. 927-948, https://doi.org/10.1080/09644016.2021.1959123. [19]

Drago, S. (2019), "No Man's Sky: Utilizing Maritime Law To Address The Need For Space Debris Removal Technology", *Santa Clara Law Review*, Vol. 389, https://digitalcommons.law.scu.edu/lawreview/vol59/iss2/3. [49]

Foust, J. (2023), *NASA Study Assesses Costs and Benefits of Orbital Debris Removal*, 13 March, https://spacenews.com/nasa-study-assess-costs-and-benefits-of-orbital-debris-removal/. [52]

Guyot, J. and S. Rouillon (2023), "Sustainable management of space activity in low Earth orbit", *Journal of Environmental Economics and Policy*, pp. 1-25, https://doi.org/10.1080/21606544.2023.2231402. [26]

Hall, R. (1991), *Letter in Response to the Announcement of Commercial Space Transportation User Fees (Apr)*. [33]

Hobe, S. (2023), *Space Law*, oHG/Hart Publishing. [42]

Hoogendoorn, R., E. Mooij and J. Geul (2018), "Uncertainty propagation for statistical impact prediction of space debris", *Advances in Space Research*, Vol. 61/1, pp. 167-181, https://doi.org/10.1016/j.asr.2017.10.009. [9]

Jakhu, R., B. Jasani and J. McDowell (2018), "Critical issues related to registration of space objects and transparency of space activities", *Acta Astronautica*, Vol. 143, pp. 406-420, https://doi.org/10.1016/j.actaastro.2017.11.042. [48]

Jakhu, R., O. Nyampong and T. Tommaso Sgobba (2017), "Regulatory Framework and Organization for Space Debris Removal and on Orbit Servicing of Satellites", *Journal of Space Safety Engineering*, Vol. 4/3-4, pp. 129-137, https://doi.org/10.1016/j.jsse.2017.10.002. [39]

Jones, B. and A. Doostan (2013), "Satellite collision probability estimation using polynomial chaos expansions", *Advances in Space Research*, Vol. 52/11, pp. 1860-1875, https://doi.org/10.1016/j.asr.2013.08.027. [7]

Kessler, D. and B. Cour-Palais (1978), "Collision frequency of artificial satellites: The creation of a debris belt", *Journal of Geophysical Research: Space Physics*, Vol. 83/A6, pp. 2637-2646, https://doi.org/10.1029/ja083ia06p02637. [4]

Kotha, A. (2023), "Earmarking of taxes for disruption and recovery", in De Cogan, D., A. Brassey and P. Harris (eds.), *Tax Law in Times of Crisis and Recovery*, Hart Publishing, An Imprint of Bloomsbury Publishing. [57]

Lambach, D. and L. Wesel (2021), "Tackling the space debris Problem: A global commons perspective", Proc. 8th European Conference on Space Debris (virtual), European Space Agency Space Debris Office, https://conference.sdo.esoc.esa.int/proceedings/sdc8/paper/230/SDC8-paper230.pdf. [11]

Limperis, P. (1998), "Orbital Debris and the Spacefaring Nations: International Law Methods for Prevention and Reduction of Debris, and Liability Regimes for Damage Caused by Debris [Note]", *Arizona Journal of International and Comparative Law*, http://hdl.handle.net/10150/659313. [23]

Liou, J. and N. Johnson (2006), "Risks in Space from Orbiting Debris", *Science*, Vol. 311/5759, pp. 340-341, https://doi.org/10.1126/science.1121337. [3]

Lucas-Rhimbassen, M. (2019), "Conceptual Model for a Profitable Return on Investment from Space Debris as Abiotic Space Resource", Proceedings of the 8th European Conference for Aeronautics and Space Sciences, Madrid, Spain. [13]

Macauley, M. (2015), "The economics of space debris: Estimating the costs and benefits of debris mitigation", *Acta Astronautica*, Vol. 115, pp. 160-164, https://doi.org/10.1016/j.actaastro.2015.05.006. [24]

Macauley, M. (2004), "Regulation of the Final Frontier", *Regulation*, https://ssrn.com/abstract=505624. [30]

Macauley, M. (1994), "Close Encounters of the Trash Kind", *Journal of Policy Analysis and Management*, Vol. 13/3, pp. 560-564, https://doi.org/10.2307/3325392. [31]

Mark, C. and S. Kamath (2019), "Review of Active Space Debris Removal Methods", *Space Policy*, Vol. 47, pp. 194-206, https://doi.org/10.1016/j.spacepol.2018.12.005. [14]

Morin, J. and B. Richard (2021), "Astro-Environmentalism: Towards a Polycentric Governance of Space Debris", *Global Policy*, Ltd 2021)., pp. 568-573, https://doi.org/10.1111/1758-5899.12950. [38]

Nordhaus, W. (2015), "Climate Clubs: Overcoming Free-riding in International Climate Policy", *American Economic Review*, Vol. 105/4, pp. 1339-1370, https://doi.org/10.1257/aer.15000001. [17]

OECD (2022), *Earth's Orbits at Risk: The Economics of Space Sustainability*, OECD Publishing, Paris, https://doi.org/10.1787/16543990-en. [1]

Oltrogge, D. et al. (2018), "A comprehensive assessment of collision likelihood in Geosynchronous Earth Orbit", *Acta Astronautica*, Vol. 147, pp. 316-345, https://doi.org/10.1016/j.actaastro.2018.03.017. [6]

Ostrom, E. (1990), *Governing the Commons: The Evolution of Institutions for Collective Action*, Cambridge University Press. [41]

Pecujlic, A. and S. Germann (2015), "Global Cap and Trade System for Space Debris: Putting a Price on Space Hazards", *Journal of Space Law*, Vol. 40/1-2, https://airandspacelaw.olemiss.edu/wp-content/uploads/2020/07/JSL-40.12.pdf. [29]

Rao, A., M. Burgess and D. Kaffine (2020), "Orbital-use fees could more than quadruple the value of the space industry", *Proceedings of the National Academy of Sciences*, Vol. 117/23, pp. 12756-12762, https://doi.org/10.1073/pnas.1921260117. [16]

Salter, A. (2016), "Space Debris: A Law and Economic Analysis of the Orbital Commons", *Stanford Technology Law Review* 19, p. 221, https://law.stanford.edu/wp-content/uploads/2017/11/19-2-2-salter-final_0.pdf. [12]

Scheraga, J. (1986), "Pollution in Space: An Economic Perspective", *Ambio*, Vol. 15/6, pp. 358-60, www.jstor.org/stable/4313302. [22]

Scuderi, E. (2024), "Tax Incentives for the Space Economy and the Potential Impact of Pillar Two", *Air and Space Law*, Vol. 49/1, pp. 69-94, https://doi.org/10.54648/aila2024006. [58]

Scuderi, E. (2022), "Provisions Primarily of a Fiscal Nature: Time to Dispel Doubts", *EC Tax Review*, Vol. 31/5, pp. 273-285, https://doi.org/10.2139/ssrn.4119635. [35]

Skinner, M. (2017), "Orbital debris: What are the best near-term actions to take? A view from the field", *Journal of Space Safety Engineering*, Vol. 4/2, pp. 105-111, https://doi.org/10.1016/j.jsse.2017.02.002. [15]

Spacewatch Global (2023), *ClearSpace to launch the first active debris removal mission with Arianespace*, 10 May, https://spacewatch.global/2023/05/clearspace-to-launch-the-first-active-debris-removal-mission-with-arianespace/. [50]

Stewart, M. (2022), "The Budget", in *Tax and Government in the 21st Century*, Cambridge University Press, Cambridge, https://doi.org/10.1017/9781316160701. [56]

Surrey, S. and P. McDaniel (1985), *Tax Expenditures*, Harvard University Press. [55]

Tanzi, V. (2016), "Lakes, Oceans, and Taxes: Why the World Needs a World Tax Authority", in Pogge, T. and K. Meht (eds.), *Global Tax Fairness*, Oxford University Press. [37]

Tapio, J. and A. Soucek (2019), "National Implementation of Non-Legally Binding Instruments: Managing Uncertainty in Space Law?", *Air and Space Law*, Vol. 44/Issue 6, pp. 565-582, https://doi.org/10.54648/aila2019035. [10]

Taylor, J. (2011), "Tragedy of the Space Commons: A Market Mechanism Solution to the Space Debris Problem", *Columbia Journal of Transnational Law*, p. 253, https://heinonline.org/HOL/LandingPage?handle=hein.journals/cjtl50&div=9&id=&page=. [27]

Undseth, M. (2021), "The Economics of Space Debris in Perspective", Proceedings of the 8th European Conference on Space Debris (virtual), https://conference.sdo.esoc.esa.int/proceedings/sdc8/paper/12/SDC8-paper12.pdf. [8]

Weinzierl, M. (2018), "Space, the Final Economic Frontier", *Journal of Economic Perspectives*, Vol. 32/2, pp. 173-192, https://doi.org/10.1257/jep.32.2.173. [60]

Weitzman, M. (1974), "Prices vs. Quantities", *The Review of Economic Studies*, Vol. 41/4, p. 477, https://doi.org/10.2307/2296698. [20]

Yamamoto, T. and H. Okamoto (2017), "Cost analysis of active debris removal scenarios and system architectures", 7th European Conference on Space Debris, https://conference.sdo.esoc.esa.int/proceedings/sdc7/paper/660. [53]

Notes

1 UNOOSA, Space Debris Mitigations Guidelines of the Committee on the Peaceful Uses of Outer Space (2007); Inter-Agency Space Debris Coordination Committee, IADC Space Debris Mitigation Guidelines, (2007); Inter-Agency Space Debris Coordination Committee, IADC Space Debris Mitigation Guidelines (2020); European Code of Conduct for Space Debris Mitigation (2004).

2 The per-launch fee for suborbital launches did not vary by vehicle payload capability because the benefit accruing to the licensee was considered to be modest. Also, performance capability comparisons were difficult to quantify for such launches and the variance among different launch vehicles was not significant for the purposes of the activities to be conducted by the OCST. See Proposed Regulations: Commercial Space Transportation; User Fees No. 56 FR 8301 5 (Feb. 28, 1991).

3 Rephrasing the words of Hon Melissa Price, Address to the Australian Space Forum | Ministers for the Department of Industry, Science and Resources, https://www.minister.industry.gov.au/ministers/price/speeches/address-australian-space-forum (last visited Aug. 25, 2023); See also: Isabella Richards, Launch Application Fees Slashed, New Strategy for 'Cohesive' Space Industry, https://www.spaceconnectonline.com.au/launch/5328-launch-application-fees-slashed-new-strategy-for-cohesive-space-industry (last visited Aug. 25, 2023); Thomas Jones et al., The Space Law Review: Australia, https://thelawreviews.co.uk/title/the-space-law-review/australia (last visited Aug. 25, 2023).

4 This chapter assumes that tax policy options that hinder free access to outer space should be avoided. Under Article I of the Outer Space Treaty (OST) '[o]uter space, including the moon and other celestial bodies, shall be free for exploration and use by all States without discrimination of any kind, on a basis of equality and in accordance with international law'. The interpretation of this provision might constitute an obstacle to the implementation of tax measures that *de facto* make accessing outer space too costly, thus preventing an equal use of space resources.

5 Limiting the number of space launches is not an intended goal of the measure as, first, diminishing/pausing space launches would be economically and socially unsustainable as the space economy produces a value to the general public and, second, because even assuming a complete stop of

new launches the number of debris would continue to grow. See European Space Agency, Active Debris Removal, available at: https://www.esa.int/Space_Safety/Space_Debris/Active_debris_removal (accessed 22 November 2022).

[6] Similar to the design of the American 'Invest in Space Now Act' of 2003'.

[7] From a legal perspective, the state where the object is registered retains jurisdiction over the space object and the persons aboard (quasi-territorial jurisdiction). Any removal operation carried out by another State requires the specific prior consent of the state of registration. Suppose there is an international body carrying out ADR services. In that case, it might be necessary to amend the liability convention and the OST to allow such international body to conduct debris removal operations.

[8] Article III of the United Nations, Convention on International Liability for Damage Caused by Space Objects (1972), which reads: "In the event of damage being caused elsewhere than on the surface of the earth to a space object of one launching State or to persons or property on board such a space object by a space object of another launching State, the latter shall be liable only if the damage is due to its fault or the fault of the persons for whom it is responsible". This type of "fault" liability differs from the "absolute" liability posed in the hands of states by Article II of the same Convention that reads: "A launching State shall be absolutely liable to pay compensation for damage caused by its space object on the surface of the earth or to aircraft in flight".

8 Addressing earth-space sustainability: An incentive-based mechanism for satellite infrastructure under three scenarios by 2030

Xiao-Shan Yap, Swiss Federal Institute of Technology Lausanne, Switzerland

Emmanuelle David, Swiss Federal Institute of Technology Lausanne, Switzerland

This chapter focuses on challenges related to the socio-economic dimension of the "earth-space sustainability" concept, more specifically the safety of the orbital environment for the long-term operation of space infrastructure and how it might affect technological competition in the orbital region and the diffusion of sectoral services on Earth. It further explores the role of an industry certification programme – the Space Sustainability Rating – in contributing to earth-space sustainability in three future scenarios and uses the findings to formulate policy recommendations.

Introduction

Space infrastructure has gained increasing socio-economic importance in recent years due to the capabilities of satellite services in shaping manifold earth-bound sectors. However, the exponential rise in space activities has exacerbated space congestion and the generation of space debris that results in the increasing risks of collision in space (ESA, 2022[1]). An increasingly congested orbital environment might eventually prohibit access to critical space-based infrastructure and the socio-economic benefits it might offer.

Research scholars have recently proposed the concept of "earth-space sustainability" as a guiding notion for managing the uses of space in a sustainable manner while addressing earth-bound challenges (Yap and Truffer, 2022[2]). More specifically, this concept calls for addressing earth-bound and space-related sustainability challenges in an integrative manner so that developments in space do not bring negative consequences to earth-bound developments, and vice versa (Yap and Truffer, 2022[2]). Implementing this goal is, however, challenging and there is only a limited set of policy options available that can potentially address earth-space sustainability in a simultaneous manner. While the meaning of sustainability becomes vague due to increasingly complex developments in space, this chapter is among the first attempts to add clarification to the concept by focusing on earth-space interdependencies. In this chapter, the authors delimit the empirical scope of sustainability to the long-term provision of satellite services for sustainable development purposes on Earth (i.e., in terms of socio-economic benefits and green sectoral transitions), as well as the environmental conditions for Earth's orbit including space safety for satellite operations in the geostationary (GEO) and non-geostationary (NGSO) orbits (Yap et al., 2023[3]).

Against this background, the "Space Sustainability Rating" (SSR) is a potential policy option to help address earth-space sustainability. The SSR aims to ensure that increasing space missions worldwide will be managed safely and sustainably by assigning tiered ratings to satellite operators based on a series of technical metrics. It is the result of a multi-stakeholder effort initiated by the World Economic Forum Global Council on Space in 2016 in collaboration with the Massachusetts Institute of Technology, the European Space Agency (ESA) Space Debris Office, Bryce Tech and the University of Texas at Austin, and is currently implemented at the Ecole Polytechnique Fédérale de Lausanne Space Center. As an incentive-based mechanism, SSR encourages space operators to adopt practices deemed more sustainable for the orbital environment (Rathnasabapathy and David, 2023[4]). The SSR is a potential policy option considering the lack of a strong, legally binding governance regime at the international level (IRGC, 2021[5]; Buchs and Bernauer, 2023[6]).

However, empirical analysis is needed to better understand under which conditions stakeholders, policy makers, and satellite operators will be driven to adopt the SSR, in particular within the next several years during which the number of satellites in the NGSO is expected to grow tremendously (United Nations, 2023[7]). To understand these conditions, the authors constructed three plausible scenarios by 2030 based on how global space governance might evolve. The authors specified the contextual factors that might shape each of these scenarios and analysed under which conditions (national and international institutional environments, market conditions, geopolitical situations) the SSR should be adapted or configured and in which forms (e.g. integrated with financial and economic incentives, creating business legitimacy in terms of corporate reputation) in order to safeguard the long-term socio-economic benefits that space infrastructure can provide. The authors first elaborate on their research methodology and subsequently present the results, including the narratives used to construct the three plausible scenarios. The authors then discuss the potential implications of these scenarios on future earth-space sustainability and derive policy implications in terms of the role of SSR.

Research methodology

In foresight studies, scenarios act as mental models that offer a structured and practical avenue for analysis, communication and learning, by revealing alternative possibilities about the future of the problem studied. The fundamental use of scenarios is a way of navigating times of uncertainty (Bohensky, Reyers and van Jaarsveld, 2006[8]), particularly in terms of proactive policy making (Wright et al., 2019[9]; van Dorsser et al., 2020[10]). Several scenario exercises have been conducted for the space sector in the past, including on the future of space applications (OECD, 2004[11]), the associated opportunities and challenges to policy (OECD, 2005[12]), space traffic management (Secure World Foundation, 2017[13]), and the futures of governing space as a commons (Yap et al., 2023[3]). In this chapter, the authors construct the future scenarios of global space governance by following the analytical steps described below.

Discourse analysis: identification of contextual factors

As a first step, the authors conducted a discourse analysis to identify the contextual factors that could shape global space governance by 2030. This was used to distil the set of policy, regulatory and business strategies pursued by key actors (i.e. state actors, private actors, and intergovernmental organisations) in three space infrastructure sectors critical for enabling socio-economic development and green sectoral transitions. The three space infrastructure sectors are satellite navigation (e.g. efficient navigation of transport, shipping, and agriculture systems), earth observation (e.g. industry application services using carbon monitoring data), and broadband satellite constellations (e.g. connectivity services across industries).

Over the last decade, there has been growing global competition in navigation, earth observation and broadband satellite sectors. In the navigation satellite sector, the Chinese BeiDou system came into full operation in 2020, and the European Union (EU) Galileo system began operation in 2016 and is expected to fully operate by 2024. In addition, the EU earth observation programme Copernicus began operation in 2014. The internet satellite sector, meanwhile, observed the installations of large satellite constellations by companies such as OneWeb, Starlink and Amazon Kuiper. Taken together, the three space infrastructure sectors provide a comprehensive view of policy, regulatory and business strategies pursued by key actors. This allows us to anticipate the set of factors that will shape global space governance in the near future, particularly with regard to the development of space infrastructure.

The secondary data used in the discourse analysis was sourced from a reliable database system - Lexis Nexis - which is a database that provides legal, governmental, business and technical information from newspapers, journals and magazines in English. The selection of the period was based on "critical moments" during which major shifts in development were observed. This was indicated by the sudden increase in news articles reporting on the development of specific sectors. Based on preliminary studies, the authors identified the few years after the introduction of the United Nations Sustainable Development Goals (UN SDGs) to have played a crucial role in boosting the development of the three selected space infrastructure sectors. For instance, some key actors promoted the potential of the satellite broadband constellations sector in closing the digital divide by offering global connectivity services. News data therefore reported on how actors expressed their opinions on the values of satellite infrastructure in terms of sustainable development, and their respective strategies to promote, develop and regulate the space infrastructure sector. The final selection period fell mostly within 2016 – 2020, with slight variations for the broadband satellites sector which only began to increase from 2018 following the rapid launch of satellites by companies such as Starlink. The latest development trends (from 2021 to early 2024) were identified through a scenarios workshop and in-depth interviews.

Actor statements in the news were coded based on a systematic coding scheme using Nvivo. The coding scheme was derived abductively, based on the conceptual framework of "institutional logics" (Thornton, Ocasio and Lounsbury, 2012[14]) while inductively identifying new elements based on the empirical data analysed (see Yap, Heiberg, and Truffer (2023[15]) for an application on the case of space debris management). Institutional logics, a concept derived from the field of institutional sociology, – allows actors to subscribe to a finite number of alternative but internally coherent combinations of value positions like the state, market, or community logics (Thornton, Ocasio and Lounsbury, 2012[14]). Each of these logics is associated with specific interpretations of fairness, success, collaboration or competition, which in this case operate in relation to the value of satellite infrastructure for sustainable development. The coding of actor statements for the navigation satellite and earth observation sectors was extracted from an earlier study by Bandau (2021[16]), whereas the one for the satellite broadband constellations sector was extracted from Coyle (2021[17]).The coded data was subsequently reorganised and compiled by the authors of the present chapter based on the major actor types (i.e. international organisations, state, and private actors) as well as their geographical regions. This discourse analysis overall derived a comprehensive view of the different strategies (e.g. state and/or geopolitically-oriented, market-oriented, or global community-oriented) pursued by different actor types.

Scenario building with experts and stakeholders

The exploration of alternative futures of global space governance was based on contextual factors identified from the discourse analysis above. More specifically, the aggregated groups of coded concepts based on the three key actor types informed us about the major logics that delineate the different scenarios in this chapter. Accordingly, the authors identified three plausible scenarios of global space governance by 2030: (i) one that is state-led and strongly driven by geopolitics; (ii) one that is led by private actors and strongly driven by market values; and (iii) one that is led by international fora driven by sustainability concerns and global community interest. Corporate stakeholders, policy experts, and technical engineers were invited to a scenario workshop in collaboration with the Politecnico di Milano on 8 June 2023.

The scenarios were jointly discussed and validated with the workshop participants. A total of 24 participants were divided into three break-out groups, each of which focused on one scenario. Individual visions and expectations were discussed and collected, which were aggregated to become collective expectations. Within each group, an expert on the topic led the discussion on how the different scenarios "perform" (Truffer, Voß and Konrad, 2008[18]). In the context of this study, this means the potential implications of those scenarios on future earth-space sustainability, e.g. the state of the orbital environment (e.g. highly congested, well maintained, under strict regulations) and the long-term use as well as the diffusion potentials of space infrastructure for socio-economic development and sectoral transitions on Earth. Subsequently, the authors discussed the opportunities and challenges for SSR to contribute to earth-space sustainability under each of these scenarios.

Triangulation through in-depth semi-structured interviews

The authors conducted ten in-depth semi-structured interviews with selected stakeholders to triangulate the above results. More specifically, this step ensured the study captured the latest development trends and asked focused questions in terms of how they perceive the value of space infrastructure for sustainable development and which configurations of SSR might be effective in the different scenarios. Examples of SSR configuration include the provision of financial and economic incentives, supporting existing and potential regulations, altering procurement processes, benefiting corporate reputation and public perception, as well as supporting environmental, social, and governance corporate reporting (Rathnasabapathy and David, 2023[4]). Table 8.1 lists the interviewees, including their respective areas of expertise in relation to the scenario building.

Table 8.1. List of interviewees

Area of expertise	Organisation	Interviewee
Geopolitics and international relations	Primakov National Research Institute of World Economy and International Relations, Russian Academy of Sciences	Dmitry Stefanovich
	Secure World Foundation	Victoria Samson
	United Nations Institute for Disarmament Research (UNIDIR)	Almudena Azcárate Ortega
Market	Planet	Anonymised
	Maxar	Doug Engelhardt
	Amazon Kuiper	Anonymised
	OneWeb	Anonymised
General scenarios	L'Istituto di Fisica Applicata Nello Carrara, Consiglio Nazionale delle Ricerche	Alessandro Rossi
	United Nations Institute for Disarmament Research (UNIDIR)	Anonymised
	Space Policy Institute Washington	Scott Pace

Results

Discourse analysis on global space infrastructure sectors

In this subsection, the authors present the results of the discourse analysis of the three global space infrastructure sectors. For each sector, the authors show in Figures 8.1-8.3 the relative distribution of institutional logics subscribed by different actor types, i.e. the percentage of one logic over all the other logics that the same actor type refers to.

In the navigation satellite sector (Figure 8.1), actors adhered to the logic of "market development" as they referred to the role of governments and private players in growing the markets for navigation services (Bandau, 2021[16]). Meanwhile, actors referred to "market competition" when discussing competition between state and non-state actors to gain higher market shares in potential service segments. In the field of satellite navigation, "national self-interest" appears to be a prominent logic, as they expressed the importance for nations to gain independence and technology supremacy in these critical services for national security, power and welfare purposes. Some actors would mention the importance of bilateral agreements with other states due to geopolitical, geo-economic, or geostrategic reasoning (coded as "geopolitical [bilateral]"). Here, states seek partners with, for instance, other states with complementary technological capabilities or infrastructure components. There are also actors adhering to the logic of multilateral co-operation (coded as "promote multilateralism") as they emphasise the importance of having multilateral co-operation (including scientific collaborations) among powerful space actors in order to have appropriate institutions to address collective action problems. Actors also adhered to the importance of "co-operation for sustainable development", in particular when referring to the potential of space infrastructure services in facilitating sustainable development on Earth. The "science (professional)" logic was coded when actors mentioned the importance of scientific competence and reputation as well as new technologies. Finally, "governance and regulation" refers to the need for legal mechanisms and appropriate political institutions as space intertwines with peace, security and social and economic development.

After the compilation according to actor type and geographical region, Figure 8.1 shows that international organisations, in particular the United Nations Office for Outer Space Affairs (UNOOSA), emphasised the importance of promoting multilateralism in view of the rising potential of space infrastructure in promoting sustainable development on an international level. The authors see that state actors highly value national self-interest when associating with the development of satellite navigation infrastructure, particularly in the United States, the People's Republic of China [hereafter 'China'], India, the Russian Federation [hereafter 'Russia'] and to a certain extent Europe. State actors of Russia, China and India tend to strongly mobilise their bilateral relationships with allied nations to reach geopolitical goals. In the context of developing countries, states tend to also form bilateral agreements with states that offer satellite navigation services to ensure the continued diffusion of those services in their nation-states. Adherence to market-oriented values among private actors was particularly high in China, possibly induced by the introduction of the Chinese BeiDou services in this period. Here, discussion in the media hovers around the importance of creating market competition between state and non-state actors, as well as the need for the Chinese government to promote market development especially also within the nation itself.

Figure 8.1. Relative distribution of logics over actors: navigation satellites sector 2016-20

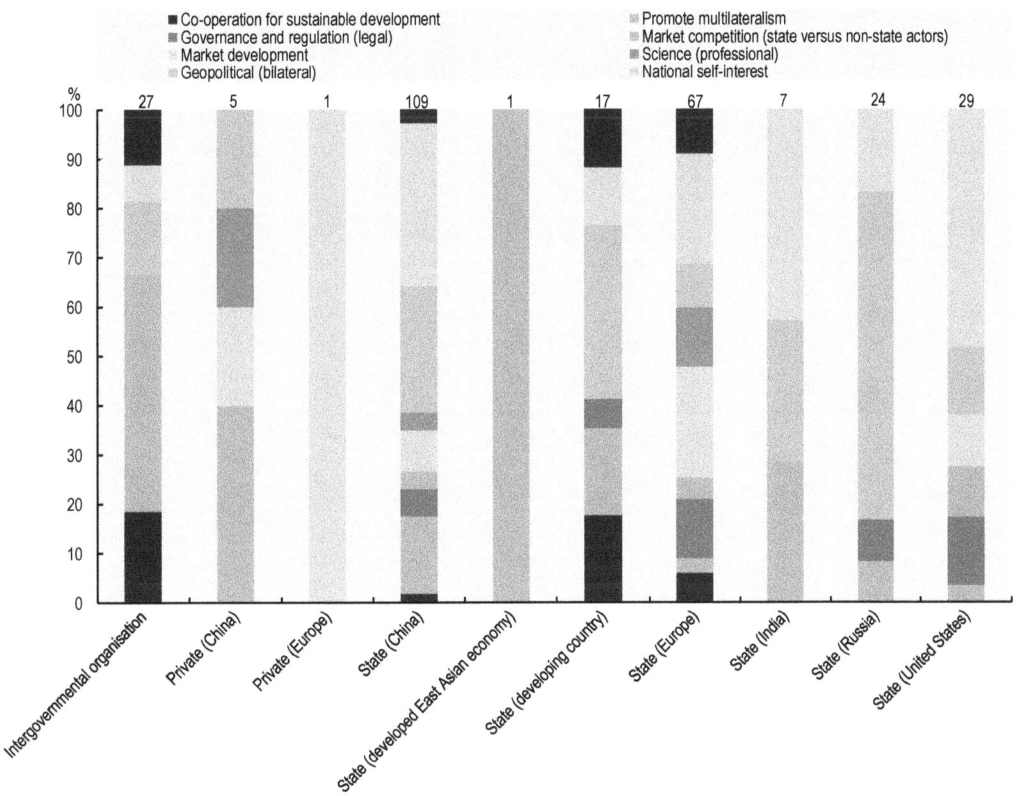

Notes: The number above each bar indicates the absolute number of coded logics. Although the category of state actors from developed East Asian economies has a 100% subscription to the logic of promoting multilateralism, it is insignificant when compared to other bars that have a higher frequency of coded logics.

Source: Author's compilation based on Bandau (2021[16]), "Emerging Institutions in the Global Space Sector: An Institutional Logics Approach", Master's thesis at Utrecht University.

For the earth observation sector (Figure 8.2), the code "government supports market development" refers to actors emphasising the role of government in shaping the market development of the sector through monetary and fiscal policies, subsidies and taxes. "Private players drive market development" was coded when actors referred to the role of business entrepreneurs and small-medium enterprises in growing the space industry via upstream and downstream services. The codes for "national self-interest", "promote multilateralism", "bilateralism" (or geopolitical and/or bilateral), "multilateral collaboration for sustainable development" (or co-operation for sustainable development), "science (professional)", as well as "governance and regulation" share similar interpretations as in the case above (Bandau, 2021[16]). The logic for "societal development" refers to using space technologies for sustainable development that can help address social challenges. Meanwhile, "sustainability (ecology)" refers to using space technologies for sustainable development that address ecological challenges. Finally, the logic of "community" mainly refers to unity as well as community-based values and arrangements in the context of diffusing earth observation services.

Figure 8.2. Relative distribution of logics over actors: earth observation satellites sector 2016-20

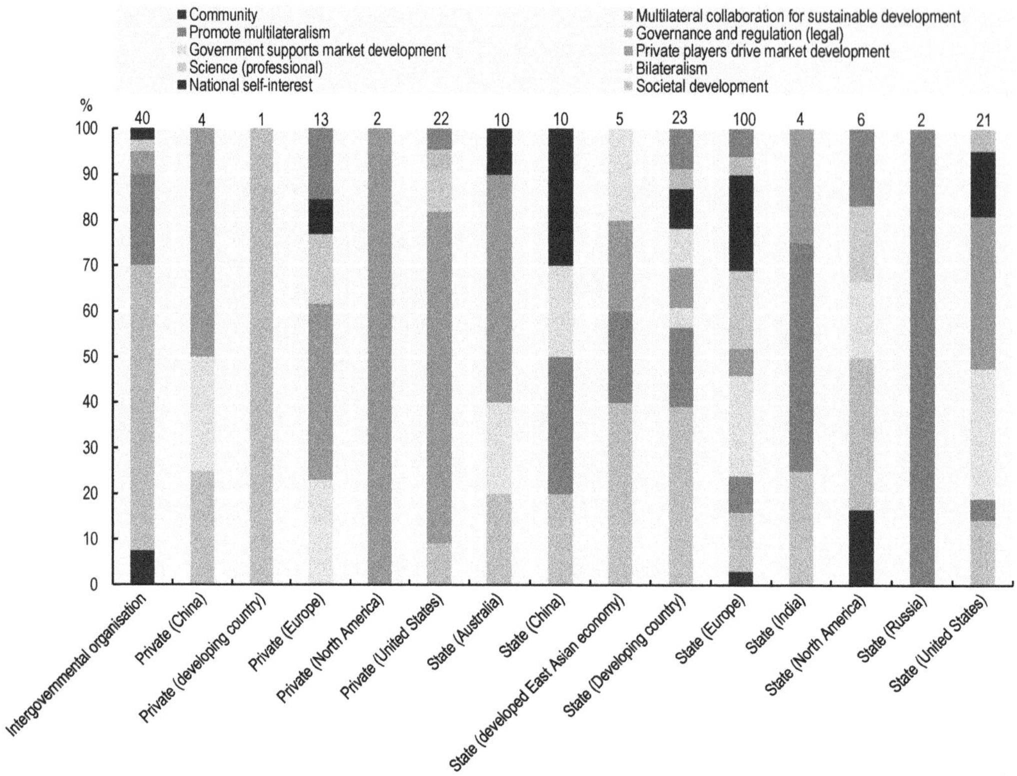

Note: The number above each bar indicates the absolute number of coded logics.
Source: Author's compilation based on Bandau (2021[16]), "Emerging Institutions in the Global Space Sector: An Institutional Logics Approach", Master's thesis at Utrecht University.

As shown in Figure 8.2, there was a strong push from international organisations such as the UN COPUOS in the earth observation sector in this period to use observation services for sustainable development purposes through multilateral collaboration. In this context, the pursuit of a multilateral agreement was also emphasised. Similarly, the authors see state actors in developing countries resonated with the idea of diffusing earth observation infrastructure through multilateral collaboration for sustainable development. European state actors own a sharp rise in the number of coded statements in this period, potentially following the roll-out of the Copernicus – the European earth observation programme. Most of the state actors in Europe pointed to the importance of government support for market development but also how earth observation capabilities may bring advantages to European countries such as technological supremacy. State actors in the United States also emphasised the role of both governments and private actors in driving market development. Private actors in the United States, Europe and Australia heavily emphasised the role of private industries in driving market development in the sector, such as in terms of rolling out different application services through observation data. Private actors in the United States and Europe shared similar opinions and emphasised the potential of the private sector, with the latter also pointing to the importance of government support.

For the satellite broadband constellations sector (Figure 8.3), the code "governing orbital sustainability" refers to actor concerns for orbital governance in particular in relation to spectrum frequencies and physical orbital slots (Coyle, 2021[17]). "International co-operation" refers to states balancing different needs and striving for co-operation with other nations. The logic for "diplomatic tool or international relations" was coded when actors referred to the importance of states maintaining or increasing their national power including by having their own satellite broadband constellations as a strategic asset. "National economic gains" refers to the potential of satellite broadband constellations in fuelling the national economy, including by supporting a nation's rural residents as well as by collaborating with private actors in commercialising services. In addition, the code for "societal development" refers specifically to the potential of satellite broadband in bridging the digital divide and addressing global connectivity. Meanwhile, "profit" was a prominent logic that actors refer to in the satellite broadband constellations sector, including discussions about market segments, industry competition, cost and prices, as well as financial support from the state. Looking at the rapid development, actors also adhere to the logic of "space as a common resource", arguing for democratising space access and space governance so that all nations including developing countries will have access to space and more actors have a say in how it is governed. Meanwhile, there were also actors adhering to the logic of "science and innovation", which argued for not just more science and innovation, but the need for less regulation to ensure quicker commercialisation of products and services.

Figure 8.3. Relative distribution of logics over actors: satellite broadband sector 2018- early 2021

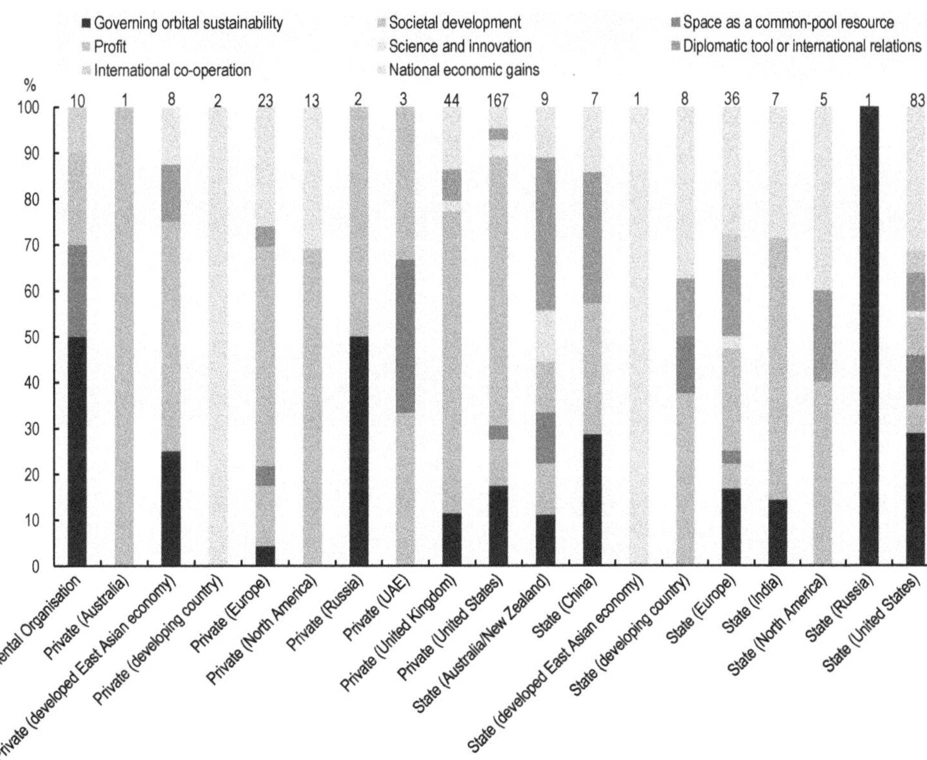

Note: The number above each bar indicates the absolute number of coded logics.
Source: Authors' compilation based on Coyle (2021[17]), "The rise of the global internet satellite mega-constellation sector: Opportunities and challenges for a sustainable transition", Master's thesis at University of Utrecht.

As shown in Figure 8.3, international organisations such as the UN COPUOS and the International Telecommunication Union (ITU) emphasised the importance of ensuring orbital sustainability through more effective governance while also mentioning the enormous market and economic values the satellite broadband constellations sector could bring. State actors in general value the potential of the sector in generating economic gains within individual nations, particularly in terms of how connectivity services might stimulate the growth in other sectors. Market values are significantly high among private actors in the

United States, the United Kingdom, Europe, and North America (Canada), with the latter two also valuing highly the national economic gains this sector could bring.

Three plausible scenarios for global governance by 2030

The discourse analysis above identified the set of contextual factors (or logics of the key actors) in terms of policy, regulatory and business strategies that could shape global space governance by 2030. Informed by the analysis, the derivation of the scenarios is based on two major dimensions identified as most critical in delineating future development trends, i.e. between state-led and private-led (non-state) governance on the horizontal axis, and between highly internationalised or highly nationalised on the vertical axis (see Figure 8.4). Accordingly, the authors derived three scenarios each of which is dominated by a different rationale: Scenario A is dominated by a state rationale; scenario B is dominated by an economic and market rationale; and scenario C is dominated by a global community rationale. Each of these scenarios consists of a mixture of state and non-state actors but may be primarily driven or led by certain actor types operating in a national or an international regime.

In this subsection, the authors will present the narratives constructed for the three identified scenarios, which were further developed and validated during the scenario workshop and through follow-up interviews to incorporate the latest developments.

Figure 8.4. Scoping of scenarios on space governance by 2030

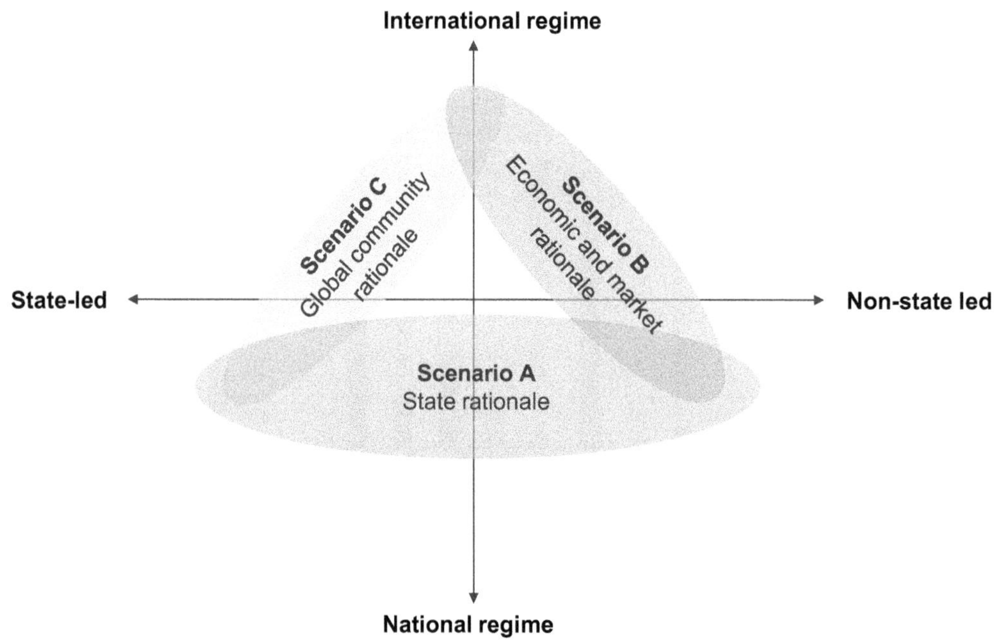

Source: Adapted from Secure World Foundation (2017[13]), "Summary of the 2017 AMOS Dialogue", https://swfound.org/media/206083/2017-amos-dialogue-report.pdf.

Scenario A: state governments take control and compete to lead space governance

This future in 2030 is strongly dominated by geopolitics (i.e. the state logic), as state governments compete for hegemony and technological supremacy in the orbital environment in the absence of new international agreements. While still operating under the 1967 Outer Space Treaty (OST), groups of state governments have gained leadership in controlling the environment of low-earth-orbit (LEO).

Within individual countries, national policies and regulations are powerful and effective in this scenario. The United States (Federal Communications Commission - FCC) further imposed its five-year post-mission disposal rule on all operational satellites launched from the United States and received strong compliance from all operators. However, given the intense geopolitical competition in space, there are also states that pursue contradicting national strategies, such as allowing leniency for companies in their respective countries in terms of the disposal rule to accelerate the accumulation of national technological capabilities and induce industry growth (e.g. by having their nationally-owned satellite constellations).

The environment of LEO therefore becomes unsustainable in this scenario as strict policies pursued by the United States are offset by the strategies of other nation-states, allowing longer post-mission disposals (e.g. the typical 25-year rule). Meanwhile, leading spacefaring states also take on the leadership role of further developing active debris removal technologies and continue to fund space debris cleaning missions. These missions, however, remain expensive and debated among countries and stakeholders in terms of financial feasibility and cost distribution.

Geopolitical interests intensify in particular in the medium-earth orbit as the major global navigation satellite systems (GNSS), i.e. GPS (owned by the United States), Galileo (owned by the EU), BeiDou (owned by China), and GLONASS (owned by Russia), compete in technological development to strengthen their state military power while at the same time aiming to diffuse their respective navigation systems widely to economic sectors on Earth. Due to rising geopolitical tension, states in major spacefaring nations also substantially upgrade and effectively manage their tracking, cataloguing and response to space debris in particular through their military facilities, potentially also with support from private actors that have strong capabilities in tracking space objects. However, rival countries tend to operate based on their own set of tracking systems, leading to different versions of the status of the orbital environment.

In line with the duty of due regard under Article IX of the OST, anti-satellite testing (ASAT) is effectively banned by certain leading states such as the United States, EU, Canada and Australia in this scenario. However, certain nation-states continue demonstrating their space capabilities through ASATs. This leads to certain regions in the orbital environment being left with debris clouds. In this scenario, the authors might see more alliances forming among nations with similar values and interests, such as between Russia and China, or between the United States and the EU. This scenario therefore observes increased examples of minilateralism that define technological and system inter-operabilities among like-minded countries, causing global institutional fragmentation.

Scenario B: state governments take control and lead space governance

This scenario in 2030 is dominated by the market logic, mostly driven by actors in the private sector in interaction with state actors. The private actors take the lead in governing LEO in the form of self-co-ordinated activities or setting strong influences on the state actors in terms of the interpretation of treaties and/or the implementation of policies and regulations.

In this future, LEO becomes an area open for market competition with commercial companies competing for low costs and high service performances. Following a first-come-first-served principle in the occupation of orbital slots, satellites of large satellite broadband constellation projects such as Starlink, Eutelsat OneWeb and Project Kuiper proliferate LEO by 2030. These large private actors are however required to undergo more scrutiny and meet more debris mitigation requirements imposed by government agencies such as the FCC in the case of the United States, in accordance with Article VI of the OST which asserts that states are responsible for the actions of their nationals including the commercial industries. Despite so, constellation companies that have become strategic space assets for their respective state such as Starlink tend to have high bargaining power when negotiating with their government agencies by 2030, e.g. the United States Federal Aviation Administration (FAA), and are particularly effective in influencing policies and regulations.

Certain technological implementations become effective, as private actors have developed their own market-based instruments to incentivise sustainability-oriented behaviour in space to ensure the safety of their own operations. This has induced rapid technological innovations and cost efficiency in the realm of active debris removal and other on-orbit servicing that help address the issue of space debris. This scenario also observes alliances among satellite companies that share similar interests and values to co-maintain orbital sustainability by incorporating disposal rules into their satellite missions. As a result, technologies such as passivation and de-orbiting technologies become well-developed among these companies.

However, there are private companies that disregard the importance of orbital sustainability and only aim for short-term profits in this scenario. Certain private actors self-co-ordinate their satellite activities and their interactions with the others in LEO in terms of physical manoeuvres and system compatibilities. In line with Article VI of the OST, state actors in this context generally seek to enact regulations to ensure their national commercial actors are still in compliance with the OST.

Overall, given that the OST is a set of general principles leaving room for the interpretation of the states, large private actors in this scenario have a strong influence on the state actors when negotiating with them and international bodies, such as the ITU on radio spectrum allocation or the International Astronomical Union (IAU) on satellite manoeuvres. This scenario therefore observes effective strategies pursued by different private actors operating in national and/or international regimes.

Scenario C: international fora succeed in global space governance

This 2030 scenario is dominated by a global community rationale that places the interests of all nations at the forefront, such as in the recent case of the High Seas Treaty (UN News, 2023[19]). Scenario C in this present study is most actively led by international fora or international organisations advocating for the benefits of inclusivity and multilateralism, as well as having a powerful say in defining international norms for space activities with support from state and non-state actors operating in the international regime.

The Inter-Agency Space Debris Coordination Committee (IADC) Space Debris Mitigation Guidelines became effective as the IADC member agencies conform to the principle of due regard (pursuant to Article IX of the OST) by preventing explosive and collisional on-orbit break-ups and ensuring post-mission disposals. The Guidelines for the Long-term Sustainability of Outer Space Activities of the UN COPUOS are also adopted at the national level across spacefaring countries due to their interest in showing good behaviour in space to foster their international co-operation with others. The United Nations Office for Disarmament Affairs and the UNIDIR become more inclusive and effective platforms through which national representatives from developing and less developed countries provide their suggestions on peaceful uses of orbital resources and equitable socio-economic development.

Moreover, the UN Space 2030 Agenda – "a forward-looking policy document for reaffirming and strengthening the contribution of space activities and space tools to the achievement of global agendas" and "to reach the Sustainable Development Goals" was successfully implemented (UNOOSA, 2024[20]). In particular, the adoption and implementation of the Space 2030 Agenda involved the international adoption of principles that space is a global commons, explored and used for the purposes of the global community, especially among less developed countries. Here, intergovernmental partnerships such as Group on Earth Observations (GEO) become instrumental in maximising the potential of space infrastructure for sustainability transitions across multiple sectors on Earth, such as transportation and agriculture (Group on Earth Observations, 2024[21]).

Other international organisations also play a decisive role in this future scenario. The ITU works closely with the national delegates from different countries to re-strategise the allocation of radio spectrum in the NGSO to ensure equitable access for countries across all developmental stages. In addition, international initiatives that place the interests of the global community at the forefront become influential in this scenario. The International Dark-Sky Association (IDA) and the IAU become influential platforms for advocating and negotiating for dark and quiet skies. For instance, the IDA becomes powerful when negotiating with satellite constellation companies for satellite manoeuvres to adhere to the IDA principles, including maintaining satellite brightness to "below the threshold for detection by the unaided eye", in the interests of indigenous communities and the biodiversity that depends on natural light cycles (Scorzafava, 2022[22]). For more details on the scenarios, please refer to Annex 8.A.

Discussion: Potential impact on earth-space sustainability

Participants of the workshop jointly discussed how each of the different scenarios may pose opportunities and challenges to future earth-space sustainability. They discussed whether the physical environment in space would be stable (i.e., the collision risk is controlled, satellites can be operated without significant risks in the orbits); how the different scenarios impact the diffusion of space infrastructure; and whether a scenario is desirable and for whom (which actor types while taking into account less developed countries).

Intensified geopolitics in scenario A will potentially lead to weaponry tests and installations by states that do not adhere to the principle of Article IX of the OST, causing more space debris in the orbital region. This scenario is deemed the least desirable, particularly for commercial actors as their operations in the orbital region will be impacted. There would be fewer private investments in new satellite constellation projects due to higher collision risks as a result of more geopolitically induced activities such as ASATs. In addition, a state-led logic also reduces the likelihood of a commercially efficient diffusion of active debris removal technologies and other on-orbit servicing. Overall, this scenario can be desirable for individual nation-states that prefer higher global institutional fragmentation and therefore prevent the likelihood of, or, delay the progress in creating effective multilateralism. This scenario is deemed highly undesirable for less developed countries as they rely heavily on space infrastructure services provided by the powerful spacefaring countries and more intense geopolitical battles between the space powers may lead to disrupted access to their respective services.

Similarly, scenario B is expected to lead to a less sustainable orbital region, in particular in LEO, as the increase in satellite operators does not guarantee all operators would follow sustainable practices. For instance, participants drew the example that 5,000 satellites of large private players could pose fewer risks than other 2 000 satellites of smaller private players that do not have the technological maturity to implement best practices. In addition, smaller private actors may not be able to invest in additional technological development, e.g. adding propulsion to their small satellites, as they have limited funding enough to only prove their short-term business plan. At the same time, the first-come-first-served principle currently favouring the larger companies in terms of occupying orbital slots is limiting fairness for smaller players or latecomers from developing or less developed countries, as orbital slots already occupied by the larger companies are de-facto not usable by others in the future.

Considering the lack of effective international regulations at the moment, participants in this break-out group still believe that scenario B – a scenario primarily led by private actors – is perhaps capable of inducing sustainability-oriented behaviour among operators in LEO. This is because private actors reach decisions based on cost-benefit analyses – in this case collectively ensuring orbital sustainability is critical for the long-term functioning of their own satellite operations. Therefore, scenario B could lead to two opposing outcomes in terms of the distribution of socio-economic benefits: (i) competition among private actors in more advanced countries prohibits the participation of companies from developing and less developed countries that might enter the market in the future; and (ii) advanced private actors could offer satellite infrastructure services that bring high socio-economic benefits to developing and less developed countries (such as global connectivity as an enabling technology), while effectively managing orbital sustainability among themselves.

The NGSO environment is deemed to be relatively sustainable by 2030 under scenario C, as space traffic management rules and practices are well co-ordinated at the international level. Meanwhile, the ITU continues to review and revise its regulatory framework through the World Radiocommunication Conference. The distribution of space infrastructure services is likely to be more equitable under this scenario; these space infrastructure services facilitate sectoral transitions while some of them become critical space assets that countries and economies will heavily rely on. Despite scenario C being deemed the most desirable for the global community among a majority of the workshop participants and interviewees, it is also discussed as being rather unrealistic or progressing too slowly given the current state of international affairs. The challenge therefore lies in navigating between the two probable futures (scenarios A and B) in order to move towards scenario C.

Policy derivation: the role of SSR

In this section, the authors discuss the opportunities and challenges for SSR under each scenario. Some guiding questions during the workshop and follow-up interviews include what might be a potential incentive package that SSR could offer (e.g. integrating SSR into the licensing process at the national and international level, integrating SSR into the procurement policies for space infrastructure). For instance, national procurement policies of space infrastructure can incorporate earth-space sustainability considerations, and SSR can be used to help assess the performance criteria of those infrastructure service providers.

High geopolitical tension in scenario A is likely to prohibit any international governing body from taking on an active role in advocating for the adoption of an incentive-based option such as the SSR. Given that individual nation-states might be competing or pushing forward their own set of policy and regulatory frameworks, the formulation of SSR in this scenario will have to be adaptable to fit the policy context and settings of different countries. In addition, given that this scenario might see a higher level of global institutional fragmentation, the rating assessments carried out by the SSR have to be made transparent and shared among the global space community so that comparisons can be made across countries in terms of the performance of different operators.

In the event that private actors become more influential by 2030 as described in scenario B, the SSR assessment criteria and procedure will have to be strengthened in order to prevent data manipulation by private actors. It is also anticipated that, under this scenario, the SSR should work together with space agencies in order to incorporate the rating system as a requirement for satellite operators. In both scenarios A and B, ensuring more transparency in SSR assessments would incentivise state and private actors to adopt the best practices in space, therefore presenting an opportunity for SSR to facilitate the space community transition from scenarios A and B towards scenario C. In scenario B, however, it is crucial for the SSR to improve on the value it could provide to the operators that adopt the rating system. A better quantification or measurement of economic value is critical here.

Effective international fora under scenario C will provide a solid ground for the SSR to be implemented, as it is more likely for member states to reach a consensus on sustainability-oriented behaviour in this scenario following the global community rationale. Besides transitioning the space community towards scenario C, the challenge for SSR here is to develop a first set of understandable operational rules and guidelines based on the standards of the SSR, while incorporating the best guidelines available on an international level (e.g. the recent introduction of the five-year disposal rule by the US FCC). These rules and guidelines should then be clearly communicated to international bodies such as UNOOSA to gain institutional endorsement. In addition, the technical standardisation by SSR has to proactively consider that the rules and guidelines are fair to all new spacefaring nations (including less developed countries). Transparency in SSR assessments is therefore also important here to facilitate cross-country comparisons. In this scenario, SSR should also initiate communications with the public (i.e. users and consumers of space services) about the importance of knowing the sustainability performance of infrastructure service providers in space.

The discussion furthermore derived general implications for the SSR, crosscutting the three alternative scenarios. Here, participants of the study (both workshop and interviewees) raised their opinion that SSR as an incentive-based policy option is encouraging given that SSR can serve as a transparent and credible third party. Improving the transparency of SSR assessments may moreover entail combining objective facts from publicly verifiable tracking data. This could facilitate credible and effective comparisons, which might foster competition among states to gain national pride by becoming leading exemplars that keep space sustainable for future generations (such as by deploying advanced technologies). A similar trend is observable among private actors, with Starlink's automated on-board collision avoidance system being held in high regard among satellite operators.

A few participants, however, raised the concern that companies might be conservative in adopting the SSR as they are unsure whether the rating system would impact their corporate reputation. This could happen if an operator overlooked certain operational aspects despite the heavy financial investment a company has put in place to improve the sustainability aspects of its operations. In this context, participants consistently emphasised the importance of incorporating an insurance model into the SSR package as well as creating more financial incentives such as access to corporate loans or other public funding. Table 8.2 provides a summary of the three scenarios in terms of desirability and the opportunities and challenges for SSR.

Table 8.2. Summary of policy implications from the different scenarios

	Scenario A	Scenario B	Scenario C
Desirable for whom	Desirable for individual nation-states that favour global institutional fragmentation	Desirable for private actors considering the low likelihood of effective international fora	Desirable for the global space community, considering that formal regulations will facilitate the uptake of active debris removal (ADR), de-orbiting, etc.
The role of SSR	• No international governing body to implement • Comparability within and across different SSR modules • SSR should be adaptable to each country • Shared ratings to facilitate transparency • Seek UN recognition • Seek complementary ratings such as fairness	• Data manipulation by private companies • High bargaining power of private actors • The need to involve space agencies • How can SSR provide financial value to operators • Simplify SSR to make it more understandable	• How to create awareness among end users and/or consumers • Developing a first set of (understandable) rules • Incorporating best practices on an international level • Conveying clear and effective messages • Enable all new nations in the space sector • Educating end users
General implications for SSR	SSR can act as a transparent and credible third-party rating body, which facilitates effective comparisons among countries and private actors. It would be important to incorporate an insurance model or other financial incentives such as access to corporate loans and public funding.		

Note: SSR=space sustainability rating.

Conclusions

Addressing earth-space sustainability is a rapidly growing challenge (Yap and Truffer, 2022[2]). In view of the exponential rise in satellite activities by the end of this decade, the international space community is confronted with a narrowing policy window to find practical solutions for the long-term provision of satellite infrastructure services on Earth, while ensuring safe and environmentally sustainable conditions in Earth's orbit. In this chapter, the authors presented three plausible future scenarios on how global space governance might evolve by 2030 in order to explore how an incentive-based mechanism like the SSR may serve as a policy option to help address the growing challenge.

Drawing from a discourse analysis of three different critical satellite infrastructure sectors, a scenario workshop and in-depth semi-structured interviews, the authors derived clear narratives for the three alternative futures driven by: strong geopolitics; market values; and the logic of multilateralism in the interests of the global community. Such distinguishable scenarios can serve as a basis for further learning, in particular aiding different actors in anticipating major development trends to navigate their policy, regulatory and business strategies. In addition, the authors derived concrete policy implications concerning the opportunities and challenges for the SSR under the different scenarios, including the provision of financial and economic incentives, support for existing and potential regulations, altering the procurement processes for space infrastructure, and the association with corporate reputation and public perception (Rathnasabapathy and David, 2023[4]).

As mentioned in the introduction, the present chapter delimited the empirical and analytical scope of "sustainability" to focus on socio-economic development, sectoral transitions and the safety of the orbital environment. Follow-up studies should however be more comprehensive when addressing earth-space sustainability to take into account a broader set of environmental and social challenges, especially when considering space as a commons (Yap et al., 2023[3]; Janssen and Yap, 2024[23]).

Annex 8.A. Scenario development

Indications that Scenario A is underway

- Signs of individual states taking a proactive role in governing orbital sustainability: The new five-year post-mission disposal rule recently imposed by the US FCC.
- Signs of intensified geopolitical competition in space include the set-up of the US Space Force. The US Space Force has announced plans to invest in an ambitious effort to build a new "integrated operations network", through which the US Space Command could mobilise the data gathered through this network to update space domain awareness to conduct on-orbit operations (Gill, 2023[24]).
- Signs of differing values and interests among nations: The US government declared in 2020 that space is not a global commons while the EU Council recently declared in May 2023 to recognise space as a global commons (Council of the European Union, 2023[25]).
- Signs of more fragmented governance through alliances: The Artemis Accords led by the US government is an example of minilateralism, although this was intended for activities on foreign celestial bodies. In addition, Russia and China are finding increasing technological interoperability in their satellite navigation systems (GLONASS and BeiDou).

Indications that Scenario B is underway

- Signs of large private companies becoming important strategic assets for the states: The use of Starlink services to aid the Ukrainian warfare; competition between satellite projects in monitoring (Humpert, 2022[26]) and connecting the Arctic (Roulette, 2021[27]).
- Signs of large private companies gaining high bargaining power when negotiating with the states: The US FCC dismissed claims from several companies against Starlink's placement of satellites in a lower orbit. The FAA was also sued for allowing SpaceX to launch its Starship Super Heavy in April 2023, without a comprehensive environmental review (Kolodny, 2023[28]).
- The ADR industry is progressing and innovating steadily, driven by companies such as ClearSpace and Astroscale. New companies for space logistics services also entered the field. More private services for Space Situational Awareness services also emerged in the last years, e.g. LeoLab, Privateer Space, etc.
- Leading consultancy companies such as McKinsey & Company released positive market outlooks on the satellite sector, potentially incentivising more business investments into the satellite sector (Brukardt et al., 2023[29]).

Indications that Scenario C is underway

- The ITU revises its policy agenda every four years, for instance through the World Radiocommunication Conferences (WRC). The ITU is actively working towards deriving allocation policies that are fair and equitable for all nations.
- Signs that multilateral formal agreements might still be effective: The recent agreement reached by delegates of the Intergovernmental Conference on Marine Biodiversity of Areas Beyond

National Jurisdiction – referred to as the High Seas Treaty - builds on the UN Convention on the Law of the Sea (UN News, 2023[19]).

- International initiatives centring the interest of the global community are increasingly active: The IDA lodged an appeal with the US Court of Appeals in response to the FCC authorisation approving SpaceX to deploy 7 500 satellites in LEO (Hartley, 2023[30]).

References

Bandau, S. (2021), "Emerging Institutions in the Global Space Sector: An Institutional Logics Approach", Utrecht University, The Netherlands. Master's thesis supervised by Xiao-Shan Yap. [16]

Bohensky, E., B. Reyers and A. van Jaarsveld (2006), "Future Ecosystem Services in a Southern African River Basin: a Scenario Planning Approach to Uncertainty", *Conservation Biology*, Vol. 20/4, pp. 1051-1061, https://doi.org/10.1111/j.1523-1739.2006.00475.x. [8]

Brukardt, R. et al. (2023), "Space: The missing element of your strategy", in *McKinsey & Company*, March 27th 2023, www.mckinsey.com/industries/aerospace-and-defense/our-insights/space-the-missing-element-of-your-strategy (accessed on 30 January 2024). [29]

Buchs, R. and T. Bernauer (2023), "Market-based instruments to incentivize more sustainable practices in outer space", *Current Opinion in Environmental Sustainability*, Vol. 60, p. 101247, https://doi.org/10.1016/j.cosust.2022.101247. [6]

Council of the European Union (2023), *Preparation of the Council (Competitiveness (Internal Market, Industry, Research and Space) on 22-23 May 2023 Draft Council conclusions on "Fair and sustainable use of space" - Approval*, 5th May 2023, https://data.consilium.europa.eu/doc/document/ST-8962-2023-INIT/en/pdf (accessed on 30 January 2024). [25]

Coyle, A. (2021), "The rise of the global internet satellite mega-constellation sector: Opportunities and challenges for a sustainable transition", Utrecht University, The Netherlands. Master's thesis supervised by Xiao-Shan Yap. [17]

ESA (2022), "ESA's annual space environment report", ESA Space Debris Office, www.sdo.esoc.esa.int/environment_report/Space_Environment_Report_latest.pdf. [1]

Gill, J. (2023), "Unified and integrated: How Space Force envisions the future of data-sharing for space operations", in *Breaking Defense*, 24th May 2023, https://breakingdefense.com/2023/05/unified-and-integrated-how-space-force-envisions-the-future-of-data-sharing-for-space-operations/ (accessed on 30 January 2024). [24]

Group on Earth Observations (2024), "Earth Observations for Impact", https://earthobservations.org/ (accessed on 30 January 2024). [21]

Hartley, R. (2023), "IDA appeals FCC approval of SpaceX Gen2 satellite constellation", in *Dark Sky*, 6th January 2023, https://darksky.org/news/ida-appeals-fcc-approval-of-spacex-gen2-satellite-constellation/ (accessed on 30 January 2024). [30]

Humpert, M. (2022), "Russia Plans to Launch Nine Polar-orbiting Satellites to Monitor the Arctic by 2026", in *High North News*, 7th November 2022, www.highnorthnews.com/en/russia-plans-launch-nine-polar-orbiting-satellites-monitor-arctic-2026 (accessed on 30 January 2024). [26]

IRGC (2021), "Policy options to address collision risk from space debris", *International Risk Governance Center (IRGC), EPFL*, International Risk Governance Center (IRGC). EPFL - Lausanne École Polytechnique Fédérale de Lausanne, https://infoscience.epfl.ch/record/290171?v=pdf. [5]

Janssen, M. and X. Yap (2024), "Governing Outer Space as a Commons is Critical for Addressing Commons on Earth", *International Journal of the Commons*, Vol. 18/1, pp. 32-38, https://doi.org/10.5334/ijc.1378. [23]

Kolodny, L. (2023), "FAA sued over SpaceX Starship launch program after April explosion", in *NBC News*, 1st May 2023, www.nbcnews.com/news/amp/rcna82289 (accessed on 30 January 2024). [28]

OECD (2005), *Space 2030: Tackling Society's Challenges*, OECD Publishing, Paris, https://doi.org/10.1787/9789264008342-en/. [12]

OECD (2004), *Space 2030: Exploring the Future of Space Applications*, OECD Publishing, Paris, https://doi.org/10.1787/9789264020344-en. [11]

Rathnasabapathy, M. and E. David (2023), "Space Sustainability Rating in Support of the Development and Adoption of Regulatory Guidelines Related to Long-Term Sustainability", *Air and Space Law*, Vol. 48/Special Issue, pp. 155-178, https://doi.org/10.54648/aila2023036. [4]

Roulette, J. (2021), "OneWeb and SpaceX are racing to beam internet to the Arctic", in *The Verge*, 26th March 2021, www.theverge.com/2021/3/26/22350643/oneweb-spacex-racing-broadband-internet-arctic-military (accessed on 30 January 2024). [27]

Scorzafava, L. (2022), "Who Owns the Night Sky?", *Dark Sky*, 22 March, webpage, https://darksky.org/news/who-owns-the-night-sky/ (accessed on 30 January 2024). [22]

Secure World Foundation (2017), "Summary of the 2017 AMOS Dialogue", https://swfound.org/media/206083/2017-amos-dialogue-report.pdf. [13]

Thornton, P., W. Ocasio and M. Lounsbury (2012), *The Institutional Logics Perspective. A New Approach to Culture, Structure, and Process*, Oxford University Press, USA. [14]

Truffer, B., J. Voß and K. Konrad (2008), "Mapping expectations for system transformations", *Technological Forecasting and Social Change*, Vol. 75/9, pp. 1360-1372, https://doi.org/10.1016/j.techfore.2008.04.001. [18]

UN News (2023), "UN delegates reach historic agreement on protecting marine biodiversity in international waters", in *United Nations*, 5th March 2023, https://news.un.org/en/story/2023/03/1134157 (accessed on 30 January 2024). [19]

United Nations (2023), "Our Common Agenda: Policy Brief 7. For All Humanity – the Future of Outer Space Governance", www.un.org/sites/un2.un.org/files/our-common-agenda-policy-brief-outer-space-en.pdf. [7]

UNOOSA (2024), "Committee on the Peaceful Uses of Outer Space Working Group on the "Space2030" Agenda (2018 - 2021)", *Committee on the Peaceful Uses of Outer Space*, United Nations Office for Outer Space Affairs, www.unoosa.org/oosa/en/ourwork/copuos/working-groups.html (accessed on 30 January 2024). [20]

van Dorsser, C. et al. (2020), “An integrated framework for anticipating the future and dealing with uncertainty in policymaking”, *Futures*, Vol. 124, p. 102594, https://doi.org/10.1016/j.futures.2020.102594. [10]

Wright, G. et al. (2019), “Scenario analysis to support decision making in addressing wicked problems: Pitfalls and potential”, *European Journal of Operational Research*, Vol. 278/1, pp. 3-19, https://doi.org/10.1016/j.ejor.2018.08.035. [9]

Yap, X., J. Heiberg and B. Truffer (2023), *The emerging global socio-technical regime for tackling space debris: A discourse network analysis*, Acta Astronautica, https://doi.org/10.1016/j.actaastro.2023.01.016. [15]

Yap, X. et al. (2023), “Four Alternative Scenarios of Commons in Space: Prospects and Challenges”, *International Journal of the Commons*, Vol. 17/1, pp. 390-410, https://doi.org/10.5334/ijc.1272. [3]

Yap, X. and B. Truffer (2022), “Contouring ‘earth-space sustainability’”, *Environmental Innovation and Societal Transitions*, Vol. 44, pp. 185-193, https://doi.org/10.1016/j.eist.2022.06.004. [2]

www.ingramcontent.com/pod-product-compliance
Ingram Content Group UK Ltd.
Pitfield, Milton Keynes, MK11 3LW, UK
UKHW051504290926
15471UKWH00008B/1414

9 789264 777804